THE
KIDS
ON THE
CORNER

THE KIDS ON THE CORNER

PAT JENKINS

LEVEL

T R U

For Kiely and Steve

Chapter One

1979

Manhattan's Upper West Side

Before crack and meth, when prescription drugs were used for medical purposes only, marijuana reigned supreme.

Detective Jack Kuchinsky pushes open the glass door that separates his two worlds. On it, the words NEW YORK CITY POLICE DEPT. 24th PRECINCT. As he climbs the worn linoleum steps the attaché case full of textbooks pulls heavily on his arm.

This morning's wake-up call from his ex contained the usual litany of his daughter's latest transgressions. Cigarettes found in her book bag again, ignoring another curfew, talking back to her mother. What else is new? And, as always, it was followed by the painful reminder, it's all because there is "no father in the house."

She's got a point. Jenny never misbehaved like she is now when he lived there. He misses being there in the morning to see her off to school, misses helping her with her homework at night. Misses her.

Halfway up the staircase, he shifts the attaché case to his other arm and with it, his thoughts shift to a very different conversation—the one he had after last night's class when Professor Ford took him aside and told him that, not only was Jack one of his best students, but he actually suggested that

Jack consider becoming a teacher himself. He said that Jack's eighteen years of police work would bring "an added dimension of reality" to students of criminology. Now, in Jack's last year of night school, the suggestion from someone he admires comes as a real compliment as Jack had never considered teaching before.

With only two more years before he can retire, he had started wondering what retired cops do for the rest of their lives. Open a liquor store, a bar? Take some bullshit security job, or like many he has known, end up spending their days sitting on a park bench feeding the fuckling pigeons. Those few dreary realities had been, until last night, his only retirement options. But now, Professor Ford has offered up a far different possibility, opening a new door and letting Jack look through it.

At the top of the stairs, a red neon arrow underlines the words DETECTIVE SQUAD. A faulty connection makes the once solid letters flicker and fade.

Approaching the top of the stairs he loosens his tie, and leaving the cerebral world of academia behind him, Jack once again steps into the harsh reality of a New York City squad room. Newspapers, open files, and departmental mail litter the cramped desks. In/out boxes overflow with paperwork. Swivel chairs and wastepaper baskets block the aisles, and typewriters click noisily away like the applause of a shadowy audience. Male voices with rough-edged New York accents punctuate their phone conversations with four letter words and an occasional double negative. Noticeably absent are any personal objects. No family photos, no humorous desk novelties. No green plants flourish here.

A half dozen or so large, burley, black and white men, all without their jackets are gathered around the coffee machine. Laughing and cursing, arguing the pros and cons of the Giant's new quarterback, debating whether their union is fighting hard enough for an increase in retirement benefits. The whole noisy scene is muted by a thin veil of cigarette/cigar smoke.

Jack strides through the familiar maze. At the coffee machine he pours himself a hot and steamy cup, then greets his colleagues with a matter-of-factly, "What's doin' guys?" No response is given, and none is expected.

At his desk, Jack blows some paint chips, fallen from the ceiling, off his blotter before setting his cup down. Then he begins the daily ritual of flipping through his phone messages. One from mom, another from a witness on that bullshit assault case. His garage called. The part he ordered for his car must have come in. Probably costs an arm and a leg. Somebody named Linda wants him to call her. He doesn't know any Linda, but it might be that redhead he sat next to at the West End Bar the other night. Jack had too many Tequila Sunrises to remember any names, but he does remember that one's ass was a bit too wide for his liking. He crumples up the little pink Linda slip and moves on.

The last three messages are all from his ex, all about Jenny again, all marked urgent. That was another of this morning's complaints. When she leaves messages for him, he does not get back to her in her conception of timely fashion. He closes his eyes and rests the bridge of his nose between his fingers. No, he's not going to call Paula right back like she expects him to do. But damn she knows how to flaunt how right she almost always is.

"So, Jackie, whaddya got planned for Thanksgiving?" a tall black detective with movie star good looks asks as he eases his butt onto the corner of Jack's desk. Holding a coffee mug in one hand and unbuttoning his vest with the other, he adds, "You're not gonna find a better cook than Tracy, and the kids would love it if Uncle Jackie showed up with his ever-welcome slight-of-hand coin tricks."

"Hey, Randy, I really appreciate the invitation, bro, but you know I gotta be with mom this year," Jack tells his partner. "This'll be the first holiday without my dad." He sucks in a quick mouthful of hot coffee to flush down the unexpected lump that rises up in his throat.

"Jenny's going over to my in-laws, so I'm the only family mom's gonna have." But Jack is touched by the invitation. After seven years together, through good times, tough times, and life-threatening times, Randy is family, too.

Randy flashes that wide, easy smile of his. "I figured, but if things don't pan out for you for some reason, you know we always got an empty chair."

An older man sporting a bad polyester jacket and an equally bad comb-

3

over stops to stir his coffee at Jack's desk. His eyes focus on the books Jack has just taken out of his attaché case. He picks up one and reads the title aloud, *Deviance-The Interactionist Perspective*, and shows his disdain with an exaggerated grimace.

"Your head's up your ass if you think this bullshit's gonna up your clearance rate." He laughs sarcastically and tosses the book back onto the desk. "Lotta liberal mumbo-jumbo if you ask me."

Jack and Randy exchange looks of wilted amusement. "Who's askin'?" Jack takes no offense at the familiar ribbing. He understands that his pursuit of a college degree is an anomaly to the squad room's aging veterans.

The older detective tosses Jack a quizzical glance. "You're not gonna turn into one of those long-haired freak shows on us, are ya?"

Jack brushes back a loose strand of his blond hair and laughs. "I'm gonna get it cut this afternoon."

The man smirks, but as he starts to walk away, he stops and says over his shoulder, "Hey, buddy, you're workin' this afternoon."

Jack laughs, calling after him, "It grows on city time, I get it cut on city time."

With the jarring ring of a telephone the room's multiple conversations come to an abrupt halt. All eyes are on the detective that picks up the receiver saying, "Detective Marino." Then after a brief pause asks, "Where's the body?"

"Fuck it," Jack mumbles more to himself than to Randy. "We're catchin'."

Next case is Jack and Randy's, and Jack knows homicides always run into overtime. With only hours before a holiday, the timing couldn't be worse.

Randy shrugs and starts to rebutton his vest. "Maybe it'll be a ground ball," he says with that easy-going way he has managed to maintain in times of stress.

"Yeah, right. Ground ball my ass. When's the last time you saw one of those?" With a humorless laugh Jack shakes his head. "Day before Thanksgiving some mutt hadda go get himself ghosted. I'll be lucky if I make it to mom's in time for a slice of her pumpkin pie."

Detective Marino hangs up the phone and asks the room, "Who's up?"

Extending his arms as limply as his interest, Jack acknowledges, "Wadda we got?"

"Male. White. D.O.A," Marino says, reading from his notes. "An apartment at 410 West one-0-five. Looks like it might be over drugs."

"Drugs." Jack stands up and tightens the tie he had just loosened. "Fuckin' assholes are gonna bore me to death before they finish killin' each other off."

In alleys, car trunks, in seedy apartments, face up, face down, standing on their heads, Jack's seen it all. One after another they just keep popping up like targets in a shooting gallery.

Randy laughs. "Another headliner, 'Mutt kills mutt.'"

Pad out, pen poised, Jack asks, "Where we goin'?"

"Name's Scholfield. That's S-C-H-O-L-F-I-E-L-D. 410 west one-0-five, third floor rear and watch it. They tell me this one's really ripe. Eyeballs already runnin' down his cheeks and so bloated it looks like he might just up and float away like a Macy's balloon."

Randy picks a piece of lint off his blazer. "Had one like that up in the two-six. Tried to take an ID outta his pocket, and the fucker blew up all over me."

"Don't suppose we got a perp on this one?" Jack asks Marino, fully expecting the negative response he gets.

But Marino does add, "Uniformed guys are holding a couple of kids on the scene. Friends of the deceased. Might have something for you."

Might. Might not. Jack wishes he could still care like he started out doing, but the deaths now all blur together into one big fuzzy homicide case folder with a dreary sameness. He looks down at the dead body of what was once a human being and all he sees is yet another case folder waiting to be filled.

The perps, too, have become interchangeable now. Convicted or not, day after day, he finds himself arresting the same faces, taking the same fingerprints over and over again. How many times has he made a collar in the morning only to see the same mutt back on the street the next day, robbing, raping, murdering all over again? Only the victims change. It's the mutts' fucking shyster lawyers who get them off on minute legal technicalities, though they should be locked up.

Then there are the victims. Jack started out caring about the fatalities and their families. But too many of them turned out to be scumbags themselves, deserving, in Jack's opinion, of what they got. And their families? Yeah, he once felt for them, for their losses. But no matter how much effort he puts into a case, sometimes even putting his own life on the line in his relentless quest for justice, there's always some fuck-head family member ready to blame Jack for whatever legal loophole got the perp off the hook. "Shabby police work." How many times has Jack heard that one whispered behind his back?

Jack shrugs on his coat and adjusts the gun shoved into the back of his belt to a more comfortable position. "Let's go," he says to Randy with a resigned sigh.

As Randy makes a right off Riverside Drive and onto one-o-five, Jack scans the buildings for number 410. Randy talks about his kid's last softball game, but Jack's attention is focused on the neighborhood.

On both sides of the street well-kept brownstones display window boxes still bursting with flowers in the colors of summer. Shiny brass-rimmed doors hover over freshly scrubbed steps. Along the curbs, thriving London plane trees, each circled with a lush skirt of green ivy, further add to the scene of affluence and elite. An immaculately groomed, middle-aged woman dressed like she just stepped off the cover of this month's Vogue, walks a pair of meticulously trimmed Yorkshires, each sporting a little pink bow on its head. Two black nannies pushing white babies in high-end strollers, chat and laugh as a young man in a Columbia sweatshirt jogs by. There is not a speck of litter anywhere and all the trashcans have lids. 105th Street appears to be the ultimate scene of peace and serenity.

Up until last month's transfer, Jack and Randy had always worked out of Harlem precincts. Up there when somebody got blown away, word went out like a shockwave. Old ladies sitting on the stoops, kids playing stickball in the streets, even winos lying flat-out in the gutter knew what went down, who got it, who did it. They all knew, and the fear, the tension, and the excitement could be seen on every face and felt in the air.

6

But here on picture-perfect 105th Street, what Jack sees is not what he knows he is going to get in house number 410. It makes him uneasy, makes him feel like now he has to watch his back more than ever. Makes him wish he was back in Harlem.

Chapter Two

In her new office on the 57th floor overlooking Columbus Circle and the vast, green rectangle of Central Park, Kate Palmer looks out the window and feels like she is sitting on top of the world. And she literally is.

She couldn't ask for a better job than art director at a top-of-the-line ad agency, couldn't ask for a better son than her nineteen-year-old, A-student, Casey. None of the usual teenage problems were present in the Palmer household through four peaceful high school years and now into college life. No smoking, drinking or, God forbid, drugs to trouble Kate's years of teenage parenting. No petty shoplifting or even class-cutting in her son's first year of college to challenge the Palmers' peaceful home.

And the household? She couldn't ask for a better place to call home than her six-room, rambling, pre-war apartment on Manhattan's trendy Upper West Side. Kate had lots of friends and even an amicable relationship with her ex-husband for the sake of extended good parenting.

And now this promotion. She's grateful that her talents have been recognized by the suits upstairs, grateful for the substantial pay raise that goes along with that recognition, but maybe most of all, as she sits here today, Kate is grateful to finally have a room with a window. So what if her drawing board still takes up most of the floor space. It is all her floor space now. She no longer has to share it with other graphic designers. And the promotion was rightfully so. After all, it was the storyboards that Kate drew that won over the pricy new client, the burger account that the firm was pitching for.

She turns her head to glance out at Manhattan's majestic view, across those countless rooftops and the impressive rectangle of Central Park's moss green carpet to try to locate her own building on the corner of 108th Street and West End Avenue, but the tall gothic spires of Saint John's Cathedral on 112th are as close as she can come to home.

Being able to enjoy the majesty of this incomparable cityscape rolled out before her like a gigantic Yves Tanguy canvas is invigorating even under this morning's sudden switch to a cold, grey sky. But the abrupt weather change has left Kate feeling oddly uneasy.

Up until yesterday, New York City had enjoyed unseasonably warm, sunny weather. A temperate Indian Summer had flowed on through September, October, and most of November, right up until yesterday. But this morning, on the eve of Thanksgiving, one of her favorite holidays, Kate awoke to a startlingly dark, dismal, and cold autumn day.

Whenever the weather turns bad, it always clears up eventually. She sighs and shifts her attention back to her work, testing a few markers on her scratch pad before choosing one to color in the little cartoon character she just sketched across the white panels of her black storyboard. Then she pauses, marker held up in the air, and frowns. Something is missing from the little sugar-pop, cartoon-guy's expression.

Kate turns to view a variety of her own expressions in the small, round make-up mirror attached to the side of her drawing board, letting her lips form ooooh's and ahhhh's until she gets just the right amount of glee. That's it. That's what her sketch was missing.

With her eyes darting from mirror to storyboard and back again, her fingers steer the marker as it quickly captures just the expression she had been looking for. Her very own rendition of joy.

Kate turns back to the mirror to take a moment to critique herself. Her girlish face has no need for make-up, a little lip gloss, a touch of blush on her high cheekbones, and she's out the door each morning. With a satisfied smile she gives her hair a little complimentary bounce and returns to her work.

After she finishes the storyboard, Kate sits back and takes a moment to connect with her son by looking up at his photo prominently pinned on her bulletin board, and she can't help but smile at him.

His picture smiles back at her. Dressed in a red jersey, number 23, and holding a football under his arm with his blond, shoulder length hair, bright blue eyes and an easy smile, Casey is the very essence of a cereal box's rendition of the all-American kid.

An hour later, Kate's phone rings, and she reaches for the receiver without taking her eyes off what she is drawing.

"Kate PA-lmer," she sing-songs in her usual cordial manner.

"Ma, something's happened," her son's voice tells her. But this voice is not familiar.

She frowns. "Case, sweetheart, is that you?" she asks, his somber tone so unlike the always upbeat son she's used to. "What's the matter? Why do you sound like that?"

"Scott's dead."

"What do you mean he's dead?" she asks with a touch of annoyance. This better not be some stupid teenage prank or be related to the conversation Casey had with Kate about thinking of moving in with Scott. A thought Kate quickly forbids. She doesn't have time for this nonsense.

"Ma, I saw him. He's dead." Casey insists, his voice flat and detached.

Casey rambles on as though he hadn't heard his mother's question. "Scott's dad called me this morning as I was getting ready to leave for class. He asked if I would go check out Scott's place to see if he was away. You know, newspapers by the door, unopened mail, that sort of thing. Scott hasn't been answering the phone for days and his dad was gettin' kinda worried. We all were. Taking off without telling anybody, that's not like the Scotto we know. I ran into Bobby on the way over to Scott's place," his words begin to quiver now, "and when no one answered the downstairs bell, Bobby and me, we went and climbed up the fire escape to look in the window, and that's when we saw...when we saw...saw..."

"Saw what? And more importantly, Casey, what the hell were you doing climbing up a fire escape? Don't you know how rickety those things are?"

He interrupts her sharply with, "He's just sitting there, Ma, on the sofa by the window and his head is all...all twisted, weird-like...Mom, trust me, the guy's dead."

She shakes her head as though he can see her denial. "Case, hon, he's probably just asleep," she says, but what she really means is, probably passed out from a night of heavy drinking. A kid living alone in a big city like New York is vulnerable to a lot of bad influences. Kids don't die, not the kids Kate knows. There's too much violence on TV, in the movies, and yes, even in the news. It has fed Casey's ample imagination. She glances at her watch. "You're going to be late for class. What have you got this morning? Trig?"

"Ma, I told you he's fucking dead," he shouts back at her, his words piercing her like rapid fire bullets. "There's blood all over the window, all over him." His voice drops to a near whisper, flat and emotionless again. "He's really dead, Mom."

"Oh my God. There must have been an accident. I'll call 911. They'll get him to the hospital, get him help..." She tries to assure her distraught-sounding son.

Nineteen-year-old Casey's voice breaks into the painful sob of a wounded child as he chokes out the words, "Nobody can help him anymore. The blood's all dried. He's turned this bluish-black...Ma, his head's all blown up like a balloon."

The memory of the last time Kate saw Scott Scholfield flashes across her mind. That ever-present red bandana wrapped around his forehead, his ponytail dangling over an out-of-date, tie-dyed tee shirt. Kate, balancing a big bag of groceries on her hip, Scott comes up to her with his arms extended. "Let me help you with that, Mrs. Palmer."

She smiled a "Thanks, Scott, but I can manage." Then for the umpteenth time she'd told him, "Please, you can call me Kate. Everybody does," and she'd given her heavy bag a little bounce to display that Kate, a women's lib advocate, was more than capable of the carrying task. Now, remembering the minor incident, she feels a twinge of guilt for not accepting his offer of help, and she hears herself whisper into the receiver, "I should have let him help me."

'What? What are you talking about, Mom?"

"Nothing, Case, nothing. I was just thinking out loud. Thinking about Scott. Oh God, Case, his poor parents. They have to be told. Are you home, Casey?"

"No, I'm in the pay phone on his corner, and, Ma…it wasn't an accident. There's a gaping hole on the side of his…I think somebody shot him."

Shot him. Shot means a gun…means a killer. "Oh Jesus, Casey. Get away from there. You hear me? Get the fuck away from there right now!"

"It's okay, Mom. It's okay," he says, becoming the pacifier now. "Cops are already here. Bobby and me, we called them right away. Whoever did this is long gone. Cops want us to hang around until the detectives get here."

The iron vice of panic that had gripped her stomach released its hold on her. Cops are there. Her son is safe.

"Bobby, oh, poor Bobby. Is he okay?"

"We're not fuckin' babies. We're both okay," he shouted, then back to a calm, almost a whisper, he said, "I'm sorry, Mom. I'm sorry."

"It's okay, Case. It's okay. Do you know if they called his parents yet?"

"No. Cops asked us if we knew how to reach them. Thing is, this morning, Scott's dad gave me his work number when he called me. He wanted me to call him after I…I just wanted to ask you first, Mom…what do I say to him?"

"God, Casey, you don't have to do that, honey. Give me David's work number and I'll call him."

"No. Scotto would want me to be the one to tell him. And I'm gonna have to do it real soon. Once the cops get the number…ah, jeeze, that would be so cold if Mr. Scholfield heard it from them. I just don't want to make it any worse."

"You can't make it any worse, Casey."

Chapter Three

Lazy, falling snowflakes cling to Jack's hair and to his broad shoulders. He brushes them off, turns up his collar, and shoves his fists into his pockets. "Fuckin' weather's unreal. Yesterday felt like July, today we get a damn blizzard."

Randy snorts a little laugh. "So you know, when we get back to the office, you can expect the air conditioning to be on."

Jack laughs, too. "Wouldn't surprise me a bit. They send up heat in the middle of the summer. I was roastin' in that hell-hole last August. City's run by a bunch of half-assed idiots." He turns to the uniformed officer in front of 410. "Where's the body?"

With a glance up at 410 the officer tells Jack, "Apartment 3C. Drug paraphernalia all over the place, and in case they didn't warn you, watch out pokin' around this one. Sucker's so blown up he's ready to go off like a firecracker. Glad I'm not one of those morgue guys. I'd hate to have to stuff this one in a bag."

"You're really makin' my day, guy."

Jack couldn't begin to estimate how many of these firecrackers he's seen all in a day's work. All with the ever-present stink of piss, from clothes soaked with that one last violent release of muscular control. Maybe that's why urinals always make Jack think of death.

"Any indication we got an O.D. on this one?" he asks. With drug paraphernalia present there's always the possibility. But his hope for a quick clearance is just as quickly squelched.

"Not really. Guy's got a hole in his head you could put your fist through.

But those two kids over there by the pay phone might have something for you. Say they're friends of the deceased. Seems like they're willing to cooperate."

Randy frowns. "Look like a couple of pasty-faced, liberal shitheads to me."

Jack checks them out. "At least they don't look strung out. Randy, you wanna go see what they got while I go up to the apartment?"

The 410 lobby door groans as it scrapes against the marble floor, and Jack's nostrils instantly fill with the stench of decaying flesh. The acrid smell, he knows, will soon invade his clothing—a cleaning bill not covered by the city. He turns to fill his lungs with one last breath of clean, fresh air, then hurries up the stairs to the third floor.

The inside of this brownstone is quite different from its affluent exterior. The vestibule, staircase, and landings along the way have not seen a paint job in decades. The wallpaper is faded, the carpeting is soiled and patched. On west 105th Street, what is on the outside is certainly not what is on the inside. Yet this seediness has a comfortable familiarity for Jack, and for a moment he is back in Harlem.

On the third-floor landing, another officer slouches against a graffitied wall where big colorful letters brashly proclaim that C-R-U-N-C-H has been here.

"This way," the officer says, one hand directing Jack to a door marked 3C, the other continuing to cover his nose and mouth. "I'll never get used to this stink," he says through his fingers.

They enter through a small foyer passing an open closet. The doorframe has been weather-stripped, which is odd for an interior door. The empty shelves are all marked with rings of dust like someone has just packed up and moved out. Jack knows better. He's seen closets where dealers have stored moisture-proof jars of pot many times before.

But the apartment is much more in line with what Jack had expected to find in a posh neighborhood like this. The décor, tastefully done in beiges and browns, is accented by a grouping of old Japanese prints that look like they may be the real thing. A large potted palm in a brass caldron sits in one corner, and an oriental rug that definitely looks like the real thing is on the floor. On one wall, the shelving is filled with an elaborate stereo and

14

speaker system and an assortment of records and tapes Jack's salary could never afford. The big screen TV is still on, a jubilant contestant just being given the okay to "Come on down." In the middle of it all, the body of a young man, seated on the couch, is slowly decomposing.

Pad and pen in hand, Jack walks over to the body. His eyes scan the face, the neck, the bare arms all swollen and bubbled by the gasses trapped beneath the surface. The bloated mass is a deep bluish-black, like a giant sausage. "I thought this guy was white?" Jack says to the uniformed officer, referring to his notes.

"I thought he was black when I first walked in, too," the uniformed cop says. "But he's not. Look at his hands."

He's right. Hanging limply from each darkened wrist, his chalky-white hands are in stark contrast. "Never saw that much discoloration before. That radiator in back of the couch probably did it. Looks like he's been fryin' here for days."

"Who found him?" Jack asks for the record.

"Kids outside. Said the father was worried when his kid stopped answering his calls, so he sent them over to check it out. Father's some big shot TV producer."

Jack shakes his head. He sure as hell wouldn't be asking anyone else to check on his kid if she went missing. He snorts. "Guess he was too busy to do it himself."

He looks down at the body; another son, another father who will not be sharing tomorrow's holiday together…and he is looking at his father's face…

Eyes closed but not in sleep. Hands folded unnaturally across a chest that no longer rises and falls. Clothed in a suit so formal, dad would not have been caught dead in it. White hair plastered down and made shiny like they poured shellac on it. Why did they do that to his hair?

But it is not dad's face that he is looking at now. It is hardly a face at all. The officer points to the corpse's right temple where a gaping hole has torn through a red bandana. "Has to be a bullet in there somewhere, but with all that brain matter oozing out, it's probably down around his foot by now."

On the coffee table, in front of the body, are a couple of record albums.

15

Talking Heads, Grace Slick. A copy of a current girlie magazine, and a small, silver scale surrounded by a handful of glassine envelopes. The picture couldn't be clearer.

"We got a number for the father?" Jack asks, looking down at somebody's druggie roadkill.

"My partner's got it. Crime Scene is on the way. Maybe they'll wrap it up for you."

"Yeah sure, and the check's in the mail."

Using the end of his pen, Jack begins flipping through a stack of letters on the D.O.A.'s desk. It's all junk. He opens one drawer, using the corner of his coat to avoid touching the handle. There are paper clips, rubber bands, a few rolls of unused film, and a handful of sharpened pencils with the points all lined up in the same direction. It's neat and tidy, the way Jack keeps his desk. He doesn't like to find himself having something in common with a low-life.

In another drawer, he finds a collection of college catalogs from The New School, NYU, City College, and the Germain School of Photography. There are a couple of take-out menus, all vegetarian, and a listing of old movies scheduled to play at the nearby Thalia theatre with the Marx Brothers, W.C. Fields, and someone called Ben Hecht all circled in red. Then, he finds something worthwhile—an address book and a small notebook titled *Money Owed Me*.

Jack puts the two books and a letter postmarked Paris in his pocket, and takes an envelope full of black and white photographs over to the window. He flips through the batch of professional-looking contact sheets with a lot of teenage girls. They're fully clothed, nothing sexy here. They're innocent poses, looking like they were taken in nearby Riverside Park with traffic on the Henry Hudson Parkway making dramatic streaks in the background. There are also a few shots of a group of young males, raising beer cans at a ballpark, and hamming it up at the beach. Jack recognizes the two individuals waiting outside. They're clean-cut, wearing baseball jackets, no long ponytails here. Hell, Jack could be looking at photos of his own high school days, which is not what he is used to finding in the home of a drug dealer. It's another 105th Street illusion.

But these wholesome looking kids outside were palling around with a scumbag. He stuffs the photos back in the envelope, adding it to the collection in his pocket, and leaves the apartment. There's a limit to how much of this putrid air he can inhale on an empty stomach.

It doesn't take long for Jack to canvas the five-story building. At 10:30 on a weekday morning, few tenants are home. Those who are, give him the usual didn't see anything, didn't hear anything, didn't know the guy. Only the tenant in the apartment next door shows concern for the death that occurred in 3C.

"I'm new in the building so I didn't know him very well," the young man in the doorway of 3B tells Jack. Clad in skin-tight black leather pants, he stands shaking his head and tsk-tsking his neighbor's demise. "He was a lovely person. When I told him that my vacuum cleaner had broken, he offered to loan me his. I haven't had a chance to return it." He smiles, pointing to his prominent suntan. "I've been in the Keys for the past ten days. Maybe you could find out who I should return it to?"

Yeah, sure, buddy. That's going to be tops on his priority list.

The neighbor also asks Jack to do something about the smell. "I've been trying to call the super, but he hasn't come up yet." He holds out a can of air freshener and encases himself and Jack in a cloud of floral mist. "I couldn't believe it when I came back last night. You'd think with the rent they charge us…" He tsk-tsks again.

Downstairs, Jack steps out onto the stoop and pauses to fill his lungs with a cleansing breath of cold air. The only thing worse than the stench of death was the fucking floral mist.

The snow has stopped falling, leaving a faint dusting of powder on the hoods of the parked cars, on the lids of the garbage cans, and a thin white blanket over the wilted, window-box flowers that bloomed so colorfully only a day ago. The sky has turned shades of grey. The world, too, like the pictures in Jack's pocket, has become a black and white photograph.

A few yards away, Randy is still questioning the two youths. From a distance, they may look straight as an arrow, but straight arrows don't hang out with drug dealers. As he approaches, Randy throws him a look that tells him these kids haven't come up with shit. Jack responds with a little shrug of his shoulders, letting his partner know his building canvas struck a similar zero.

Randy tells the kids, "Look, fellas, we're not interested in who was buyin' from him. We just want to find out what happened here." The two kids shuffle from foot to foot, exchanging guilty glances. Randy smiles and further assures them, "You guys got nothing to worry about from us."

With that, the blond kid's cheekbones begin to throb, and the other kid quickly folds his arms across his chest.

Randy points his notebook at Jack. "My partner, Detective Kuchinsky."

"We're all on the same side, guys," Jack also assures them with a fake, friendly smile.

Randy flips his notebook open and reads to Jack, "We got a Casey Palmer and a Bobby Ardsley here. Friends of the deceased."

"You gotta find the scumbag that did this," the blond kid says through clenched teeth.

"Okay, guys, first things first. Which one are you?" Jack asks the blond kid who looks like he's going to start blubbering like a baby any minute and checks him out at the same time. Pupils not dilated; speech not slurred. Kid's sneakers had to cost a bundle, expensive clothes and clean-cut looks.

"I'm Casey Palmer. Ah man, he'da given them anything they wanted. Why'd they have to go and kill 'im?"

"That's what we're here to find out. That's what we need your help for," Randy tells them like they are all partners in this.

The other kid offers Jack the useless piece of information that the D.O.A. was such a good guy. He shares a look with Randy that says yeah, right.

Jack's voice drips with sincerity. "I can see this individual was somebody you cared about." He one-ups the punks with, "I got a gut feeling we can trust you guys, so I'm gonna do something we don't usually do in a homicide case 'cause I think we're really going to need some help on this one. I'm going to let you in on this investigation." Their eyes widen with unexpected glee. "Your buddy Scott Scho...? What's his name?"

"Scholfield," they both pipe up, all ears now, just like Jack knew they would be.

"Yeah, Scholfield." Jack gestures to the building behind him, and with a dead serious expression he looks at the boys, first one, then the other. "Your buddy's sitting up there and right now it looks like he's been the victim of a shooting. He can't tell us anything, but if you guys really want to help, you might be able to do the talking for him."

"We're starting from scratch here," Randy chimes in. "Anything you can tell us about what was going on in his life, who he was hanging out with, if he had any disputes with anyone lately. Girlfriend problems. Anything."

"You guys are in a better position to talk to his friends than we are," Jack adds to further emphasize the "we need your help" approach. Then, laying a consoling hand on the blond kid's shoulder, he soups up the credibility by promising, "No strings, fellas, or my daughter should die of cancer." He reaches into his pocket and pulls out a couple of business cards.

DETECTIVE JACK KUCHINSKY
24th Homicide
212-606-6631

Jack sums it up with, "You never can tell, the smallest thing could end up nailing the shooter."

"We will." "You bet," they eagerly respond, accepting the cards as though he were handing them a fistful of cash.

Although Jack has indicated that the interview is over, the Palmer kid looks like he doesn't want to leave. It couldn't be more obvious that he knows more than he's saying.

Palmer stands there shifting his weight from one foot to the other. His head bowed, he says, "Um" and "Aah" and "Oh man, oh man, this is so fucked up. I can't believe this is happening." Then, "This wasn't supposed to happen."

The other kid frowns uncomfortably. These kids definitely know more than they are letting on, but what did they expect, playing around with drugs and hanging out with a low-life dealer?

Ardsley holds his head, like he has a world-class headache. "They just left him sitting there like he was waiting. Oh God, we were the ones he was waiting for." He turns his back to Jack and Randy, looking up to the sky, and rails, "Those motherfuckers."

Jack lays his hand on Ardsley's shoulder, cashmere for sure, soft, like petting a rabbit. "I know it's hard," he commiserates, "but you give us something to work with, and I promise you we'll do the right thing by your friend."

"We will. We'll ask all his friends." Palmer jumps in like he can't wait to get started.

Ardsley doesn't look so optimistic. "Thing is, he didn't have that many friends. Me and Case, maybe a half dozen more. He was a quiet kinda guy."

That's about all Jack had seen in the photographs.

"But maybe if we get everybody together somebody will remember something, like you said, some little thing," Palmer argues persuasively enough to make Ardsley shrug a reluctant agreement to try.

"That's just what we need from you guys," Jack tells him. These kids sound sincere, and that kind of help is just what Jack and Randy do need. If they are giving him a stroke-job, it's the best Jack's ever seen.

But when Randy tells them to bring these friends down to the office this afternoon, the excuses begin to flow. A kid named Jeremy has classes until four, one named Brad, until eleven. Then there's Rich who plays soccer on Wednesdays, and a Johnny G. who's likely hanging out at some girl's house if he's not playing Frisbee somewhere in Central Park. "It's going to take a while," Palmer informs Jack and Randy, as though he's just taken over the investigation.

Palmer says something about how they will look for a clue. If these assholes want to play Colombo, fine, but getting suckered into overtime on Thanksgiving Eve is just what Jack was afraid might happen. If a child is molested, a young girl raped, God forbid a cop killed, okay then, Jack has no problem with overtime. But for the death of some mutt dealer? No way.

Problem is, these punks have him by the balls. His tour should end at four, but if there is even the glimmer of a chance something might break, Jack is obligated to wait it out. He forces a smile and hears himself capitulate, "Whatever, guys. You got our number."

Chapter Four

K ate sits on the sofa, the cup of tea in front of her untouched. Her watch says it's been nearly an hour since Casey called and she'd rushed home to meet him. She drops her head back on the couch, her eyes staring blankly into the ceiling's white emptiness. *Where is he?*

He's talking to the detectives, of course. The police have to question anyone who finds a dead body. It's not like Casey is in any trouble or anything. It's just taking longer than she'd expected.

A fat, orange cat sleeps soundly beside her, its warm body pressed up against her thigh. She strokes the soft fur and tries to close her eyes, but it is an effort to even hold her lids shut. She takes a deep breath and tries to focus on happier times, looking around her eclectic living room as though she were seeing it for the first time. And what she sees comforts her.

On a shelf of framed photos, a cluster of baby pictures makes her smile. There are more recent ones of Casey wearing a hockey uniform, winter shots of Kate and her son skiing in Vale, and a ten-year-old Casey sledding down Riverside Park's famed Suicide Slope. A picture of a smiling Kate and Casey riding a London bus sits next to a beach shot from last year's trip to Portugal.

But the reality of Scott's death aggressively pushes aside her good memories. Snippets of her small talk with him only days earlier come to mind. "So, Scott, your mom tells me you've become quite the photographer." He seemed so happy to hear that.

She has visual memories, too, like how Scott's face lit up when Kate told him that his mom was so proud of him. It was sidewalk chatter with a boy who had only days, maybe only hours, of life ahead of him.

She remembers Scott telling her how much he was looking forward to photographing Paris on the family's next vacation there. It was trivial small talk, but Kate likes maintaining a cordial relationship with her son's friends. When she said goodbye to Casey this morning, there was no hint of the horror that would follow. She looks at her watch again. *Where the hell is he?*

Murder? That only happens on the six o'clock news. It happens in places like Harlem, the South Bronx, and Bed-Sty. Murder doesn't happen on west 105th Street.

She gets up and walks to the window.

Arms folded, she looks out at the building across the street. It's like peeking through a dozen keyholes; each window offers a glimpse of a neighbor's life. They are neighbors Kate knows and likes: Mrs. Solomon's lace curtains frame her ample hanging plants, the Andersons' bamboo shades, and the Caplivitzs' flowered drapes. A cat sleeps soundly in one window, a green bird sits patiently in its cage in another. Kate's anxiety lessens. Life is still all around her. Then her eyes lock onto Scott's parents' apartment. In one window a gooseneck desk lamp peers back at her, its chrome twisted at a jaunty angle as if this household didn't have a care in the world. *Why doesn't Casey call?*

Kate's eyes drop to the street below. The group of kids, mostly teenagers who commandeered the corner of 108th and West End Avenue to be their own three ring circus are nowhere to be seen this morning. No skateboarders zooming by, no Frisbees flying. No one straddling the mailbox, blasting a boom box or occupying the phone booth. The only movement is the swaying of a cluster of sneakers tied together and playfully tossed over the corner streetlamp.

The combination of kids whose parents owned posh brownstones, only blocks away from kids whose welfare families lived in bare-bone's city projects, delighted Kate. White, Black, Hispanic, Asian—the group blended together with a wonderful equality. Kate understands the noise complaints of her neighbors on lower floors, but she genuinely likes these kids. She has known most of them since they were toddlers playing in the park's sandbox. "Hi, Kate" they greet her when she passes by. Kate sees this unique combination of backgrounds, color, and creed more like a rainbow. To her, their cross-racial friendships were a microcosm of the way she believes the whole world should be.

With a small shudder, Kate turns away from the window. The emptiness below only heightens her anxiety. *What is taking him so long?*

The click slam of the front door answers her question, and a moment later a breathless Casey stands in front of her.

He looks drained. "I talked to the detectives," he tells her in that same disturbing flat voice.

She hadn't meant to assault him with questions, but the words just burst out of her. "Do they think it was a robbery? Do they know who did it? What did they ask you?" She leaps to her feet and tries to put her arms around him. "Are you okay, honey?"

He pulls away, his body dropping heavily onto the couch. Legs parted, arms flung out along the sofa back, head over to one side, like a tossed rag doll come to rest. But his hands, rolled into tight, white-knuckled fists, tell a different story.

"I'm fine, I'm fine," his lips tell her, but his eyes tell her he is not.

A distant memory from the black and white newsreels of Kate's childhood flashes back to her. Her son's eyes are hauntingly the same as she remembers those young World War II soldiers returning from battle.

She sits down next to him and asks as softly as she can, "How did it happen, Case?"

"They shot him in the head." The flat voice continues. "Cops think it happened days ago. That's about when he stopped answering his phone." Casey sits quiet and still for a moment, but the fingers of one hand tap rapidly on the armrest beside him. "I knew it. I knew something had to be wrong."

Shot. She struggles to find words but there are none.

"When we stepped into the vestibule the first thing, we noticed this...this smell. We were making jokes about it. When I looked in his window, I didn't know what I thought I'd see. I hoped it would be something that would mean he had just been there. Maybe food on the table, a smoking cigarette in the ashtray. I don't know…" His jaw begins to tremble. "Mom, the TV was on, and he was just sitting there like he was watching it. Ah man, the only way I knew it was him was by what was left of the red bandana."

Kate wants to be there on the fire escape blocking his view. She wants to sweep away his memory of this nightmare that is clearly overwhelming his young brain. "Oh God, it's alright, Casey. It's alright," she says, but she knows it is not. Not for Casey. Not for David and Maggie Scholfield. Kate reaches out and wipes away the tears of her living, breathing son. At this moment that's all that matters to her and the reality of the safety of her own flesh and blood momentarily relieves her.

"Did you call David?" she asks, hoping her son was spared that terrible experience.

"Yes. Right after I called you. I think maybe he was expecting bad news. After the detectives left, we walked away and Mr. Scholfield got out of a cab with Scott's mom. Ma, you know what he did? He came over and put his arm around me and asked if I was alright. He asked if I was alright."

"Those poor people." These are the only words she can offer. "How was Maggie?"

"She was crying but kind of quietly. We stayed with her while he went upstairs with one of the cops."

"David went in there?"

"What assholes those cops are. The minute he stepped out of the cab they hit him with a description of the body. Reading out of a little notebook like it was a shopping list. Just cold like that. Using words like oozing and brain matter."

"The detectives made David go in there?"

"No, the detectives, they were cool. They left before Scott's parents got there. It was the guys in uniform. They told him he had to go up there to identify the body. How fucked up is that? They knew it was his son." He forces his eyes and lips to close tightly for a second, then says, "No father should have to remember his son that way. I told the cops I'd do it, but they said it had to be a relative."

"It was a good thing, Case, you offering to do that," but she is thankful they didn't take him up on it.

Casey shakes his head. He suddenly looks uncomfortable, licking his lips and folding his arms across his chest.

"Do you know if he kept money in the house?" How much money could a kid who clerks in a health food store have?

Casey leans forward, but his eyes do not meet Kate's. "Mom, I never said anything to you about his business because it had nothing to do with me."

"Business?" She frowns. "He worked in a health food store. I've seen him there."

"He only did that so his parents wouldn't wonder where his rent money was coming from." He looks her square in the eye now. "You didn't really think he was supporting himself on the chump change they paid him, did you?"

"Are you telling me he had another source of income?" she asks, sensing she is going to regret hearing the answer.

He looks at her with a face as placid as the one on his school ID. His lips barely move, but the words are unmistakably clear. "Scott was a dealer."

The image of Scott Scholfield dressed in a snappy black cutaway and red silk cummerbund, deftly flipping cards onto a green felt tabletop, flashes across her mind. But Kate is painfully aware that is not the kind of dealer that her son is talking about. Her face and her voice do nothing to conceal her rage. "A dealer? You're telling me Scott Scholfield was a drug dealer?"

"I knew you wouldn't understand. It was just grass, a little hash, Mom," he reveals in a far too nonchalant tone. "He was doing real well, too. He paid his rent, paid for his clothes, food, even concert tickets. He never asked his parents for a cent. And he was real generous with all of us."

She knew Casey had experimented with marijuana; he'd told her that years ago. Kate was proud of the fact that she and her son had always maintained an open relationship. They could talk about anything. Kate viewed Casey's minor drug usage as a rite of passage. But now, he is showing admiration for the kid who probably gave the dope to him, and with that revelation another wave of relief washes over her. Scott, she now knows as a potentially damaging influence, has been removed from her son's life. *Maybe Scott Scholfied's death is a blessing in disguise.*

Before she can catch that breath of relief, a sharp pain, like an electric shock, explodes inside her. Scott was a kid she'd seen grow up. He was the son of friends of hers. Her stomach twists in the stinging grip of guilt. Feeling as transparent as glass, she tries to sound calm, but she can't help but angrily ask, "Damn it, Casey, why didn't you tell me what Scott was into? You know you can always talk to me." She realizes as soon as she hears her words, that telling her would have been, for Casey, the betrayal of a friend.

Casey thrusts his jaw towards her, the words shooting out rapid fire. "Where do you get off being so righteous? You said it was okay for me to smoke weed."

Her heart pounds. "Never. I never told you to do it." She thought he'd understood their conversation about brief experimentation, but now this is coming out all wrong. She presses her fists to her temples and forces a calmer tone. "That time I found a joint in your room I didn't punish you. We talked about it, Case. Don't you remember?"

Casey's eyes bore into hers, his lips curling up in a faint smile of victory. "Oh, I get it, Ma. It's okay for me to smoke an occasional joint, but the guy who gives it to me is some kind of a low-life."

She takes a deep breath, and with her voice a near whisper now, she tells him, "You're not stupid, Casey. You knew I wasn't telling you to smoke grass. When we first talked about drugs you were what? Twelve, thirteen? I wanted you to know you could always talk to me about anything. You have to know whatever I told you back then, it was only to protect you." She hears her words coming out sounding insipid. For the first time in her life, Kate feels helpless.

Casey slumps back in his seat and quietly gives her what she needs. "I did know I could talk to you, Mom, and I love you for that. I never said anything because I just didn't want you to be worrying about me. And, Mom, I never told you this, but I really respected you for not freaking out when you found that joint in my room, not like some other kids' parents did." She nods knowingly. Casey adds, "Bernie's mother," he manages a weak grin, "poor sucker, they find one joint, and they send him off to Day-Top rehab. Lotta good that did. He's one of Scott's best customers." They sit in strained silence for a moment, then he tells her, "I never wanted to deceive you, Ma. I was just afraid you'd think I was hanging out with some sleaze." Thin wet lines divide his cheeks. "Scott was a really good guy, Mom."

"He always called me Mrs. Palmer," she says softly.

"That's the way he was, always trying to say the right thing. But he really liked you, you know. He told me once he envied me, being able to talk to you." He shakes his head sadly. "Thing is, he was just starting to have that kinda relationship with his dad."

"Did his parents know what he was doing?"

"No, no he never wanted them to find out. He was going to go back to school. He was going to pay for it all by himself. He was going to study photography. That's what he wanted to be, a photographer. He wanted his parents to be proud of him. Ah, shit. I'm sure the cops have told them by now. The detectives knew. They found the remnants of his stash. Bobby and me, we're thinking maybe that's what he got killed for."

Casey is doing exactly what she wants, being open and honest. Is this the same straight-A son she is so proud of? She suddenly feels like she is meeting the real Casey for the first time.

He jumps up like he has suddenly had an epiphany. "I gotta do something. I promised."

"Do what? You called the police. You called Scott's father. You talked to the detectives. You've done everything you could do."

"You don't understand. I promised the detectives. I would call everybody, try to find some, some little…Scott's sitting up there all dead and here I am doing nothing." He pulls a small address book out of his pocket and reaches for the phone. "I'm gonna get who did this."

Chapter Five

Later that afternoon, Casey Palmer, Bobby Ardsley, and a tall, black youth with handsome chiseled features approach the 100th Street precinct. Packed together like a solid unit, they move swiftly, their conversations hushed, visibly intense, their gestures animated, and arms jutting out with their heads shaking earnestly.

"I can't believe those assholes," Casey hisses angrily. "All of a sudden nobody wants to admit they even know him."

"Believe it, man," Bobby says, his voice more defeated than bitter. "Bottom line is everybody's lookin' out to protect his own ass."

Casey shoves his fists into his pockets. "Cops told us they weren't lookin' to bust anybody over a couple of stupid jays."

"Yeah, but Johnny G., Mark, and the rest of them weren't there to hear that. They're all scared."

At the precinct door the black kid abruptly turns to block their way. With palms up, he momentarily holds them at bay by saying, "In there, my name's Eddie. Eddie Burke. Got that?"

"Ah, man. You can't start pullin' that shit, now, Brad. You start playing games with these guys and you're gonna fuck it up," an exasperated Casey responds. "They're not after us. Tell him, Bobby."

"It's true, Brad. I didn't get any bad vibes," Bobby concurs, but Brad doesn't look convinced.

"Fuck it, man. You agreed we gotta find the dude that did this," Casey reminds him. "You agreed."

"Yeah, well, I'm here, right? Nobody else showed up." Brad smacks his fist into his palm. "Don't you think I wanna see that motherfucker pay for what he did, too?" Then his voice drops to a near whisper as he quickly adds, "Just 'cause I wasn't hangin' out with Scotto for a while, doesn't mean I don't care."

Bobby's hands shoot up like a shield. "Hey, what happened back then was between you and him."

Without comment, Brad steps aside and Casey hurriedly starts up the steps. Looking back over his shoulder he reinstates, "If we're gonna keep on top of this, we can't be wasting time worrying about getting busted."

Brad's eyes dart around the stairwell. "Jeez, shut the fuck up," he murmurs softly. "This whole place is probably bugged."

Jack sits at his desk methodically sorting through the articles he took from the D.O.A.'s apartment. He flips through the scrawled pages of the *Money Owed Me* book. "Christ," he says to himself. It looks like this sucker loaned half the city money. The address book is full, too, but without some more information, it's not of any use yet. He starts to read the letter from Paris, dated a year earlier.

Dear Scotty,

I'm writing from Paris. Staying in the same old hotel where you and your brother got stuck in the 2-man elevator. Your mother's spending most of her time shopping. No surprise there. Last family trip here you had just turned twelve. Now, seven years later, still seems like only yesterday. I guess you could call that trip the calm before the storm.

We miss you, but mom and I understand you couldn't take off from your job on such short notice. We do respect your sense of responsibility on this one.

Switzerland was marvelous. Wish I could have skied it with you. The shoot went well. A topnotch crew and some of the best stunt work I've ever seen, Just the kind of thing you'd have loved to photograph.

Scotty, I still don't fully understand where things went wrong with us, but I do think that now that we, as a family, have Dr. Alling to hash it out with, we are finally on the right track. Believe it or not, I still remember how tough those teenage years can be.

I've been talking to Alling a lot about the things I should have said, like telling you how proud I am of you, of your talents and your intellect. Dyslexia has nothing to do with intelligence. They don't come any smarter than you, buddy.

Wish we could have figured out what was missing before you moved out. I want you to know an education is still there for you any time you want to jump back in. I accept some of the blame for the wall that grew between us, but I have to say, kiddo, you were never one to reveal your true feelings either. It's water under the bridge now.

We're planning another trip here next year, Scotty. It would mean so much more if you came with us. I know Brian would love to have his big bro to hang out with again. I'm giving you a lot more advance notice on this one.

Think about it.

Love,

Dad

They're parents who would give their kid anything, and the mutt still flimflammed them. The father must have been wearing some heavy-duty blinders.

It's not the way Jack handled his daughter when her mother expressed concern there might be drug use. He asked Jenny, flat out, if she ever smoked dope. She looked him straight in the eye when she said no, and that meant, case closed to him. You've got to stay on top of things with kids these days.

Jack stuffs the letter back in the case folder. He immediately gets up when three youths arrive, two white, and one black, and with a smile and an extended hand, he greets them like he's really happy to see them. "Casey and Bobby. Right?"

"Yeah, right," they say as one.

"Glad to see you, boys. Let's talk over here." He gestures toward his desk and pulls up a couple more chairs. When everybody is seated, Jack asks, still smiling, "Where's the crowd you promised?" He'd hung around for the same two kids plus one. Shit, they better have something for him.

Before they can respond, a ringing phone cuts in. "Fuckin' phones never stop around here," he tells them like he's accepted them as colleagues, and answers briskly, "Detective Kuchinsky. Can I help you?" A moment of silence and then, "That's Detective Perez's case. He'll be in on Friday." As he jots a hasty note, Randy joins the group without greeting the boys.

Jack looks up. "We got a new face here so let's start with introductions. I'm Detective Kuchinsky and this is my partner, Detective Watts. And who might you be?"

The black kid looks as spoiled and pampered as the white ones, with an expensive jogging suit, top-of-the-line sneakers, and nice haircut. No Afro here. There are no dreadlocks dangling down this pretty boy's face.

"Eddie. Eddie Burke," the kid pipes up a bit too quickly, as the other two make uncomfortable eye contact. These weasels are up to something.

"Okay then. Casey, Bobby, and Eddie. Whadda you guys got for us?"

They shift uneasily in their seats. One coughs, another clears his throat. Seems like nobody wants to start. So, Jack gets the ball rolling.

Opening the Scholfield case folder, he takes out a piece of paper. "You guys interested in what the coroner had to say?" With deadly serious faces, the three heads bob up and down, and Jack begins to read, "Cause of death massive internal bleeding in the brain caused by two 22-caliber bullets."

"Two? God," they mutter, as though the second bullet was worse than the one that killed their buddy.

"You better get the motherfucker that did this," the black kid orders, like Jack works for him.

Jack's eyes narrow ever so slightly. *Yeah, sure kid*, he thinks to himself, like collaring the guy who ghosted your dope dealer buddy is going to get me a commendation from above. The shooter should get a good citizens award for helping clean up the neighborhood.

But what criminal activity the victim was into can never be a part of the equation. If Jack wants to keep his batting average up, and he does, like it or not, he will do his best to fulfill the Burke kid's demand. "Okay, guys, let's get down to business. Did he have any enemies you know of?"

There were three no's, followed by a round of what a good guy he was, generous, and he'd give you the shirt off his back. To hear them tell it, he was a regular Boy Scout. Palmer ices the cake with, "He wasn't in it just for the money, you know."

"Let's cut the crap here," Randy breaks in with a shot of reality. "He wasn't giving his dope away."

Jack holds up a pacifying hand. "Let's talk this one out. You boys think this was over drugs, or something else? A woman maybe?"

"Definitely not a woman," Burke responds with certainty.

"He liked girls, but he got real quiet when he was around them," Palmer concurs.

A wimp with the women? This isn't like any of the Harlem drug dealers Jack has known.

"It had to be the weed," Ardsley concludes.

The Burke kid glares back at him, quickly adding, "Scotto kept that aspect of his life private. There was never any weed around when we were at his place."

Yeah, right. Jack wasn't going to buy that one.

Randy is clearly becoming irritated. "Hey, bro, don't try to bullshit us here," and like the clash of two stubborn rams, he and the Burke kid lock eyes for an uncomfortable moment.

"Whoa, guys," Jack cuts in to cool things down, assuring them, "We're all on the same side here. The only arrest my partner and I are looking to make is for homicide." He needs this crew to trust him if he's going to get anything out of them. "We told you boys that down on the street." The white kids look convinced, but the black kid doesn't. Jack picks up the victim's address book and starts thumbing through it. "How about we go over some of these names? Let's see, who's this Michael Echart?"

Burke dismisses Echart with a quick, "He's away at Dartmouth."

Figures it would be Ivy League. He tosses the little black book onto the desk. "Come on," he says, palms up, fingers urging information out. "Gimme something, some names of people who might know something about his dope dealing."

After an exchange of eye contact, Ardsley shrugs. "Like Eddie said, he never talked to us about his business."

Like hell he didn't. Jack tries another path. "How about friends? Any disputes there?"

"No, none," Burkes pipes up a bit too quickly again.

Palmer's eyes squint like he is grasping at straws. "There are all those fringe people, but," he contradicts himself, "they're nobodies. No-nothings. A buncha kids."

Jack's pen is poised over his pad ready to grasp at the slimmest straw. "Got any names for these nobodies?"

Palmer waves him off with a negative. "Just kids who bought joints offa him. Little jerks. They wouldn't know shit."

Randy lights a cigarette and tosses the burnt match in Palmer's direction. "If he was sellin', he was buyin'. Those are the guys we're interested in."

If the Burke kid slouches down much more, he's going to disappear into his chair. But Palmer's response is causal, making it sound legit. "Like we said, he never had any of those dudes come up when we were there. Once he said something about them being from Jersey. He said, "I gotta handle those guys with kid gloves, or I might find myself floating down the river in a cement canoe." And with the prophetic memory, the three wince like someone just punched them in their collective stomach. "It was a joke, ya know. A joke. He was only kidding," Palmer hastily explains.

"Welcome to the real world kid," Randy mutters as he loosens his tie.

This is what they brought him? Some guys from Jersey? What's Jack supposed to do, interrogate the whole state? He tries backtracking a bit. "Can you give me the names of any of these nobody-kids who were buying from him?"

"Yeah," Burke finally contributes. "There's a David, a Sammy with some Jewish last name. Liza and Billy." He shakes his head. "There are a lot of them. Maybe twenty or more, but they're just neighborhood kids, airheads who hang out on the corner. Scotto never had anything to do with them, I mean socially."

"How old are these kids?" Randy asks.

"Fourteen, fifteen. Couple of twelve-year olds," Palmer answers, seeming to be the one most interested in cooperating. "They bought so much from Scotto that he hired one of 'em to handle that aspect of his business. A gofer, someone to take orders, make deliveries, an employee. He worked for free joints."

Employee? Sure, your Harlem kingpins have their boys to make runs for them, but Palmer makes it sound like Scholfield should have been offering Blue Cross insurance. "This gofer kid got a name?"

"H.G., H.G. O'Connor," one of them says, finally giving Jack something to write down.

Palmer feigns a shudder. "Jeez, that little punk gives me the creeps."

"Scholfield have any problems with him?" Randy asks, giving Jack a glimmer of hope.

"No. H.G.'s too spacey to be involved in anything," Ardsley says quickly bursting Jack's small bubble of hope.

"A loser's loser," Burke confirms.

Palmer leans forward, talking to his pals like Jack and Randy aren't there. "Ever notice how H.G.'s got this grayish, rodent skin, like he's never seen the sun? Like there isn't any blood flowing through his veins." He laughs. "I think the little twerp is half bat."

Ardsley and Burke chuckle, but Jack is not amused, and Randy looks like he is ready to give these three a tune-up. Jack takes the *Money Owed Me* book out of the case folder.

"Let's get down to the root of all evil, guys. We got lots of names in here. He ever mention having trouble collecting from anybody?"

As if he's touched a nerve, Burke responds immediately, "Absolutely never." He then crosses his legs and folds his arms like he is closing down for the day.

Jack runs his finger down the first few pages. "Let's see. Here's a big one. Your buddy loaned a Brad Hillrich five hundred last May. No note any of that's been paid back. Seems like he kept pretty good records." Jack tries to make eye contact with all three. "Any of you guys know this Hillrich character?"

Only the Burke kid chooses to return the eye contact. "I heard Brad was planning to pay it all back by Christmas. I heard that from a lot of people. I heard he's been saving it up to pay it back all at once." Burke rambles on, concluding with, "Brad's away, out of town, for a while."

Jack makes a mental note to follow up on Hillrich and Burke's obvious connection to him.

Palmer is staring at the floor, looking as uncomfortable as hell. "It wasn't Brad. Who else is in there?"

Jack turns a page. "Howie Glickman. He's in here for a hundred." Heads shake negatively. "How about Julio Ortega for one seventy-five?" More negative responses. Jack runs his finger down the list, turns the page. "Lotta these are nickel and dimmers. Your buddy loaned a lot of people money." He puts the book down. This is going nowhere.

Palmer says softly, "He was like that. People knew it and they took advantage."

A drug dealer who can be taken advantage of? Now that's a new one on Jack.

Ardsley looks like he's about to bail. "But if you did anything for him, any little thing, he'd be so grateful."

"A real sweetheart," Randy says, getting up to answer a phone at an empty desk.

Palmer smiles with a fond reminiscence. "Like the time he got dragged down into the underworld."

"What underworld?" Jack asks with renewed interest.

Ardsely interprets. "The subway. Scotto told that story a million times, and every time he'd make it sound more dangerous."

Dangerous? Maybe Jack is finally going to get something. "Was somebody threatening him?"

"No, no, no," Palmer says, dashing Jack's moment of optimism. "Not dangerous like somebody wanted to hurt him. Dangerous, like fun dangerous. He liked to talk about it."

"Ah, the Golden Age of Writers," Burke muses. "Them was the days, me boys."

Where the fuck are they going with this? Jack looks at his watch. An hour into overtime and he's listening to gibberish. "One of you boys want to enlighten me here?"

Palmer is the only one eager to volunteer. "Graffiti writers, but we're not talking bathroom walls here. Those guys made the whole fucking subway car into a work of art. Pictures of those cars are in art books now." He informs Jack, as if Palmer is some kind of patron of the arts. "Some of those guys are showin' in big Soho galleries. We knew them from the neighborhood when they were just starting out: Dondi, The Fab Five, Futura 2000." With the mention of each pseudo-celebrity's name, the other two nod reverently.

"Man, when those guys bombed a car it was top to bottom. Now that they're off the subject of drugs, Burke is eager to contribute, too. Apparently, these kids don't understand that vandalizing city property is also a crime. Jack notices they are being careful to keep their own names out of it and their knowledge of these graffiti events in the past tense. "I'm talkin' about the outside of the car. Only toys ever messed with the inside."

"Bombing a car could get pretty intense," Ardsley tells Jack as if Jack cared. "It's real dark down in those tunnels. They got to deal with Transit Authority Cops; they got to watch out for the third rail. The rats."

"I was never into it myself," Palmer lets Jack know. "None of us were. We just knew some of the guys that were. Most of the guys we knew were into Safe Haven graffiti piecing. Station walls were their primary canvases. They kept away from the trains."

"Couple of years ago a kid was piecing up at the lay-ups between 137th and 145th," Burke offers.

Ardsley interprets to explain, "Painting a subway car parked in the train yard for the night."

"Yeah, bout three, four in the morning, and T.A cops just blew the kid away. Twelve, that's all he was, just a little kid." Burke informs Jack with indignation as though Jack had some culpability in the shooting.

Sure, blame the cops who were doing their job. Where were the parents when their twelve-year-old was running around in the subway tunnels in the middle of the night?

Burke rambles on. "Never made the news 'cause it was just some little black kid. Name was Paco. He went to P.S. 145 with my brother."

Jack's had enough. Coffee klatch is over shitheads. "One case at a time, fellas. We were talking about your friend being in danger."

Palmer picks up where he left off. "So, Scotto's walking down Broadway with these guys, and they're trying to describe this wall that one of them bombed the day before. It was on the abandoned station at 91st. Uptown side."

"That was some juice piece," Burke reminisces with Ardsley agreeing. "We're not talkin' any cheap, two-color throw-ups here."

Palmer lounges back in his chair, thumbs tucked under his armpits and beams with pride. "A lot of time was put into that one," he says, making it pretty obvious he was the vandal who put in the time. "The whole station wall was like a twenty-foot canvas. Since trains don't stop there anymore there were no T.A.'s to worry about so the writer could take all the time he wanted."

Jack frowns. "That station's been sealed off from the street as long as I can remember, paved over long before you guys came along." The punks better not be jerking him around.

Palmer smirks knowingly. "On the island in the middle of Broadway at ninety-first, there's an old service entrance. A hole in the ground with a grating over it and a ladder that goes down to the tracks. Got bushes all around it, you hadda know it was there." The arrogant, little motherfucker looks like he's getting a kick out of telling the cops something he knows that they don't know, and before Jack can ask, Palmer candidly reveals that, like everybody else, he too had a key to the grating.

"How'd you punks get a key?" Randy asks, showing his first sign of interest.

Ardsley shrugs. "Nobody knows where the first one came from, but man did it multiply. Half the kids in the city had that key swinging from their belts."

Burke adds, "Most of them never used it. It was a status thing just to have it."

Palmer sits back in his chair, feet stretched out, hands in his pockets like the squad room has become his domain. He gazes off into the distance like an old man recalling his youth. "Those were good times."

Randy loosens his tie. "This story got an end? Or a beginning?"

"What my partner means is we got bad guys to catch. How long ago did this incident with your buddy take place?"

"Two, three years ago." Palmer leans forward, like a team huddling to hear the next play. His friends do the same. "As I was sayin', Scotto was walking down Broadway with these guys and they're trying to describe the 91st Street piece, but Scotto's just not seeing it…"

"Doc Rowdy," Ardsley interjects, his fingers drawing the letters in the air. "Bet you can still find that tag around."

"…so, 'bout then somebody notices they're right across the street from the service entrance."

"Let's get more specific here boys. These guys got names?" Jack wants to know, his pen ready for something. Anything.

"I think it was Hector and um, Billy, and maybe Henry D…" Palmer begins to offer.

But Burke quickly puts a stop to the roll call. "We're not really sure. Scotto never said."

Ardsley agrees. "Scotto talked mostly about his part in going down there."

"He was always too scared to go down there before, but this time he had a little buzz on," Palmer continues, "and he kept telling these guys how he wished he had the nerve to go and see the piece himself." Ardsley and Burke chuckle softly in the background, looking like they can't wait to hear what they already know is coming. "So, they say okay, let's go, and they start pushing him across the street. They are just kidding around at first, and he's laughing so hard he can hardly choke out, 'You're not getting me down in that dirty little hole, with trains zooming by and the third rail and the rats,' but he's not fightin' them off either…" Palmer is laughing so hard he can hardly choke out his words.

Jack looks at his watch. 4:30. He's already on overtime, and Palmer shows no signs of slowing down.

"And then Scotto starts calling them a bunch of maniacs, but by now somebody's got the grating open..."

Burke is laughing, his fingers juggling the air in front of him. "It's broad daylight, broad daylight and here they are stuffin' this big guy down a hole in the ground in the middle of Broadway, the busiest street in the world. People must have noticed a commotion in the bushes around the hole, like first you see a guy's head sticking up and then it's gone. But nobody got involved."

"Next thing Scotto knows, he's down on the tracks and they're edging him along the tunnel wall up to the dim lights on the abandoned platform. You gotta realize it's really dark down there, but they can still make out Scotto's face, and they said he had this 'Ah, shit, what did I get myself into look,' plastered all over it. I swear to God, they said you could hear his heart pounding."

Jack remembers hearing it, too, the pounding of his own ten-year-old heart.

...when he chose to explore the empty tenement, his father had forbidden him to ever enter. A place of such purported danger, Jack had been made to promise he would cross to the other side of the street when passing by. But dad's comment that there were "Things in there little boys weren't meant to see," proved more of an enticement than a danger. His little brother was an easily enlisted cohort. They'd squeezed their small bodies through a hole in one boarded-up window, crept silently through the dark rooms. There was empty wine bottles, beer cans and the stench of urine. They climbed the creaking staircase, Jack feeling the pull of his brother's little hand on the corner of his jacket and heard the pounding of his own heart. At the top of the steps, an open door draws him to it like a magnet. A dirty mattress is on the floor, two feet hanging off one side. A slurred voice wants to know "Whodafucksdere?" In their frantic retreat, schoolbooks flying, Jack and his brother tumble over each other, tangling in a sobbing ball of twisted arms and legs, they manage to get down the stairs, and out the window. He'd had to lie to mom about how he got a tear in his new blazer. He had to make his little brother lie,

too. The sin further compounded by the story he made up to explain to
the nuns what happened to his schoolbooks, but the thrill of adventure
superseded everything.

The old memory reassures Jack that there was a time when kids knew right from wrong, and he finds himself smiling. He rubs his eyes and tunes back to Palmer who rambles on with...

"...so, because they only have ten-watters down there, the writer used day-glow orange and hot pink. It made the tag look like it was hanging in the air when trains went by."

"Is there a point here?" Jack asks, making his irritation clear with a slap of his pen on the desk.

"I'm getting to that," Palmer tells him, sounding a bit irritated by Jack's interruption. "They were standing there, down on the tracks looking up at the piece, like they were in a museum or something, when all of a sudden they hear it." He rubs his hands together and his two-kid audience slides to the edge of their seats for the ending they obviously already know. "The rattling of keys."

Ardsley breaks in, "They said Scotto's squinty, little eyes bulged out like a couple baseballs."

Burke takes over, suddenly not nervous about relating the story anymore. "Next thing they know, a flashlight is shining in their faces, and this T.A. cop up on the platform yells hold it right there or I'll blow your fuckin' heads off. I mean they were stunned. T.A. never hang out down there on closed-down platforms."

"All of them start running like crazy, and in the dark they know they'd never find the ladder they came down in time. The only hope they had was getting to the 96th Street station."

"Man, those station lights were a long way off," one of them remembers.

"A long way," Palmer chuckles, "but everybody's runnin' as fast as they can, tryin' to keep away from the third rail, tryin' not to fall in the middle of the track, and they look back at Scotto 'cause this is real foreign territory for him, and they see him, half stumbling, his arms flapping all over the place, lookin' like some kind of stupid ostrich cartoon."

Ardsley shakes his head good-naturedly. "Scotto was never gonna go for the gold."

Palmer agrees. "They said he had this panicky grin on his face, excited and terrified all at the same time. Everybody's yelling for him to run, run, and that's when they heard the train, coming right up behind them. Horn blowing like crazy."

"Talk about runnin' for your life." Burke manages to chuckle.

Jack is not amused. The gnawing pang in his stomach says he is overdue for a meal.

"So, they get to the 96th Street station," Palmer goes on like it's just him and his buddies talking old times, "jump over the local track, and hoist up onto the platform. Everybody but Scotto. When they look back, oh shit. There he is running right up the middle of the express track, those long gangly legs of his stumbling all over the place and right behind him, right behind him, that big motherfucker barreling down, whistles blaring, motorman waving his arms and screaming God only knows what."

"And a second before the express zooms by, Scotto hoists himself up on the platform."

Burke cuts in, "A second before."

Palmer drops back in his seat like he'd just been running with them. "They all whiz past these gawking people on the platform, like it's Bowling for Dollars 'til they hit the street laughing so hard everybody collapses on the sidewalk."

"Scotto swore he'd never go down there again, but, man, he sure got a juice rush out of it."

"He called it, 'The days of the sewer rat patrol,'" somebody concludes.

"Okay, boys. We got way off the track here, no pun intended," Jack reminds them. Have these assholes forgotten why they are here? This fun-and-games buddy of theirs is now a ripe D.O.A. and reminiscing about what Palmer thinks were good old days isn't going to get Jack a collar on this one. He slips the two little black books back into the case folder and poses the question he often asks in homicide cases. "If you boys were in my shoes, where would you start?"

The laughter comes to an abrupt halt with Palmer wanting to know, "First, can I ask you something?"

"Shoot."

Palmer crosses his legs, uncrosses them. "Well, um. It's about what you found in his apartment." The question drops a somber cloud over the three boys.

"A little pot. Scales." Jack keeps his tone matter-of-fact, sensing something might finally be breaking. Kid looks nervous as hell. "I want to reinforce; we're only looking for the shooter. The merch, the buyers, we couldn't care less."

Palmer looks like he is about to bawl again. "Ah shit, they *did* kill him for the weed."

This confirms Jack's gut feeling. From the beginning, these kids knew more than they were letting on. Mom used to tell Jack, "Patience brings roses." Mom would have made a damn good detective.

Randy looks skeptical. "Blown away for a fuckin' spoonful of grass? 'Cause that's 'bout all we found in the apartment."

"It was in a lot of glass jars. He kept them in a special closet," Palmer explains. Ardsley squirms, Burke shoots daggers at him, but Palmer's opened the door and looks like he's going to go through it. "He just got a shipment of weed," Palmer goes on, "but it was new, primo stuff. It's called sinsemilla, it's a…"

Jack has to cut him off here. It's Jack and Randy's job to know what shit like sinsemilla is. "We know what sinse is, kid."

Jack's eyes shift from boy to boy. Can't judge a book by its cover never rang more true. Palmer, with his blond hair and blue eyes could pass for a son Jack might have. Even the baseball jacket is like one Jack used to wear. Ardsley looks like he just came out of the shell. Burke looks like he stepped off the front of a cereal box, but now that they are back on the real topic of drug dealing, Burke is fading into the woodwork again.

Palmer, on the other hand, has no hesitation now talking about his buddy's business. "The way Scotto kept his weed, it was sort of his trademark. First, he'd put it in a plastic baggie, seal it, then put the baggie in an airtight mason jar. He kept his stock at peak potency that way. He had more than twenty jars full of sinse like that."

"Where'd he keep these jars?" Jack hadn't seen any in the apartment.

"In the foyer closet. He even put weather-stripping around the door to keep it extra dry in there. That way he got top dollar right to the end."

Jack remembered the curious weather-stripping on a closet. Nice to have that little detail cleared up. But coming from such a wholesome looking kid? Has drug exploration become today's rite of passage? In Jack's youth it had been sex. Getting a girl to climb into the backseat, getting to unhook her bra for the ultimate goal, a handful of warm, firm breast. Retelling the encounter over beers with the guys was like Palmer's relating his drug expertise.

In Jack's teenage years using weed was called reefer madness. Not a part of Jack's crowd. Something only ghetto blacks and jazz musicians indulged in. Maybe it's time for another talk with Jenny.

"Top dollar means he was raking it in," Randy says with raised eyebrows.

A large quantity of high-priced dope missing from a homicide scene puts a new spin on the case. "Who else knew about the sinse?" Jack asks hopefully.

"Everybody," is the discouraging response.

Palmer agrees. Palms up, shoulders raised, he states the obvious. "He wanted people to know. He was selling it."

Ardsley frowns. "What about that sleazy dude who sold him the stolen bike?"

"You got a name on this dude?" Jack asks, pen raised and ready again.

Burke snickers. "Guys like that don't have names. They have nicknames. I think it was Poppy. I met him once. He might look sleazy, pock-marks, nasty tattoos, but that P.R.'s got the heart of a chicken. I guarantee the only thing he's into is ripping off bikes. Anyway, Scotto was real pissed when he found out the bike was stolen, and he dumped that guy. That was more than a year ago. I haven't seen Poppy around the neighborhood since then."

Palmer scowls. "I knew it was dangerous keeping all that shit in his apartment when everybody knew he lived alone. I told him to get a roommate. It's a two-bedroom apartment, for God's sake. I was thinking of moving in, but at the last minute he'd always say, 'I like having my own place all to myself.' So, I'd tell him, get a dog, a pit-bull." Palmer throws up his hands in disgust. "Then he tells me he likes cats."

They all nod in agreement. "A dog, that's what he should have had. A big nasty dog."

Ardsley shakes his head somberly. "He was such a baby when it came to trusting people. He'd fuckin' let anybody who rang the bell in."

Then Palmer solves the case. "Trust. That's what killed him."

Jack puts the pen back in his pocket and closes his notebook. Thanks for nothing, kid.

Chapter Six

On the afternoon of Thanksgiving Eve, Kate's hands are busy—cranberry sauce to make, a pumpkin pie to bake, and things to peel and mash as the big, pink, turkey carcass slowly defrosts itself in the sink. But there's no escaping from the only thing on her mind. What this terrible experience of Scott's death will do to Casey. How can she help him deal with grief at such a young age? At nineteen, he's legally an adult now. She can't force him to see a therapist. How can she persuade him to get help?

At least there is no need to worry about Casey's safety any longer. He's already talked to the detectives. He clearly is not in any trouble with the police. Rounding up Scott's friends and bringing them to the precinct is the right thing for him to do. Maybe it's his way of grieving.

Kate starts to set the table, this time adding a place for her ex, Charlie Palmer. By coincidence, Charlie's Los Angeles ad agency job had left him stranded in New York over this holiday weekend. With Charlie's friends three thousand miles away, Casey agreed with Kate's idea to invite him to holiday dinner. Now, with what has happened to Scott, she feels it's probably especially good to have both parents present.

She spills a box of cranberries into a colander. The collision fills the air with a sharp burst of metallic pings. Standing at the sink, she rinses the blood-red berries while trying to rinse her mind of Scott's bloody death. The berries sift through her fingers, allowing her to methodically discard the soft ones, but her grim thoughts are not so easily discarded.

"Ma," Case says, startling her.

"Case, I didn't hear you come in." Kate turns off the water. "For tomorrow," she says, putting the colander aside. "How'd it go with the detectives?"

"Nowhere. It went nowhere." He opens the refrigerator and stands staring blankly into it.

"Casey, please don't hold that open."

He rolls his eyes, shuts the door, and turns to slouch against it. "There's nothing to eat."

"There'll be plenty tomorrow. There's some cheddar. You can make yourself a grilled cheese. The cops, they didn't hassle you about anything, did they?"

He looks puzzled. "Why would they hassle me?"

"Honey, he was selling drugs. You were his friend."

His shoulders drop in exaggerated frustration. "I told you it was grass, Ma, grass. He was murdered. That's what the cops care about. Not who's buying a few lousy joints offa him."

She opens her mouth, but nothing comes out. There is a perverse logic to what he is saying.

"Did any of your friends know anything?" she finally thinks to ask.

He pulls out a kitchen chair and sits down heavily like an old man. "Not really. Cops are asking us for help. Like we should solve the case for them. Shows how much they care." He presses his palms to his eyes. "It's not their friend rotting up there."

Kate reaches across the kitchen table, taking hold of her son's forearms, but he resists her comforting effort, tensing under her touch. She instantly releases him.

"Case, they have to find out who did this. It's their job." But in her heart she knows he is right. No cop is going to shed a tear for the loss of a drug dealer. "I'm sure those detectives already know a lot more than they are saying."

"They don't know zip," Casey responds flatly.

For a few seconds mother and son sit in silence, both staring into the polished surface of the kitchen table as if its glossy blackness holds some magical key to turning back time, to bringing Scott back.

Kate hears herself lamely filling the air with words she thought she'd never use: fingerprints, ballistics, forensic evidence, as if these empty words will guarantee a conviction. "They'll trace the bullet," she tries to assure her son like she knows what she's talking about. She only knows what she's seen on TV dramas, what Hollywood has taught her, but she knows she has to give him something,

"Lot of people are into dealing and, no, mom, I never was."

"I didn't ask, Case." But, truthfully, she did wonder.

His blue eyes bore into her. "You asked without asking," he responds sharply. And he is right. It is what she wanted to know. His tone softens. "I guess if I was you, Mom, I'd want to know, too," he says, more like an adult than the teenager he still really is.

How easily his slightest show of understanding brings her back into his fold. How easy it is for her to trust him again.

"You never played with Scott when you were growing up," she says.

"Nobody did. There wasn't anything wrong with him, he was just a loner." Then, he chuckles. "Him and Mr. Whiskers, that odd looking hairless dog he was always walking. Never played street hockey with any of us, either."

"Did anyone ever ask him to?"

"That's not how it works with kids," he says, like she hasn't been around them for the past nineteen years. "I didn't start hanging out with him till my junior year, and he had his own place by then. Started by me buying a few joints offa him," he tells her like his own early drug use is no big deal now.

It is a big deal to Kate, but she doesn't interrupt. What's done is done.

"…an we got to talking, and it turned out he was a nice guy. He could be real funny, too. That's when he started getting friends. Me, Brad, Bobby, and a couple of others."

"Selling weed gave him a social life?" she concludes sadly. "But how did he find people to buy from him?"

"No problem there." Casey snorts. "That bunch of little kids on the corner were lined up. When we usta hang out on the corner it was fun and games, softball and skateboards, but it's been changing over the last few years. It's a pretty druggie scene now."

Kate's rainbow, the kids she had defended to her complaining neighbors, druggies. Her heart sinks. "Didn't Scott ever worry about getting arrested?" she asks to get off her sensitive subject of the corner kids she liked.

Casey looks at her like she had just asked the world's most stupid question. "Worry? Why would he? Scotto only sold to people he knew."

Oh, Case, grieve for your friend, miss him with all your heart, but for God's sake don't admire him.

But Casey clearly does. "Dealing turned out to be a smart career move for Scotto. He found out he had a good head for business. Honesty was the key to his success. He never stiffed anybody with lame stuff and people knew that. If he thought he'd gotten stuck with inferior inventory, he'd just flush it and take the loss. He was a good guy like that, and everybody knew it."

Kate swallows back her tears. The values of honesty, fairness, respect for others were all there, but it was coming out all wrong. She shakes her head and covers her ears. "You make it sound like he was selling vacuum cleaners. Didn't his parents ever suspect anything? I mean, all that money coming in?"

"He kept a safety deposit box at the bank. It kept filling up so fast he had to keep opening up new boxes. He didn't like deceiving his parents so he finally said, 'Fuck it' and got his own place."

For a few seconds, mother and son sit in silence. Their moment of fragile peace is shattered by the ring of the wall phone above Casey's head.

He grabs the receiver. "Yeah," he answers without emotion.

Then his body stiffens. "Who? Are you sure? Gimme five minutes."

Casey leaves the receiver dangling from its cord as he rushes to the front door.

"Case, what happened?" Kate shouts as she tries to reach for his arm. "Where are you going?"

"Brad found somebody who knows who did it."

"Stop. We've got to call the cops with this."

But he is already out in the hall pounding the elevator button. "Come on, come on, come on."

Running up to him she tries again, to grab his sleeve, but the silky fabric of his baseball jacket slides through her fingers. "If he did it, this guy is dangerous. This is for the police to handle. Case, call the police. Call them now. Don't go, honey."

But he's already in the elevator, shouting back at her. "It's a kid, a fuckin' little kid. If he sees cops, he'll start screaming for a lawyer," he yells as the elevator door slides shut on her. Kate is left in frightening silence again. Her jaw drops in exasperation. He must have reached the lobby by now. Only moments ago, he was safe. Safe. Sitting at her kitchen table. She walks slowly back into her apartment, but her mind is racing.

She wants to call the police, but what would she say? Her son went to meet a friend, who knows somebody, who knows something. Not enough to tell them. So, she doesn't make the call.

An hour later, Casey stands in front of her, his hair disheveled, face red and sweaty, and a long rip of cloth dangling down the front of his baseball jacket.

"We got him, we got the fucker, and we got the evidence to prove it," he tells her with breathless pride.

"What happened? Are you okay? Did you call the police?"

He drops down into a chair. "It was just like Brad said it would be. No cops, we solved the case without them. Scott would have liked that."

Chapter Seven

As he buttons his raincoat, Jack looks out through the precinct's thick glass lobby doors. A nasty night. Damn, he should have worn a sweater under his jacket. His ex-wife always reminded him to do things like that. Paula never missed a weather report. One of his buttons hangs by a thread. "Fuck it," he says to himself, snapping it off and shoving it in his pocket. Now he's gonna have a fucking tailor's bill.

He steps out into the night's cold air. A fine white dust, left over from this morning's brief flurry, covers the window ledges, railings, mailbox, and car hoods. An icy wind off the river whirls little flakes of powdery snow around his feet. He squints his eyes and surveys the muted scene. There are no sharp edges anywhere. The thought he is viewing his own life crosses his mind, and a small shudder racks the emptiness he suddenly feels.

He checks his watch. Twenty after seven. Should have left when he had the chance, but no, he had to stay and finish up the paperwork. Then the kids come, all excited, and babbling over one another. He senses a long night ahead. Support checks, mortgage payments, rent on his sublet, always something with the car, and now this morning Paula hits him with the news that Jenny needs orthodontia. He stuffs a stick of gum in his mouth and rubs his eyes. Yeah, he's gonna miss Thanksgiving with mom, but he can sure use the overtime pay.

A few yards away, two of the youths from this afternoon's bullshit session are talking to one of the uniformed officers. "They were there," one of them loudly insists. It's Palmer, the one who's agitated all the time. And the other one is? Jack flips open his notebook and reads Bobby Ardsley, Casey Palmer and slips it back in his pocket.

He approaches the boys with a friendly, "Casey, Bobby." He shakes their hands. "You got something for us here?" he asks.

Ardsley is seething. "Ah, shit. Shit. They musta got out the backa the building. I was watchin' the front." Shifting his weight from foot to foot, he frantically looks up and down the street as if to see this "they", whoever the fuck they are.

Detective Watts comes out of the precinct building, joining Jack with a look of, Oh-no, not-these-asshole-kids-again.

"Okay, fellas," Jack says. "Wanna tell us what went on?"

"Man, he didn't look like he was goin' anywhere," Ardsley stammers angrily. "He couldn't even move the way we left him. Ah, shit. And they did do it for the weed."

"Who we talkin' bout here?" Jack asks. "Couldn't move" has definitely gotten his attention.

"This kid. There were three of them," Palmer shouts like Jack has a hearing problem. "They killed Scott."

Jack opens his notebook. The conviction he hears in this kid's voice is real. "Gimme some names."

The words shoot out of Palmer's mouth like it is a machine gun. "H.G. did it. H.G. O'Connor and Garth Gaines, and that little punk, Claude Moldorf. The gun belongs to Garth's father. We know where they hid it. We gotta get to it before those motherfuckers get rid of it."

"Where are they?" Jack needs to know.

"I dunno. They were at Claude's," Palmer is quick to say.

"How'd you come by this information?" Randy Watts asks, his tone considerably less friendly than Jack's.

Palmer and Ardsley exchange nervous glances. Then Palmer looks down at the sidewalk and mutters, "We can't talk about that till our lawyer is present."

Ardsley looks as surprised as Jack and Randy.

"My mother thought we might need one," Palmer nervously explains.

Randy is livid. "We don't have time for this lawyer crap. Listen to me. You little fuckers are getting in deeper and deeper."

Jack holds up a consolatory hand. "I know these boys are going to cooperate. Scholfield was their friend." But Jack is equally taken aback. This kid is talking about getting a lawyer when nobody's so much as even inferred they are under suspicion.

When Jack and Randy worked out of the three-0 in Harlem, sure the pimps and drug dealers all had lawyers, the best their dirty money could buy. Up there, hiding behind some slick lawyer meant you had something to hide. Maybe Jack and Randy just found themselves a couple of potential perps.

"What about this gun?" Jack asks, making a grab for something substantial.

Palmer's enthusiasm returns. "We gotta get it now. That's why we're here."

"It's up at Garth's house," Ardsley blurts out, revealing he knows more, too. "In a box on the floor in the back of his father's closet."

Palmer chimes in, "Garth's house is on West End. We can show you the building."

Randy looks like he's been given an adrenalin shot. "You want to take the time to go for a warrant?" he asks Jack.

"Let's just chance it and see what cooperation we get without one," Jack responds. "If there is a gun, by the time we get a warrant, it'll be long gone," Jack concludes. "Let's check it out. Hop in the car, guys. We're goin' for a ride."

Chapter Eight

Jack and Randy exit the apartment building and walk to the car, the rifle wrapped in a white towel, nestled in the crook of Jack's outstretched arms.

Palmer and Ardsley are waiting for him, one leaning against the door, the other sitting on the hood of the department car. Jeez, Jack hates when kids do that.

"You got it. You got it," they shout like it is Christmas morning.

Palmer jumps off the hood. "It's got to be plastered with his prints."

"What makes you so sure this H.G. kid did it?" Randy asks, sliding into the driver's seat.

Ardsley pipes up, "'Cause that little jerk, H.G. said he…" but a sharp look from Palmer cuts him off, leaving a possible confession hanging midair.

Jack places the rifle on the back seat. "Look, guys, Professor Gaines is going to be coming back to the precinct with us," and he indicates the building's marble-columned entrance. "He'll be out in a minute, so I think it best if you two make yourself scarce," he slides in next to Randy, "but next time I see you we're going to talk, really talk." Then he says to Randy, "Can you believe this guy is actually a professor up at Columbia and he's got a kid in this kinda shit?"

Randy starts the motor with an angry roar. "Just another shithead parent who has no clue what his kid is doing."

Jack glares at Palmer. "Look, kid, we all want the same thing here." Both boys nod sheepishly. "We're putting a lot of trust in you two. Counting on you to stay available. Go home, stay by the phone." He knows they aren't

54

going too far from the comforts of home. Harlem kids vanish at the drop of a hat. But Palmer and Ardsley, soft and spoiled, aren't going anywhere. The affluent don't have to run as the system works just fine for them.

As Palmer and Ardsley walk away, a bearded man in a tweed jacket steps out of the building and lights a cigarette. His expression is very grim. He walks briskly to the car, climbs in the back seat, and instructs Jack and Randy. "Make sure the media doesn't get a hold of this."

Jack types, "single shot, 22 caliber, long rifle, Serial # 639821" on the property voucher. He rolls his chair back and swings his feet onto the corner of his desk. "I'm thinking maybe we misjudged these kids. Palmer and his two cronies. There's some heavy involvement here that they haven't been forthcoming about."

"You mighta. I had those fuckin' weasels pegged at the crime scene. Day one."

"I'll tell you one thing, the ole' professor is going to have to shell out a few bucks for his mutt son's lawyer."

Randy is grinning broadly now. "Streets may be cleaner down here, but a mutt is a mutt, no matter what rock he lives under."

"I think it's about time we had a more formal one-on-one with these guys. Let's start with Palmer," Jack says. Randy nods in agreement.

On a grey Thanksgiving morning, Kate wakes up to the sharp ring of her bedside phone.

She answers it with a sleepy, "Hello?"

"Detective Kuchinsky. Sorry to bother you so early in the day. Is this Casey's mom?" His speech is New Yorkese without the polish, still the rough edge is intriguingly gentle.

"Yes, Kate Palmer," she says, her voice cracking nervously. "Did you find the killer?"

"No, not yet," he informs her, "but your son's been very helpful, and we'd appreciate if he'd come down to the precinct to answer a few more questions."

"Of course. Casey's still asleep. I'll get him up and he'll be there in a half an hour."

She pauses, then adds, "Detective Kuchinsky, there's something I wanted to ask you."

"Talk to me," he says, like he's right there in bed next to her.

"Well." She pauses again. "I'm worried for Casey's safety. These people that Scott…um…well, associated with…Casey doesn't know any of them. But they might not know that, and if word gets out that he is talking to the police…"

Jack interrupts, "I can understand your concern, but if your son never met these people and wasn't a witness to the actual crime, then nobody's going to be looking for him," he tells her in his best nothing-to-worry-about tone.

This time it is Kate who leads Casey up the precinct steps and sweeps through the anteroom into the squad room.

On this special family holiday there are only two detectives on duty. One sits, eyes closed, finger locked peacefully across his chest like a benign Buddha. The other, dressed like it was his day off, wears a white, Irish fisherman's sweater and jeans. He's buried in the sports section of today's paper. Perched on the corner of his desk, a small boy of four or five is repeatedly kicking the side of the metal desk with a dull thump-thump, thump-thump. "When are we going to grandma's?" he asks the detective repeatedly.

"We're here to see Detective Kuchinsky," Kate announces, sweeping through the gate into the squad room, its clanging causing the sleeping detective to open his eyes.

Without moving anything but his lips he informs her, "He's not here right now. You have to wait on the other side of the gate, ma'am. This is a restricted area."

"He's expecting us."

"Ma'am, Detective Kuchinsky and his partner are out in the field right now," the one with the small boy says. "You have to wait on the other side of the gate till they get back."

"We're helping them find the murderer," Casey shouts abruptly.

The detective with the little boy looks up from his paper again. "What case is this?" he asks matter-of-factly.

What case is this? My God it's the case. It's the nightmare that has torn the rug out from under Kate's comfortable life.

"Scott Scholfield, the boy who was killed," she informs him, inferring he is negligent for not already knowing about the case. "My son might have information that could help find the murderer."

"Ma'am, I told you, they're out in the field," the detective tells her again, like he didn't hear a word she said. "You have to wait on the other side of the gate till they get back."

"Didn't you hear what I said?" Kate startles herself by shouting, but her outburst is only acknowledged by blank stares. "I'm telling you my son might have information that could lead to the killer, and all you care about is what part of the room we wait in. I don't believe this."

Why aren't they eager to hear any information Casey might have about these kids? Why aren't the detectives rushing out the door, guns in hand, jumping into a police car? It's their job to do that, isn't that what she has been assuring Casey of? "If this area is so damn restricted, what's that little kid doing here?" she asks indignantly.

"Lady, I don't make the rules. They could be bringing suspects through here at any time. The area has to be kept clear. It's for your own safety," he responds in an equally indignant tone.

Kate retreats to the anteroom section, sitting beside Casey on a wooden bench. It's been ten very long minutes since they were banished to that no man's land where mother and son wait in silence, Casey looking like he will explode if Kate so much as touches him.

"I can't believe we're being treated like this," Kate finally says to her inattentive son. But Casey's attention is fixed on the door and the sudden sound of multiple footsteps hastening up the outside staircase.

Suddenly the tiny anteroom area is bursting with people. Two burly detectives in trench coats usher in a disheveled Claude with a noticeable black eye, along with his parents. Kate doesn't acknowledge them nor do the Moldorfs acknowledge her, but as Kuchinsky stands holding the gate open for the Moldorf family, he makes eye contact with Kate.

The penetration of his iridescent blue eyes triggers a delicious swirl in the pit of her stomach, holding her hostage for one breathless moment, and she knows instantly that he is the voice that only a short while ago was in bed with her.

He reaches out to shake Kate's hand with a, "Mrs. Palmer, I presume? I'm Detective Kuchinsky, and this is my partner Detective Watts."

But Detective Watts is already leading the Moldorfs into a side room telling them, "Wait here. We'll be with you shortly."

"Follow me," Jack tells Kate and Casey, ushering them over to his desk and pulling up two more chairs. He holds up his hand, prohibiting Kate from saying anything but allowing her to notice there is no wedding band on it, and tells her, "We'll be right with you. Hang on." Then he turns to greet Casey with a good-buddy pat on the shoulder. "Glad to see ya, guy. Wait here with your mom. We won't be long."

He motions to the tall black detective. "Be right with you, Randy." Then to Kate, with a smile he says, "Be back in a few minutes."

Kate sits in silence. She can't hear anything the Moldorfs are saying in the next room, but when the door opens, she does hear Claude request to be given permission to call his lawyer.

Jack confers with Randy in hushed tones for a second, then returns to Kate and Casey. "My partner will be right with us, then we can get started." He turns to Casey, wrapping his arm around Casey's shoulders and turning him away from his mother. "Listen, bro. Why don't you have your mom take a seat in the anteroom and read the paper while you and I and my partner have a talk in the other room?"

"I want my mother there, too."

Kate announces that she fully intends to be present when her son is interrogated.

Jack doesn't take his eyes off Casey. With his arm still draped around the Palmer kid's shoulders, Jack stage whispers, "You sure you want your mother to hear what's been going on with you and your buddies?"

"Yes, I want her there," Casey curtly responds, though his voice does crack a bit.

Jack's arm remains wrapped around Casey's shoulders, but his eyes dart over to Kate. Squinting just enough to intensify his warning, he asks her the same question. "You sure you want to hear what your son has been into? This involves a lot of dirty stuff."

"I want to be there," she tells him emphatically.

Jack turns on his heels and with his hand, motions Kate and Casey to follow him into another small, side room where one long table and a cluster of metal chairs occupy most of the space. The shabbiness of the setting is only intensified in the harshness of the fluorescent lighting. Kate notices green walls that haven't seen a paint job in decades, a floor that looks like it's never known a mop, a few ashtrays filled with cigarette butts, and finally, the iron bars on the one window. It's the kind of room in which criminals sign their confessions.

This is a room that Kate and her son were never meant to be in. The tall black detective joins them as they all take their seats. "My partner, Detective Watts," Jack says again. Kate sits, arms folded across her chest, and Jack takes note. She is licking her lips too much. Casey, on the other hand, looks like he is carved out of stone.

Jack takes his time removing his jacket and neatly folding it over one of the chairs, the gun handle now protruding angrily from the back of his belt. As Jack sits down, his partner begins to pace back and forth behind Casey's chair.

In the small room, Detective Watts seems larger than life. Suddenly, he stops abruptly behind Casey, bending down close and spitting his words into the side of Casey's face. "Okay, Palmer, it's time you start levelin' with us."

Kate presses her lips together and doesn't say a word. She is well aware that these two bullies are in charge.

But the stone cast over Casey's face begins to crack. He shifts in his seat, his words coming out unnaturally measured. "I came here to help you find H.G."

Detective Watts straightens all the way up. Towering above Casey, his voice blasts down on the boy's captive ear. "You call the bullshit you've been handing us helping? You've been fuckin' around with this case since day one." Then with an expression of superiority, he gloats, "We know you got the weed." Kate looks stunned, Casey looks like he is about to cry.

Kuchinsky looks at Kate, his voice disarmingly calm. "Your son and his buddies are holding drugs worth a minimum of ten thousand dollars, street value, and that's probably a conservative estimate."

"I can't talk about anything until my lawyer is present," Casey responds in a steady voice, his face emotionless again, but Jack notices there is a minute twitch at the corner of his mouth.

Watts drops his voice to an icy whisper. "Remember, kid, you're in my house now."

Kate stands up resting her hands on her son's shoulders. "Is Casey under arrest?" she asks in a voice too calm to be believed.

"No," is Jack's quick response. "We just have a few questions for him."

"Then we're leaving," Kate says, urging her son to stand up with her hands.

Moments later, Kate and Casey are down at the street door, and it is Kate who is now furious. "You said you told me everything. But obviously you did not. All you said was that there was a fight, and when you left, H.G. was knocked out. Those detectives clearly found out a lot more from Claude."

Casey interrupts her, "I'll tell you everything, but not till we're outside. There might be microphones in here."

Ten minutes later they sit on opposite ends of the couch in the safety of Kate's apartment and Casey begins. "Ma, I did tell you it all got violent real fast, and we thought it was okay to leave them there because H.G. looked like he was unconscious. We only took the weed to protect the evidence. They would have flushed it for sure."

"You didn't tell me how you got to Claude's in the first place. Tell me from the beginning. Everything."

"Okay, okay. Brad heard from his little brother that H.G. killed Scott, and that Garth knew where H.G. was."

"Why didn't you call the police?"

"'Cause it was up to us to bring him in. We had to do that for Scott."

"Oh, Casey, no. It wasn't up to you, but what's done is done. Now tell me the rest of it, now."

"Brad's brother goes to Collegiate with Garth. He's in the same class, and Garth was bragging about how he knew a dealer who got shot in the head while he was watching TV. Brad's brother was waiting to tell him when he came home. That's when Brad called me."

"Casey, by now I'm sure half the neighborhood knows what happened to Scott."

"You don't get it, Ma. Garth was saying that stuff two days ago."

Her lips part, but only a silent "Oh my God," comes out.

"First, Brad's brother thought it was a joke, ya know, like Garth was making it up to look important. Brad's brother just forgot about it until today when he heard about what happened to Scott. When Brad got home after talking to the detectives, his brother told him about Garth. That's when Brad called me."

"How do you know H.G. and Garth were involved?"

With the shadow of a smile Casey answers, "'Cause we got it out of Garth."

"How do you know Garth wasn't just making that up?"

"Because we hung the little creep over the wall by his ankles, that's why." His lips look like he is straining to hold back the grin that is flickering in his eyes. "Man, he told us everything. It just poured out of him."

"You did what? What wall?"

"The park wall, down on Riverside Drive."

"That's a three-story drop down to the park. You could have killed him."

Casey calmly assures her, "We were all holding him real tight. Me, Bobby, and Brad. We weren't going to drop him, but he didn't know that. And I know he was telling the truth 'cause the little punk was so scared he peed all over himself, upside down. Then we made him take us to where he said H.G. was. He was at Claude's apartment."

Kate's heart sinks, expecting she has yet to hear the worst.

Casey paces back and forth, talking almost too fast to be understood. "We pulled him back up and made him take us there."

"Casey, slow down, I can't keep up with you. I need to know everything.

Just how it all happened."

"All right, all right." He sits down and gets right up again. "How it started, how it started. First, we went out looking for Garth and we found him right away, sitting on a stoop down the block all by himself. He was rotating the wheels on his skateboard, so we went up to him all friendly-like and invited him to go down to the park and smoke a joint with us. The little jerk was so flattered, being accepted by the big boys, ya know. When we got down on the Drive, Brad suddenly pushes Garth up against the park wall, and we confronted him with what Brad's brother had said. At first, he actually tried to tell us Brad's brother was lying. Garth got scared but he didn't get hurt. Well," he looks away, "at least not then."

"Not then." A lawsuit, a police record for assault, a jail sentence. Kate's mind is racing. "What did you do to him?"

"I'm trying to tell you that, damn it." He makes a mock attempt at pulling his hair. "Next thing I know we got him hanging upside down. Cops could never have done that to make him talk," he says with a touch of unabashed pride in his voice.

The smugness of her son's tone sends a chill through Kate. "What else did you do to him?" she reluctantly demands to know.

"We made Garth take us to where H.G. was, up at Claude's. The plan was to bring them all down to the precinct and hand them over to the detectives."

"Casey, that's what the cops are supposed to do."

He shakes his head vehemently. "You don't understand, Mom. Before all this happened, I had a funny feeling about H.G. There was just something too spacy about that kid. Scott had made him his gofer, his runner. H.G. made deliveries for him, that sort of thing, and Scott paid him in free joints. I really thought Scott should dump him and I told Scott that. Then I thought about it and oh my God, I'm such a jerk. I actually started to feel sorry for the little creep. It seemed like all he had going for him was that gofer job, and he was so proud of having the keys to Scott's place. So, I turned around and told Scott to just forget what I said." His finger pokes angrily at his chest. "Me, it was me who told Scott to keep that fucker around, Mom. If it wasn't for me, Scott would still be…"

"No, Case, no. How could you know? It's not your fault."

"You want to hear what happened or not?" he snaps, like her compassion was an attack, and he continues. "So then Garth told us H.G. was up at Claude's."

"Oh my God."

"Ma, there were so many of them in on this, that whole crew knew what was going to happen to Scott. Outside Claude's door we kept our backs to the wall when Garth rang the bell, so when Claude opened the door, we all rushed in." He holds his head. "It all got crazy so damn fast. I'll never forget the TV was on, and H.G. was lying on the couch watching a closeup of Cheryl Ladd, pointing a gun straight at us. H.G.'s eyes were all glazed over, and he was smoking one of Scott's joints. Then the fucker goes and offers us some of the joints. Can you believe that? He lay there and bragged about how he killed Scott."

"How do you know the joints were from Scott?"

"Because Scott stored the weed in these mason jars, and they were scattered all over the place. Oh, shit. The little fucks had been getting off on Scott's weed while his body was back in the apartment rotting away."

"Where were Claude's parents when all this was happening?"

"They weren't home, but it wouldn't have mattered if they were. We were taking H.G. to the cops no matter what. It just got all crazy so fast. Bobby punched Claude, and I smacked Garth so hard there was blood dripping from his mouth, and he was standing there holding a couple of teeth in his hand. Then I saw Brad pick up Claude's baseball bat and I yell no. But he starts hitting H.G. with it anyway."

"Oh, please tell me...not hitting his head."

"I don't know where he hit...we scooped up the weed and put the jars in a suitcase that was there, and we figured we better get the evidence to the cops before they made it disappear. H.G. was out like a light, and the other two were just whimpering like babies. I remember a chair got broken. That's when Brad took the suitcase to stash it in a safe place till we could get it to the cops."

"Casey, you beat up people, took evidence in a murder case. This is really bad stuff."

Chapter Nine

Kate watches as her ex, Charlie Palmer, stands up to carve the turkey. He took the seat at the head of the table like the last fifteen years never happened. That is Kate's seat now. But this holiday is tense enough with Scott's death hovering over it and an injured H.G. still missing. Is he critical? Dying somewhere? Dead? When Charlie holds up his empty glass and says, "Refill time, Katie," she takes the glass without saying a word. Same old Charlie.

When she returns with the refill Charlie says, "When is this Brent kid getting here with the evidence?"

"His name is Brad and he's really a good guy," Casey tells his father.

"He is a good guy," Kate concurs.

"Where the hell is he then?" Charlie asks, plopping a heaping spoonful of chestnut stuffing onto Casey's plate.

"Dad, I can't eat all of that." Casey protests using the palm of his hand to try to block the gluttonous portion from his plate. "I'm really not hungry."

Kate agrees. "Neither am I. Too much happening."

"Eat it. It's good for you. It'll put hair on your chest," Charlie says with a smile as Kate shakes her head with a no-you-don't have-to-eat-it look to Casey.

For a moment Kate feels as though she has come full cycle—the same family unit sharing a holiday dinner at the same old oak table, eating off the same blue China plates, with Charlie Palmer back in the driver's seat, thinking he's running the show again.

Charlie passes the platter of sliced white meat to Casey. "White meat for the white boy," he says, making both Casey and Kate wince.

"I don't know how you could let this Bran … Brad kid run off with the drugs. And where were you, Katie, when all this was happening?"

"Mom was home, Dad. I came back here right away. We had to make sure they didn't flush the evidence."

Kate looks at her son, no longer a child but a grown, young man. Charlie might sound the same, but with his thinning, grey hair and his expanded waistline, he more resembles the father-in-law she once had those fifteen years ago. It's not the same Palmer family it once was. Kate is the one in charge now, and Casey has become a young adult. As Charlie takes a big gulp of his Bloody Mary, she says, "Take it easy, Charlie. Casey's got a big night ahead of him."

"I'll say he does, and Katie, I really think I should be at this lawyer meeting."

"Charlie, we agreed. Your plane leaves at ten. Your presence would only complicate things more. You already called the lawyer to voice your concerns." Charlie's bombastic approach to problem solving, his way or the highway, is the last thing this situation, fraught with legal potholes, needs now.

"I can easily switch to a later red-eye back to L.A. I think a second opinion is called for here," and he asks Casey, "What's holding up your two buddies? If there are money problems with either of the two for this lawyer, Mel Rubinstein, I'll cover it." Charlie takes a swig of the Vodka and tonic he's switched to.

"Oh, Dad, that's great. That's really above and beyond." Casey beams appreciatively. "They'll be here soon. They're having Thanksgiving dinner at home, too."

"These kids have families?" Charlie asks, pouring more gravy on his turkey.

Kate closes her eyes for a second then opens them to inform Charlie sternly, "Yes, they do have families, and they are all friends of mine." Kate knows she has to keep focused on Charlie, especially when he is drinking. She leans forward and forces a small smile. "So, Charlie, how's your golf game these days?"

Kate serves the pumpkin pie when the boys arrive. Charlie has switched to Vodka shots. The introductions make it obvious that Bobby's habit of saying "yes, sir" and "no, sir" is making a favorable impression on Charlie. Brad, however, is a different story.

Brad isn't displaying his similar good manners. He isn't displaying much of anything. After Charlie greeted Bobby with a warm handshake, and Brad with a wilted, "How ya doin', kid," Brad withdrew to a corner chair where he sits quietly picking at the piece of pie Kate handed him.

Twirling the ice cubes in his vodka shot glass with one finger, his eyes probe Brad from head to toe. "So, you're the kid who walked off with the evidence. Must make you feel pretty important. Did you bring it with you for the meeting?" Charlie asks, seeing full well that Brad did not.

Without making eye contact Brad tells him, "It's stashed in a safe place for now." Brad then slowly puts down his fork and looks up directly at Charlie. "Yes, sir, Mr. Palmer. I got it alright, and nobody knows where I stashed it."

Charlie's drink hand shoots out, the ice cubes sloshing some of the Vodka onto the rug. "Listen to me, you little punk. If you know what's good for you, you better tell me where you're hiding those drugs. There better not be one cent of the money you found with the pot missing."

Kate is on her feet now. "Charlie. We need to be unified on this," she tells him. "Brad is only doing what the boys all agreed to." How many more of her worst dreams are going to come true, tonight?

Casey and Bobby mutter, "Ah, shit, ah, shit." But Brad is cool as a cucumber. He sets his plate down on the end table, settles back in his chair, arms spread out across its back, feet stretched out in front of him like a triumphant "T" and smiles at Charlie. It is not a warm smile. "Where are the drugs? Where are the drugs?" Brad's smile widens. "Join the club," and his hand shoots out to wave an imaginary glass at Charlie. "Where the weed is stashed is for me alone to know." He looks at Casey and Bobby. "We all agreed to that," he concludes amicably.

Charlie is on his feet now, his face is blotchy-red, and his eyes are narrow slits of rage. "You little bastard, you're not taking my son up the river with you. I got news for you, Brian or whatever your name is. Me. I'm the one who's picking up the tab for the lawyer, and I'm gonna instruct him not to represent you. Casey and Bobby will be safe, but you, buster, will be sent away to where you people belong."

Casey throws his head back and groans, Bobby sinks further into his seat, and Kate stands in the middle of it all, wondering how much more can go wrong.

Brad lets her know. He jumps to his feet, grabs his jacket, and charges out of the room, yelling back, "I don't need your faggot lawyer."

"What the fuck are you trying to do, Charlie?"

Did she really just say fuck to Charlie? Charlie's parted lips confirm her metamorphosis. With his sudden silence, Charlie relinquishes any attempt at control, and Kate takes the ball and runs with it. "These boys are not going to be divided by you or anybody. If I have to pay for the damn lawyer, I will, and it will be for all three of them." She hurries out after Brad, leaving a shouting match between Casey and his father behind her.

When she catches up with Brad at the elevator, she grabs his jacket sleeve and pleads, "Brad, don't leave like this. He was wrong to talk to you like that. You saw how much booze he was throwing down."

He shrugs his sleeve out of her hand, his voice now cracking with emotion. "My mother told me to stay out of it, to stay on my side of Broadway, the project side, and I said I had to stick by my friends. But I see now she was right. I don't need his fuckin' white lawyer money. He needs me 'cause I got the weed, and I put it where nobody knows but me."

With that, the elevator door closes, leaving Kate all alone in a deadly silence.

Chapter Ten

In the lawyer's apartment upstairs from Kate's, the chairs have been arranged in a circle. Jack is seated between his partner and the one empty seat. Ardsley is here, but noticeably, there is no Burke kid. Palmer has dragged his mother along again, but there are no other parents present. No fathers. Jack is not surprised.

Seated across from Jack, Kate Palmer is poised in a rocker, motionless and rigid, as though she were posing for a portrait. Her hands grip the chair's armrest so tightly each finger stands out, starkly white against the dark, polished wood. Her long slim fingers end in ten perfect, white tipped pink ovals. Four silver rings on the right hand. None, he is quick to notice, on the left. The fingers hold him mesmerized. He feels them encircling him, enveloping him, wrapping their soft warmth around his hardness, and he has no choice but to swell within their feathery embrace.

He shifts in his seat, crossing his legs and raising his eyes to meet hers, and the Palmer woman's eyes do meet his, latching on like two powder blue fishhooks. She is expressionless, her body stiller than death. She seems to be staring straight through him, but he notices that their eye contact triggers a slight stirring in her.

How long has it been for him? Ten days? Two weeks, since he'd brought that new waitress from the West End Bar back to his apartment? He tries to remember her name, but it escapes him. Too many Bloody Mary's before he did her. No matter, his purpose had been relief rather than passion. His focus is now on the Palmer woman and it appears, to Jack, hers is on him. Ever so slightly those pretty, pink fingertips begin to caress the armrests of her chair. Circling and stroking, they slowly trace minute rings on the dark wood. The long, thin fingers reach slightly down and curl up the armrests, slowly, with the escalating rhythm of a seductive dancer. And all the while her eyes remain locked onto his. For one breathless moment the spectacle holds him a willing captive, until Randy leans over and whispers, "I see the two little weasels got all prettied up for the occasion."

Randy is right. Palmer and Ardsley sit side by side, all decked out in their pansy suits and ties. Jack also thinks that they sit motionless like proper little monkeys. See no evil, hear no evil, but what happened to speak no evil? Burke is looking more and more like a possible perp.

The lawyer looks at his watch for the umpteenth time and says, "We'll give him a few more minutes," and with that, as if he'd cued it, the doorbell rings. A moment later the missing Burke kid waltzes in. Like his buddies, he too is all dolled up in his Sunday best topped off with a smug grin. As he is ushered in, the Palmer woman's body noticeably relaxes.

"Right here, Brad," the lawyer says, indicating the only empty seat to the kid Jack knows as Eddie Burke. "We're all present now so let's get started. You all know each other, and the gentleman next to me is District Attorney Herb Ruben. This is his case."

Jack leans forward, a pleasant smile on his lips and smoldering anger in his eyes. "Not exactly. Before we go on, I'd like to be clear on this young man's name. We know him as Eddie Burke."

The Burke kid looks at the lawyer who nods a go-ahead and then sheepishly confesses, "My name's Brad Hillrich."

Jack sits back in his chair making no attempt to conceal his expression of I knew it, but he is kicking himself. He should know better than to believe anything that comes out of a druggie's mouth.

"Okay, Herb, you want to take it from here?" the lawyer asks the D.A., as though he were handing over the baton at a high school assembly.

Unlike the boys, the D.A. has come dressed casually, wearing a dark green jogging suit and running shoes. He pinches his horn-rimmed glasses at the bridge of his nose and hikes them up a notch, signaling he's ready for business. But the low-slung canvas chair he has chosen to sit in is not cooperating.

It has gobbled up his slight frame so that his legs protrude at odd angles, and his arms flail in a futile search for non-existent armrests. He makes an inept attempt to sit up straighter, but the constraints of the chair refuse to allow him even that micron of dignity. He sinks back down, addressing Palmer, Ardsley, and Hillrich from the depths of his confinement. "I want you people to know, and I'm saying this with your lawyer, Mel, present, as long as you tell us everything and are totally honest with us, the D.A.'s office will not move to prosecute any of you in connection with the missing drugs and money."

Jack studies the woman and the three boys for even a glimmer of incrimination, but they all sit frozen like four fucking statues. Jack had to pass up mom's dinner, pass up her special, one-and-only, lemon meringue pie, for a trip to Mount Rushmore?

But when Herb adds, "That doesn't mean that if any of you, or all of you, are in some way connected with the actual homicide, we won't prosecute on that charge."

The boys react, shuffling their feet and squirming in their seats. The kid's mother, however, remains stone-cold still. She doesn't even appear to be breathing.

"Okay, Herb." The lawyer smiles in that smarmy way they all do. "I think everyone understands." He looks at his clients, one, two, three. "Now that we can all feel free to discuss the matter openly, who wants to start?"

Now, the little punks have no trouble admitting they ripped off the dope. Their rationale for their actions is some bullshit about protecting the evidence. Truth, the whole truth, and nothing but the truth? Not likely from the mouths of these babes.

There are no major surprises in their story. Their version, self-serving as it may be, does pretty much parallel the one Jack got from the Gaines and Moldorf kids.

But there is one entertaining anecdote. The three chose to conduct their interrogation of Gaines by dangling him by his ankles, over a thirty-foot park wall. Nice touch, Jack thinks. He can't help but smile. Randy is on the edge of his seat, practically salivating. If Randy and Jack ever tried to pull a stunt like that, they would not only be fired, but arrested, and the fucking mutt would turn around and sue them for every cent they had. Jack would lose his car, his house, his bank account, and his reputation. He's heard the horror stories.

But these kids pulled it off. With big grins on their faces, they can brag about it now that their shyster lawyer has gotten them an immunity deal. They pulled off the sort of shit that would bury Jack in a New York minute, and they're getting away with it. It just reaffirms what Jack has known for a long time. The scales of justice have more than tipped in favor of the mutts. They've fuckin' fallen over.

Randy doesn't say boo until Palmer finishes his narrative of the Gaines incident.

He then aims his finger at Palmer. "Now I want to tell you something, kid," he seethes. "You know you guys really screwed up this case?"

Hillrich has the nerve to mumble, "We solved the case for you."

Jack has reached his limit, too. "You thought you'd be big shots and go out and play detective. You tried to do our job and look at the mess you made. Assault. Tampering with evidence. Breaking into the Moldorfs' apartment."

The lawyer holds up his hand. "Let's keep this civil now. The boys are here because they want to help."

Randy sits back and unbuttons his vest. "They musta gone to the Eliot Ness School of Crime Detection." He smirks.

Herb joins in the recriminations with an angry, "You screwed things up so bad, these kids have a good chance of getting off."

That struck a nerve. All three, and the woman as well, look like they are in instant shock.

"What about the confession?" The Hillrich kid asks with pathetically feeble indignation.

"And his fingerprints on the gun," Palmer chimes in. "Haven't you checked that out?" he asks, as if Jack and Randy are so incompetent that it's something they would have overlooked.

Herb answers the first question curtly. "Forget it. It was taken under duress. The confession may not even be admissible. And you, gentleman, have a big surprise coming if you think they're going to find prints on a gun that's been handled by so many people. A hundred people might have handled it since the shooter pulled that trigger, and even if, by some miracle, no one else touched it, the original prints would have evaporated by now."

Jack has been watching the woman, who is not the kind he'd expect to find mixed up in a dirty drug mess like this. She looks too young to have a kid that old. She has a nice pair of tits though, on the small side, but they really stand out. This makes a guy sit up and take notice. It goes with the cute, little ass he'd noticed when she'd first showed up at the precinct. But what he likes best is that wholesome, girl-next-door look she's got. She could be a model or an actress. It's too bad if she is, though. Jack finds those snotty bitches hard to stomach.

"Evaporated," the woman pipes up, her baby-blues wide open now that the real-life limitations of detective work have reared their ugly head.

"Prints are only oil," Jack explains with deliberate placidity, smiling as he might at his daughter's naiveté. "Gone in a matter of hours, days at best." He smiles again. "Not like it is in the movies."

"The gun was picked up last night. It was fired last Friday. You figure it out, lady," Randy enlightens, with a raw edge to his words. Jack has worked alongside Randy long enough to know that he, too, is at the end of his rope with these punks' escapades.

The revelation about the confession and the prints appears to have hit Palmer the hardest. His dismay looks real. Could the punk have a touch of conscience in him after all? Clearly life's dealt him a no-show father. Maybe, Jack thinks, he should cut the kid a little slack. Cut the woman a little slack, too. A woman can't handle a boy alone. It's different with a girl. Look what a good job his wife Paula does with Jenny. She keeps on top of every little thing. God knows she phones Jack with enough complaints. But a boy needs a father present to keep him in line.

"All this bullshit has stopped our investigation dead in its tracks," Randy smolders, dumping a shitload of guilt right where it belongs. "We came for two things, the drugs and the money. Let's do it."

All eyes are on Brad now. But Brad is tight lipped. Herb holds up his hand.

"It was Mel's' intent to get this immunity thing set up before anything was said or done, and I had no problem with that. His concern for his clients is certainly understandable."

Jeez, Jack thinks, what a sniveling ass-kisser Herb turned out to be. Lawyers, they're all the same, no matter what side they're on. But then Herb stops brown-nosing. He sounds about as serious as his tinny voice will permit, and he lays another dose of reality on the three clients.

"You three young men have to understand that there is no way this case can be presented with evidence hanging mid-air." He leans so far forward his chin looks like it might graze his knees. "That would be solid gold to the defense."

"Are we going to wrap this up tonight or what?" Randy repeats in his inimitable way of cutting through the crap.

"Since yesterday," the lawyer reveals, "Herb and I have been communicating by phone, and the arrangements for that exchange have been agreed to."

With the clearing of his throat, Hillrich commands everybody's attention. He stretches his long legs out in front of him and prefaces his statement with a smile. It is the smile of someone who knows they have you by the balls. "I could probably have it here in an hour. I'll bring it to Casey's house."

"Good. Then you'll meet the detectives at the Palmer apartment upstairs for the exchange," the lawyer says, taking the liberty to speak for all present. The lawyer looks at his watch like he is pinpoint, timing a bombing mission. "Let's make it in exactly sixty minutes. Herb doesn't need to be there for this one. Jack and Randy will accept the evidence."

An hour. And yet another meeting. All to accommodate the schedule of this Hillrich weasel. Jack is livid.

Herb doesn't blink an eye. There's not even the trace of a slap on the wrist for Hillrich. Jack has testified for Herb before. He never considered the guy attorney general material, but on this Mickey Mouse case, Jack's opinion of Herbert Ruben has sunk to a new low.

This is one time Jack doesn't care if his true feelings are revealed. "Let me get this straight," he says to Hillrich. "Am I to understand that you people got us up here and you didn't bring the weed along?" Beside him, Randy is muttering obscenities under his breath.

Herb stands up. "I think you detectives can handle it from here," he says pleasantly, both ignoring Jack's frustration and adding to it.

Chapter Eleven

Seconds after she hears the bell ring, the brawny figures of the two detectives fill Kate's doorway. Kuchinsky, his face impassive except for his gum chewing jaw, holds out an empty coffee container. "Somewhere I can dump this?" He looks very tired.

"Sure, give it to me." Kate takes the cup from his hand and invites him and his partner in. "Come on in, everybody's here." For the first time since this nightmare started, she hears relief in her voice. The evidence is now safely stashed in her apartment.

As she ushers the men into her living room, Kuchinsky touches her arm, his body briefly brushing against hers. "We're all on the same side," he whispers as though they were alone together.

She turns to him and smiles. "I know that," she says and for one small moment lets her eyes tell him that she would consent to being alone with him. But as they enter her living room they are anything but alone.

Young bodies fill every seat and overflow onto the floor. Sprawling, sitting cross-legged and stretched out, they cover every square inch of seating and carpeting, making Kate's apartment more resemble a railway station's waiting room than a comfortable home.

Kuchinsky surveys the youthful assemblage. He rolls his eyes and asks the mother, "What did you do, sell tickets?"

"They're all friends of Casey's, and they liked Scott a lot. They want to see the evidence that's going to nail that little bastard. Mel said it would be okay since there's not going to be any discussion of the case. It is okay with you, I hope?" she asks Jack, making it clear Watts' opinion is of no interest to her.

"Everybody needs their pound of flesh, huh." Kuchinsky quips with a shrug. "No problem as long as they don't interfere with our business."

"It's your house, lady," Watts snaps even though he wasn't asked. "Let's get this shit wrapped up."

The crowded living room is an eerily silent and still tableau. It's an assembly of teenagers without movement, without talking or laughing or horsing around. One girl has brought her dog along, a large black mongrel. Even the dog sits still and mute. Though Kate knows that in a matter of minutes, the thorny problem of the missing evidence will be resolved, the unnatural passivity of this scene brings back her edginess.

Like a king holding court, Mel, the lawyer, is the center of attention. He is seated in a big wicker, sedan chair with his disciples, Casey, Brad, and Bobby, huddled at his feet. Mel's domination of the scene is challenged only by the large brown suitcase planted firmly between his feet. Under its handle the gold initials C.B.M. proclaim for all the world to see, that this piece of luggage did indeed belong to co-conspirator, Claude Bennett Moldorf.

Brad had delivered the crucial evidence only minutes before the detectives' arrival, and with it, a large wad of bills minus three hundred dollars. Brad explained the missing money by revealing his hiding place for the suitcase. It seems Brad paid for room number 2223 at the Waldorf Astoria, where the valuable suitcase and Brad both spent the night. Brad on the satin covered king size bed, the suitcase under the bed, paid for with a three-hundred-dollar deduction from the roll of cash that H.G., Claude, and Garth stole from Scott along with the pot. Brad grinned ear to ear as he described his chosen hiding place as his top-of-the-line safe deposit box.

When Kate heard that, she was thankful she didn't know sooner. She would have spent a sleepless night worrying some maid might be thorough enough to clean under the bed. In spite of the craziness of it all, she couldn't help but smile. Brad Hillrich does have style.

Seeing the evidence safe in her living room, safe in the possession of a lawyer, her lawyer, Kate has to admit the boys have managed to pull off what the detectives could not. She lets herself beam openly. Now, Kuchinsky and even Watts will have to appreciate what the boys did to make this case.

77

But when the detectives arrived, they didn't show even a glimmer of gratitude on their faces. They're just two weary-looking men who waved off her offer to take their coats with an apathetic, "This won't take long."

Mel picks up the suitcase and roll of money and hands it to the detectives. Without comment, they plunk it all down on Kate's coffee table and the lid is quickly popped open. In front of a transfixed audience, its contents are carefully inventoried, with Watts writing down each item as Kuchinsky takes it out. In all, there are eight mason jars, each stuffed with a plastic bag full of greenish-brown leaves. Kuchinsky keeps calling each item "alleged" marijuana. What did he think he was emptying, a bag of groceries?

The last item is a burlap-wrapped brick. Kuchinsky opens it and sets the brown brick on the table pronouncing it to be "alleged" hash. Watts signs the list, tears it out of his note pad, and hands it to Mel. "Your receipt. Look it over and give me a receipt for the receipt." Kate feels like she is watching The Three Stooges, Moe, Larry, and Curly.

Kate looks down at the prized stash and only sees a collection of garbage. There are no sparkling diamonds, no glittering gold or silver, not even a watch or a wallet. The street value of this illegal cache may be indisputable, but actually seeing the jars of dead leaves and a nasty brown brick is hard for Kate to fathom she is viewing anything more than trash.

But the reality that a young boy lost his life for this trash, a family is to forever grieve, and her son's memory irrevocably stained with the horror of what he saw through Scott's window, overwhelms Kate.

Kate's lips part but no words come out. The pile of ugly rubbish is too much for her and she turns away to wipe her eyes. She covers her mouth with her fingertips and lets a silent scream echo within her.

Chapter Twelve

At five minutes to four in the afternoon, Jack finishes up the last of the day's paperwork. Suddenly, the squad room's tiny anteroom is bursting with an agitated Palmer and his two cronies again. They tell the closest detective they need to see Kuchinsky right away. Jack stands up and waves them over to his desk. "You boys got something for me?" he asks cordially, but he sees more overtime ahead. These kids are becoming a real pain in the butt. Nevertheless, Jack has to follow up on any and every lead in a homicide case.

"Yeah, yeah, we do." "You bet," they say with excited enthusiasm.

"We think we know where H.G. is hiding," Palmer announces.

"We didn't think of it before. You gotta go there right away before he gets away again," the Brad kid demands like he is Jack's supervisor now.

"Go where?" Jack asks, throwing Randy an exasperated glance.

"The water tower," Ardsley blurts out. "The one on top of my building was his favorite."

"Yeah, yeah, that's just where he'd go." Palmer and Hillrich both agree.

Water tower? This tour has turned into a fuckin' nightmare. Are these kids for real?

"Say what?" Randy responds, throwing Jack a what now? look. "Who's this guy we're lookin' for, a fuckin' fish?"

"It's true. H.G. would think that's a cool place to hide." Palmer concurs. "That whole bunch of airheads, they all hang out up in the water towers, smoke weed up there, screw their wimpy little girlfriends up there. They even sleep there sometimes."

Randy doesn't look interested. Clearly, like Jack, he is anticipating a wild goose chase. "Who do you shitheads think you're talkin' to?" he sneers. "You think we just cracked outta the egg? Water towers got water in 'em. That's why they're called water towers."

"No man," Palmer refutes. "Yeah, they got water in them alright, but they all have this little platform built out over half the water, up on topa' the water, it's like a little room. Every water tower has to have this platform for guys to come in to do repairs or clean it out. Bet you didn't know that," he adds smugly, looking like he's getting off on showing the detectives something else he knows that they don't.

Ardsley readily explains, "There's a ladder outside on the roof, that goes right up to where the platform is," his hands demonstrate the water tower's pointed slope, "and right there, under the water tower's roof, is a little door."

Hillrich breaks in, "When you open that door you can crawl right in on the platform. It's never locked. The platform extends out over half the water."

Randy squints dubiously. "Sounds more like you're the ones who've been hangin' out up there."

Palmer rolls his eyes. "We're not idiots, ya know."

They could have fooled Jack. "Does sound like firsthand information," Jack says, agreeing with his partner.

"It is." Ardsley brazenly admits. "Everybody's checked out the water towers at one time or another. We'd go exploring on the roof when we were little kids. Nine or ten."

Palmer brushes it off. "Kid stuff. Like climbing trees. Nobody ever actually went inside. Just opened the door and looked in."

A nine-year-old climbing that ladder on top of a fifteen-story building is enough. Jack is horrified. "Where were your parents?" He has to ask, but no one responds.

Detective Jack Kuchinsky has eighteen years with the N.Y.P.D. under his belt, and he finds himself interrogating the Huck Finn Squad. Climbing trees? Yeah, that's kid stuff alright, but this water tower business? It leaves him feeling that, behind his back, these three weasels are laughing their asses off. What he wouldn't give to be back in Harlem interrogating some what-you-see-is-what-you-get street hustler.

"You trying to tell me this O'Connor kid was sleeping on a few flimsy planks suspended over what, thirty, forty feet of water? He could roll over in the middle of the night and nobody'd even hear the splash."

"I wish he had," Palmer says grimly.

Hillrich turns to his friends and tells them, "Know what H.G. told Scotto once? He said sleeping over the water made it real convenient when he had to take a piss in the middle of the night."

Now Ardsley looks horrified. "I wish I'd known that. His favorite water tower is the one on my building."

Jack doesn't even try to conceal his revulsion. "You mean to tell me people in that building were drinking that scumbag's toilet water? And no one had the decency to tell the super?" His contempt for Hillrich and the D.O.A. is coming through strong.

"All right, boys, time to go for another ride."

They are all parked in front of Ardsley's building when the back-up unit Jack called for pulls up. "We got a possible perp on one of our homicides," he tells one of the uniformed officers, pointing to Ardsley's building. "Might be on the roof."

The sky has turned dark with the budding night. Jack's back is killing him. *When are they going to give him a unit with a seat that doesn't have broken springs?* His stomach is sour from lack of a decent meal, and the seven or eight cups of coffee he'd poured down his gut to keep him going haven't helped matters any.

Overtime is good, but Jack is worried about getting all that reading done for Ford's class. Finals are only three weeks away, and he is having to waste precious time following these loony tunes around. First, they can't wait to help, then they won't talk without a lawyer. Now, they're coming on like gangbusters again.

As everybody piles out of the two cars, Jack turns and gives the boys the kind of look they've been getting from his partner. "You better not be pulling any shit here," he warns them.

"If you didn't do anything wrong, what do you need a lawyer for?" Randy wants to know. Then he zeroes in on Hillrich. "Hey, bro," he drawls with a rare smile, draping his arm around the black youth's shoulders and steering him off to the side. "What the fuck's going on with you guys? With this lawyer shit? You know that's not the way a man takes care of things. How about you start levelin' with a brother?"

Brad angrily shrugs Randy's arm away. "Ah, man, don't try to pull that brother shit on me. What the fuck's going on with you guys? We're trying to help you catch a murderer and you're wasting time hassling us." He throws up his hands in disgust and spins around, back to his buddies.

If these kids are bullshitters, they're the best Jack's ever come across. He sighs audibly and says to his partner, "Okay, Randy, let's go up and see what we got."

When the elevator reaches the top floor, Jack removes his weapon from his ankle holster. Then, in silence and with the gun drawn, he starts to climb the short, dimly lit staircase to the roof. His partner, the two uniformed cops, and the three kids follow on the steps close behind. Jack hates this part of the job. Cops get killed in places like this.

As Jack pushes the heavy metal door open, a cold wind instantly slaps across his face. He steps out into the darkness and stands huddled with the others, everybody looking up at the black water tower perched precariously high atop its scaffolding.

"That's it," Palmer whispers excitedly.

Silhouetted against the dark sky, the tower is a silent and foreboding image. Like the evil castle in a child's nightmare, it could only house something threatening. Jack laughs softly, but without humor. "You got to be kidding. You really think somebody's in that thing?"

"Yeah. It's true," Palmer's hushed voice assures him. "They all hang out in those things. H.G. and his sleazebag girlfriend, Amy. They go up there to fuck."

Ardsley's outstretched arm directs Jack's eye to the target. "Up there, right under the roof you can just make out the little door. See it? See the ladder that goes right up to it? All you gotta do is climb up, open the door and crawl in.

Sure, he can. Jack can climb up there where his back-up can't follow him, stick his head in a fucking black hole, and crawl right into a bullet. Jack contemplates his next move when one of the officers whispers, "Something moved up there."

"Stay here by the roof door," Jack tells the boys. "Don't make a sound. Don't breathe."

Jack, his partner, and the two officers begin to creep stealthily across the black tar roof, guns protruding from their hunched figures. No one speaks. The cold wind makes no sound. Even the street far below is still. Jack and his entourage are an image, etched on a piece of silent film.

The men position themselves around the base of the scaffolding. Through a hole in the clouds, the moon suddenly beams down, spotlighting the taut scene where Jack is immersed in the deathly anticipation of a curtain about to go up. He waits on his mark, his place on the dark stage, forced to play out a part for which there is no script.

His life may depend on his skills of improvisation. His breathing quickens along with his heartbeat, every nerve, every muscle poised. All his senses are on high. He can hear a feather drop, shoot a hole in it before it landed. Terror and exhilaration hold him like a vice. He is intensely alive. He is ready.

With his gun in one hand, he grabs the cold metal rungs and begins to climb the ladder. Slowly, silently. The scaffold is old and rickety, emitting an unfortunate tiny groan with each ascending step. Is someone being warned? *Careful, Jack.* His movements are measured, almost fluid. The smallest click of his gun against the metal ladder could betray him. Each step brings him higher and higher into the night sky.

Each new step he leaves his back-up farther below. Like little toy soldiers poised for combat, their shrinking faces and guns turn upward as Jack is drawn up into the darkness. The black velvet sky wraps around him, and he is now suspended in it. He is part of the heavens, part of hell. With the twinkling lights of a miniature city dotting the circular horizon, he feels like a million sparkling stars are lighting his way. He has never felt more alone.

The wind is stinging up here. It makes his ears ache. His fingers freeze against the cold metal ladder, against the cold steel of his gun. He tilts his face up and sees his hand reaching for the next rung...

... a small boy's hand reaching up into the warm sunshine, to whack the hard, little, black ball. Atta boy, Jackie. Dad beside him, looking so young. His hair is thick and blond, his face is smooth and movie-star handsome. Jack watches dad sweep agilely around the court, pounding the ricocheting ball. "You do it like me, Jackie. Swing at it hard. That's my boy, you can do it, Jackie." Laughing, panting, breathing out through every pore, their bodies aglow with the

    delicious heat of their own sweat. Just the two of them in the whole world of that concrete square. Nothing can hurt Jackie here. Dad won't let it...

And then dad is gone. The memory snaps off as abruptly as a light switch. Alone and cold, Jack's hand reaches the top rung of the ladder.

Jack takes one last deep breath and pulls himself up, waist high, his thumping heart right smack in front of that fucking, little door. With his gun hand he reaches for the knob. In a flash, the door is thrown open, Jack's arms spring forward, both hands gripping the gun as he aims it into the unknown of the dimly lit interior. "Police. Come out real easy or I'll make a fuckin' ghost outta you."

"I'm coming out. Please don't shoot me."

Inside the cramped chamber, beside a flickering candle set in a beer can, a figure wriggles out of a sleeping bag. Its eyes are enormous, its trembling apparent even in the faint light. It begins to crawl toward the barrel of Jack's gun.

With his eyes and weapon still pointed at the doorway, Jack lowers himself a few steps, the exhilaration immediately descending with him. Above, a small head pops out of the opening, and Jack is startled to see what appears to be no more than a child.

"Out, kid. Move it," Jack commands, and the small captive immediately begins to descend above him.

The second the boy's feet touch the roof he is whirled around, arms jerked backward, and handcuffs snapped on.

"What's your name, shithead?" Randy demands.

From a distance Palmer answers for him, "He's Bernie, Bernie Maisel. He's H.G.'s best friend. You better talk, you little creep. Where is he? Where is he?"

For a moment Bernie looks scared again. "I don't know where he is. I swear it."

Randy grabs Bernie by the forearm, tilting him slightly so he has to walk at an angle. "How the fuck old are you anyway?" he wants to know.

Bernie looks down his little pug nose at Randy. With new-found arrogance, he answers, "I'm fifteen, and you can't do anything to me 'cause I'm a juvenile. I know my rights. I'm gonna call my mom."

Chapter Thirteen

The day after his encounter with the police, Bernie Maisel walks down West End Avenue. After a brief interrogation at the precinct, they let him go. He didn't even have to call his mom. All they want to know is where H.G. is, and Bernie doesn't have a clue.

He is so engrossed in his quest for a joint that his legs move independently toward the corner of 108th Street. If he's lucky some of his crowd will be there, the corner not empty like it's been for the last few days. As he walks along, his fists shoved deep into his pockets and his parka pulled up to his ears, he barely feels the morning's raw chill. His eyes are fixed on the black and white sneakers that jut out ahead of him. Left, right, left, right, the flopping of their wide laces giving each step a jaunty air.

But Bernie's thoughts are anything but carefree. He thinks about how the once bustling corner turned into a ghost town overnight. How, since Casey Palmer found Scott's body, nobody hangs out there anymore. That's why he was in the water tower last night. He had hoped one of the gang might show up. Instead, it was Casey and some of Scott's stuck-up friends along with the police. He's dying to replay his cop story and how he got over on them to anyone who will listen. Maybe they'll be back on the corner, Garth, Raul, the Bernstein twins, Pogo, Claude, and if he's lucky, some of the girls.

The corner has been Bernie's refuge, his home away from home. He was never alone there, not like the home his bedroom is in. Mom is always off to one of her committee meetings. Dad is usually working late at the office, whatever that means. Bernie smelled the perfume on dad's coat, seen the matchbooks from all the different bars on his father's bureau.

Like a turtle retreating into its shell, he hikes up his parka with his shoulders. He does have a goal, though. His day started with the discovery that he's only got three puny joints left in his stash. With no telling when H.G. will be back in circulation, Bernie is on a mission to locate someone to buy, beg or borrow from.

His day went further downhill when he walked into the kitchen this morning. Before he could get to the orange juice, his mom was all over his case about the two C's he'd brought home. There was no mention of the three A's, of course. It was a typical morning in the Maisel household, only this time Bernie couldn't slam the door behind him and head for the 108th Street corner gang. Damn H.G.

Yet as quickly as his anger flares up, he is sorry for it. H.G. is Bernie's best friend. Didn't he prove that by including Bernie in the plan?

The plan. Bernie can't remember hanging out and not talking about it. It was something to knock around while they were getting high. It wasn't just him and H.G. who took part, but whoever was there. They'd huddle together, snickering like Cheshire cats when Scott walked by holding his head up like he was King Shit, too good to even nod a greeting. They'd chuckle behind his back and elaborate a little more on one or another detail. How to sneak the gun into his apartment, and how to sneak the stash out of it. When to do it, late at night, or early in the morning when no one else might be there? Where to shoot him, in the head or in the heart? They talked about it like the fine-tuning of an instrument being more important than the playing of it. The only part ever etched in stone was the name of the shooter, and nobody challenged H.G. for that role.

Bernie was elated when he was chosen to be the keeper of Scott's keys, and H.G. had a separate set made just for Bernie. He reaches in his pocket and fondles them for the umpteenth time. The role of key-keeper has a kind of white-collar importance, like being the high-priced lawyer of some important gangster. It suits Bernie to a T, a position of power, but one where he could keep his hands clean.

Talking about pulling it off had been cool, but now Bernie feels the anger flow.

With the acceptance of the corner's inner circle, Bernie's days had been getting better by the minute. He knew, after they did it, they would have an ample supply of Scott's primo weed. The whole wonderful scene was only a memory now. Bernie's three joint stash says it all.

But how can he really be mad at H.G.? It was, after all, H.G. alone who stuck up for Bernie when Claude said Bernie wasn't smart enough to handle the key part. And when it all finally went down, Bernie was handed those keys the next morning. It was his job to go back and forth with H.G. and Claude to empty out Scott's weed closet. They all, even H.G., stood and waited while Bernie stuck the key in the lock. Each time Bernie was allowed to come into the apartment, he'd see Scott sitting there all dead, like something out of Night of the Living Dead. Being right in the same room with a dead body was way more cool than he ever imagined anything could be. He owes that experience all to H.G.

He trudges onward to who knows where, trying to think of nothing, especially not his decline back to lonely nobody's land. He is watching the sidewalk unroll under each step, when suddenly it dawns on him. Each step his feet take, has never been taken before, and can never be taken again. Each of his footprints is being recorded, stored away forever, in the file cabinet of eternity under the name of Bernie Maisel.

Bernie is doing something that no one else can do again. No one can put their foot down in the exact spots that Bernie steps on. He feels what great explorers must have felt. The Columbuses, the Lewis and Clarks, the Captain Kirks.

Yet the emptiness of the corner ahead of him just reinforces the reality that there is no one to buy from or bum off of. He plays back a memory of a better time, when H.G. arrived at the corner with a pocket full of joints freshly rolled out of Scott's primo sinse and he proceeded to hand them out, free to all present, his generosity proclaiming that it was done.

Chapter Fourteen

In the weeks between Thanksgiving and Christmas, Kate throws herself into her work with a vengeance. H.G. is still missing, with the extent of his injuries still hanging like a shroud over Christmas, yet another damaged holiday. The spectacular view from Kate's office window no longer commands her attention. She manages to smile and make pleasant small talk with her co-workers, but at her drawing board the tone of her storyboards is decidedly different. Her once fanciful, little, cartoon characters have begun to choke with cartoon violence. Those lovable little sugar-pops now brandish weapons and punch each other out for a place on the spoon.

It is two days before Christmas. Red and green holiday trappings decorate the sides of buses, apartment windows glitter with multi-colored lights, and sidewalk Santas ring bells to their ho-ho-hos.

It has been a bone-chilling December. Claude is out on bail for drug possession. Garth's lawyer negotiated an immunity deal for him, dropping the weapon's charge in exchange for his testimony. And like it or not, Christmas is imposing itself upon Kate.

She sits on her bed, encircled by a border of Christmas wrappings and boxes waiting to be wrapped, tagged, and put under the tree. She made herself go out and get a tree, but for the first time in her life, trimming it was more like vacuuming or washing the dishes, a chore. She needs that fresh, clean start of a new year. The ringing of the phone interrupts her thinking.

"Hello?"

"Mrs. Palmer?" Jack asks.

The sound of Kuchinsky's voice makes apprehension and anticipation

89

collide within her. "You got him?"

"Listen to me," he says, the smile apparent in his voice. "I got a nice Christmas present for you and your son. We just got a call from the O'Connor kid's lawyer. He'll be bringing him in to a precinct in Dobbs Ferry. We gotta go there to pick him up."

She closes her eyes and falls back onto the pillows, the red ribbon in her hand unraveling like a festive streamer. But she has to hear it again, to make it real. "You really got him?"

"We will in about an hour."

"Dobbs Ferry. Is that where he's been hiding?"

"At a cousin's house."

"And his...um, physical condition?" she asks with terrified apprehension.

"I understand he has a cast on his arm," he tells her. "Look, I know what you're worried about, but in light of the crime he committed, I don't think the beating is going to be an issue."

"And you'll get his confession on record now?"

Kuchinsky laughs. "That's pretty unlikely. He's going to be with an attorney. We can ask him anything we want, but with a lawyer standing next to him, the only thing he's going to give us is his name and address. That's the way the system works. It bends over backwards for the mutts."

She is like a rag doll being pushed and pulled all at the same time. "My God, they're not going to let him out on bail, are they?"

He laughs again at her naivety. "Don't worry about that. Generally, on a homicide, there is no bail and especially on this case where the kid's already made a run for it. I guarantee the D.A. won't offer any bail."

"What happens next?" she asks warily.

"He'll be arraigned tonight, then sent to Riker's where he'll be held until the trial. If it's any consolation, you can tell your son the little weasel isn't going to be in for a pretty time at Riker's. In that hellhole, fresh, white blood gets gobbled up fast."

"I never thought I'd hear myself say this, but good. I'm glad. God, that's so unlike me," she adds, speaking more to herself than to Kuchinsky. She finds herself filled with both the sweet rush that only a just desserts can bring and the revulsion for feeling it.

"You know, I really wanted to give you this news in person, but I didn't want to just show up on your doorstep." This time his laugh is more intimate, the way close friends laugh together. "Didn't want to bump into any angry boyfriends."

"No boyfriends right now," she clarifies so quickly she surprises herself, and with a small self-conscious giggle explains, "I'm a very independent woman these days."

"Oh really," he says, making it clear she gave him what he was hoping to hear. "Look, Kate, you mind me calling you Kate?"

"Not at all."

"We should be finished with this mutt by ten tonight. If that's not too late for you, how 'bout me buying you a drink to celebrate?"

This time she makes sure her voice conveys a smile, too. "It's not late at all. I'm a night person. And I love celebrations."

As she slides into the passenger seat, Jack notices her legs. Slim and long like her fingers. He notices her thighs, so firm they look like they've been painted with the denim of her jeans. With her high, tight boots and loose, floppy sweater, she dresses more like a kid than a mother. She smells like she bathed in something tasty, too.

"You got him?" she says again, with a nervous little giggle as though she can't believe it until he tells her to her face.

He flashes his best reassuring smile, the kind he uses to put John Q. Public at ease. "We got the mutt. All locked up."

The icy reserve he'd seen on Thanksgiving is gone. She looks more fragile than he remembered, more delicate and feminine, like a woman should be.

He's got to hand it to her though, she didn't fall apart in all of this. There's not one display of feminine hysterics, and she didn't flaunt her lack of a husband to play for sympathy, like some women might do. It's pretty clear there's no Mr. Palmer in the picture. It must have been hard on her, alone and finding out her son was mixed up in all that dirty dope-dealing. Jack is suddenly flushed with the desire to put his arms around this woman, to protect her from all the shit that's out there. That's what a real man does. He reaches over and touches her shoulder lightly, telling her, "I'm gonna keep on top of this case."

Her face brightens into a big smile. A pretty smile. "Well, Detective Kuchinsky, this is certainly a lot nicer than our last meeting."

He shifts into drive and heads uptown. "This job has a way of putting a damper on first meetings, and if I'm gonna call you Kate, you're gonna have to call me Jack."

She curls around in her seat, tucking one foot under her knee, like Jenny might do, and drapes her arm over the back of the seat, "Okay, Jack, let's go celebrate. Where to?"

"You mind going to a black bar?" he asks, intending to go there whether she likes it or not.

"No." She grimaces perplexedly. "Why would I?"

The car radio interrupts with a crackle of static, then a female voice. "Sixty-five. Gas leak. Seven-0-two west nine-three." More static, now a male voice. "Twenty-four David. Ten-four." The woman again says, "One hundred west nine-eight. Female assaulted. Approached by black male. He has a possible gun. In front of location. Ten-four." Then another male says, "We have it. Three units responding."

She looks surprised. "This is a police car?" she asks like she's in some kind of vehicle from outer space.

Civilians, they're all the same. They never see what's right in front of them. "It's a department car. Unmarked. I keep mine at the precinct." The radio interrupts again. "Fifty-six. Man down in parked car. Riverside and one-o-six. Foul odor coming from vehicle." Jack shuts it off. "I'm not working now. We don't need to listen to that shit."

"Where's this place we're going?"

"Up in Harlem. Friend of mine owns a bar there. Larry, the bartender, he's good people."

Her perfume fills the car, wafting around him like a tease. Some kind of flower scent, but not heavy, like some women wear. Lilac maybe or lily-of-the-valley. It suits her.

"You have any kids?" she asks.

"I have a daughter."

"Is there a wife that goes along with that daughter?"

She's a sharp piece of work. She wants to get all the facts right up front. He likes that. She's definitely interested. With his fingers he combs back a wisp of hair that has fallen onto his forehead and laughs, answering. "You don't waste any time, do you?"

"I like to know who I'm with. So?" she persists coyly. "What's your situation?"

"Separated."

"You live in the city?"

"Not really."

"So where? Boy, you really are a Mr. Secretive," she taunts playfully.

"During the week I stay at a place I'm subletting from a friend."

"And weekends?"

"Weekends I spend with my daughter. I have a house outside the city. My wife stays at a relative's when I come over."

She feigns exasperation, asking him with outstretched palms, "So, where do you actually live?"

"I'm neither here nor there," he hears himself snap. The game has worn thin, the questions are becoming irritating. He doesn't need some jilted bimbo calling his house one day, upsetting Paula, and turning Jenny against him. Jack's business is Jack's business, and that's the way he intends to keep it, but there is the rest of this evening to salvage. "What's with all these questions?" he asks, deliberately lightening up. "That's the detective's job, you know."

She giggles, bubbly like foam rolling down the side of a mug, "Okay, okay. I give up.

It's just nice to be talking to you about something besides H.G."

Jack nods in agreement. He stops for a red light and shifts in his seat. These broken-down units kill his back, and the gun he has tucked in the side of his belt has begun to jab into him again. He reaches around and pulls it out. "Here, hold this for me," he tells her, placing it on her lap. The barrel is pointed away from her, the handle nestling down between the tops of her thighs as if it were something as inane as a flashlight. Jack likes to let a woman know she is with a man who can protect her.

The minute the warm metal touches her, Kate's hands fly up, and her whole body jumps, seeming to recoil from the gun in her own lap. But he notices her legs part like the Red Sea, allowing the gun to slip down and wedge itself between her thighs. "I hate guns," she blurts out, but she does nothing to remove it.

"You're a liberal, right?"

"It's not just liberals who don't like guns," she retorts coolly, and for a moment that bitch he met in the squad room is back.

"How many guns have you been around?" he asks her casually.

"None," is her obvious answer.

"A gun doesn't only kill, you know," he clues her in. "It protects, too."

At 158th and Broadway, they pull up in front of a Chinese restaurant. Big, neon letters in oriental style graphics proclaim it to be Chow Lees, but the flickering, near death C and L indicate that Chow Lees has seen better days.

Barely grazing her thigh, Kuchinsky reaches over and reclaims his weapon, his eyes never leaving hers.

"This it?" she breathlessly whispers like she is making a pledge to follow this man anywhere.

He answers, "Yep," as he opens his door and gets out. Her hand pops her door handle, and in an instant, she follows him across the sidewalk through a double set of glass doors. One door, she notices, is held together with a piece of duck-tape. Broken in a recent fight? They enter the restaurant together.

Inside, Kate notices the dingy ambiance is summed up in the restaurant's somber color scheme of maroon, grey, and very dark green. A low-mirrored bar leads into a large back room where she can see a handful of black families with small children and a few couples occupying the booths that line the walls. The indirect neon only further highlights the fading wallpaper and the plastic flowers that adorn the tall oriental vases at either end of the bar.

The cash register is mounted on top of a lighted tank of goldfish. A small,

Asian man rushes out from behind it to greet Jack. "Ah, my friend Jock. Is good to zee you," he says, sounding like he means what he says.

"Hey, guy, what's doin'?" Jack responds with equal sincerity as he guides Kate to the bar.

She starts to seat herself on a stool at the end, but Jack immediately stops her, taking the seat for himself, instead. "I've got to sit where I can see the front door," he tells her, moving her to the seat next to him, and to her puzzled expression he nonchalantly explains, "to keep an eye out for any mutts who might be comin' in to start something."

She nods an, "of course", as if all her dates take her to dangerous places. Before Scott's murder, such a gesture would have been a turn-off. Now having a gun-toting bodyguard is an appealing new experience. But deep inside her a small voice warns, Neither here nor there, Kate. This is a man in transition, with a woman he still calls my wife out there.

A small, wiry Asian man of undetermined age hurries down the full length of the bar. He is dressed in a white shirt, black pants, and a red bow tie. He puts two cocktail napkins down in front of Kate and Jack. "I don't see you yesterday," he says to Jack with a broad smile that almost overlaps his narrow face, revealing both unabashed affection and a set of very crooked teeth. "I fix you something special?" he offers eagerly.

"Beer and?" Jack looks at Kate.

"Wine. White wine, dry, please."

Jack introduces Kate to the waiter as, "My buddy, Larry," and Kate reaches out to shake his hand. Her imposition of physical contact seems to startle Larry, but he offers a limp handshake in return, along with another smile.

Jack says something that sounds very much like Chinese, and Larry responds with a laugh and a shrug, "Not so good," he says. "Eugene was big winner last night," then he hurries off to fill their orders.

"You speak Chinese?" she asks in amazement. Detective Kuchinsky is full of surprises.

He leans forward, looking hard and deep into her eyes, his gaze wrapping around her the way she knows his arms would feel, and all at once she is alone with him, everything else blocked out by the blueness of his eyes.

"I speak a little," he says like it is no big deal. "Larry's been teaching me. They play poker here after they close at night. The waiters and I play with them sometimes. I'm picking up a couple of words here and there," he explains, surprising her by offering some unsolicited information about his personal life. "The words I pick up during those games are not exactly the ones you'd get from a Berlitz course." He smiles at her again, and something in the pit of her stomach twists and stretches to caress her from within.

Down the bar a man looks like he's fallen asleep hunched over his beer and shot glass. Next to him, a heavy-set Hispanic woman sits sipping a tall, foamy drink with a paper umbrella in it. She lifts her glass in a salute to Jack. "Yo, Jackie, you have a good one, okay, baby?"

"Hey, Carmen, happy holidays." He salutes back with a wave of his hand. "The same to Manny, you hear." Then displaying how much at home he is, Jack leans over without looking, reaches under the bar and pulls out a fresh cocktail napkin. His full attention back to Kate, he says, "Lemme show you something," and he takes out a pen and scrawls several Chinese characters down the side of the napkin as if he'd been writing like that all his life.

Kate is impressed. Her elbows on the bar, her crossed wrists tucked under her chin, she leans close enough to feel his warm breath on her cheek. "So?" she asks softly. "What did you write?"

He translates, "The year of the rat," but his eyes tell her it could be the year of Kate and Jack.

Chapter Fifteen

Christmas came and went, and thanks to H.G.'s arrest, there was something to be festive about. The threat of an assault conviction no longer hangs over Casey's head. It turns out, the baseball bat did minimal damage to H.G. And just as Jack had predicted, the lethal trio of H.G., Garth, and Claude's own legal problems took priority over the beating they got from Casey and his crew. It was never even mentioned by any of the three lawyers. The final resolution of Scott's murder was now in the hands of the professionals, the D.A., and the judge, with a jury waiting in the wings.

Since their night at Chow Lees, phone calls from Jack have become a daily occurrence. They're usually brief, but attentive none the less, like he's checking in to make sure she is alright. In light of all the trauma she'd been through, Kate appreciates a guy who does that.

She also likes how he didn't ask to come up to her apartment that first night at Chow Lees. She didn't offer, of course. "This was fun," she'd told him as she'd opened the car door and dropped one foot out onto the curb. It was her way of telling him she doesn't do one-night stands, and she doesn't bring men back to her apartment with her son sleeping there.

Without saying a word, he'd taken her hand, holding it by her fingers, and raised it to his mouth. She'd felt his lips, firm and cooled by the December chill, brush against the smooth waves of her knuckles, as softly as if it were a memory while it was happening. He didn't ask her to come back to his place either. That left her wanting to, all the more.

But getting together for a whole evening proved to be an elusive proposition. Due to last- minute, job-related phone calls, Jack broke a string of dates. The two nights they did manage to meet for drinks at Chow Lees, the dates were cut short by Jack's beeper. Kate couldn't resist chiding, "You'd think people would be a little more considerate about the time they choose to murder somebody." The year was new, and the victims were anonymous again.

Lunch dates proved a bit easier to arrange, midday not seeming so prone to violence. He took her to Katz's on the Lower East Side for pastrami and corned beef, to Silvia's up in Harlem for ribs and sweet potato pie, and to the Central Park Zoo for sauerkraut-smothered hot dogs. A nice break for Kate from her Madison Avenue power lunches. But lunch dates had the built-in constraint of always ending with Kate and Jack returning to their respective offices.

Then one morning on the first of February, after Jack had finished his midnight shift, he called Kate as she was getting dressed for work and asked if she wanted to meet him for a quick breakfast. She did, and everything changed.

At 9 a.m., the Olympia Diner in Kate's neighborhood is bustling. The smell of coffee mixes with the pungent aroma of frying bacon. A small army of waiters rush from table to kitchen shouting their orders in Greek. An aging cashier sporting a crisp pink hankie in her apron pocket and three inches of make-up on her face, rings and dings her register to the morning rush.

Jack is devouring an order of fried eggs, hash browns, bacon, and toast, as Kate sits nibbling on an English muffin and sipping a cup of tea. They chat about some of Jack's cases, about his night school classes, and about Professor Ford's suggestion he consider teaching one day. They discreetly giggle at the pudgy couple in the booth across from them who keep ordering diet-this and low-cal that, while eating waffles heaped with mounds of whipped cream.

Jack suddenly becomes silent, shoveling the last of his hash browns into his mouth, his jaw chomping away. He looks like he is deep in thought. He puts his fork down and looks up into her eyes and says softly, "You know, I want to make love to you."

Twelve hours later, Kate stands behind Jack as he turns the key in the lock, opens the door to his apartment, and with a sweep of his hand, welcomes her in. His beeper, this time, has managed to stay silent.

Kate steps into a room that looks like nobody lives there, furnished with only the bare necessities: a tiny closet-sized kitchen, a fridge, a sink, and a stove in one small alcove, a desk, a small table for eating with a straight-backed chair pushed into it, a bookcase, and dominating front and center—a sofa bed left in the open position. Its sheets and blanket pulled flat as glass and tucked in tight like Kate would expect to find in an army barracks. Only Venetian blinds cover the one window. There is no color scheme, no sign of human inhabitation. No socks, underwear or newspapers on the floor, no coffee cups or salt and pepper on the table. On the desk, one lone pencil lies perfectly parallel to a clean legal pad and the books on the shelves stand at attention, lined up according to size like obedient little soldiers. An open door in one corner reveals there is at least a bathroom. Jack Kuchinsky looks like a man who could check out of a woman's life in a fast fifteen minutes.

Then she notices there is one small personal item in the room. On the desk, there's a gold-framed photo of a pretty, young woman with a lot of make-up and a seductive smile that screams out to be noticed. For a room this spartan to display a woman's picture, she has to be somebody pretty special. What's going on with this guy?

That she may have unknowingly infringed on another woman's territory is a turn-off. Kate Palmer is no shoplifter and suddenly she wishes she were anywhere but here.

"Who is the pretty woman?" she asks in as casual a tone as she can muster.

"That's my daughter," he beams with pride. "She's fourteen but she photographs older."

Fourteen and all that make-up? But Kate is relieved to find out the photo is not of a girlfriend, and once again, she is glad to be there.

He steps around behind her. "Lemme have your coat," he says, separating her long hair and slipping his fingers inside her collar to pull it down over her shoulders.

"Oh, fine," she says, noticing as he opens the closet to hang their coats, that there is a space between each hanger. None of his clothing hanging there, touches. The shelf above is filled with one large suitcase, the floor below with three pairs of shoes, all lined up in a straight row.

"What do you want to drink?" he asks, stepping into the tiny kitchen area and opening the refrigerator. "I have, let's see, rum? Vodka? Some Sambuca?"

"I'll have rum if you have any coke. A rum coke, please."

He laughs. "My kinda guy. One rum coke comin' up."

She looks around for a place to sit, but the apartment isn't set up for conversational gatherings. It's the bed or nothing, so she plops herself down on one corner. Her feet remain on the floor as she lets herself fall back leisurely on her elbows.

He comes out of the kitchen area with a tall glass in each hand, ice cubes clinking, and stands over her, almost up against her actually. His feet are planted on the floor between hers, his knees pressing into the side of the bed, his thighs pressing out against her spread thighs, and he hands her a cold, wet glass, its clinking ice-cubes inviting her to partake. But when she takes a sip she wrinkles her nose and he asks, "Too strong?" immediately reaching down to take her drink back.

"No, no, not at all. Really, it's good like this."

And it is. Strong, yes, but just what the moment calls for. Sweet tentacles of rum roll through her body like the unraveling of a soft, hot wave. It immediately relaxes her, warming her from the inside out, taking the edge off this first time.

"So, I see this is the only place to sit in your house," she says with a coy smile, and with her eyes still on him, she takes another longer sip of the tangy-sweet coke.

"Want some music?" he asks, popping a cassette into the tape player and filling the room with the melancholy strains of Barbara Streisand's *You Don't Bring Me Flowers Anymore*.

He sits down beside her, putting his drink on the floor next to the bed, and without taking his eyes off her, simply removes the glass from her hand and places it on the floor next to his.

"You're a beautiful girl," he tells her, grazing her cheek ever so lightly with his knuckles. Then, allowing his fingers to slip around to the nape of her neck so tenderly that microscopic lightning bolts begin exploding across her skin, she feels his fingers slowly make their way down through the smooth intimate curve of her shoulder blades.

"Gi-rl?" she hears herself giggle as a girl would.

"No more talking," he whispers huskily, leaning close into her until, by covering her lips with his, his command of her is ensured. She willingly reaches up into him, into the strong folds of his arms, feeling like a piece of slow-motion film, the two of them ease back down onto the bed as one.

They lie together from head to toe rocking gently, kissing gently, their mouths rapt in the wonderful newness of their individual explorations, as their hands deftly unbutton, unhook, and unzip each other.

Their clothes have quickly melted away, strewn uncaringly wherever they fell and now she feels the coarse hair of his chest pressing against her bare breasts. His body deliciously hard against hers, like warm malleable steel. His muscular arms around her make her a part of him, make her feel his flesh as though it were hers, too. It is hers now in this forever moment that has none of the constraints of time. The heat of him runs down the whole naked length of her body, down to where his feet hold hers in an ultimate act of joyful imprisonment. She is his completely, as she wants to be.

He kisses her long and hard and soft, the palms of her hands held out in a futile arrest against the strength of his broad chest. In the sweet torment of her imprisonment, she can hear herself making soft moaning sounds.

He, too, is breathing heavily now, looking down at her small breasts cupped in his large hands, kneading them as though he were molding her out of clay. Recreating her. He exhales into her ear, "God, look how they stand up," he says, "like a twenty-year-old's tits." His lips slide down her body until they fasten onto one taunt nipple. His fingers skillfully twirl and twist the other as though he were fine-tuning a delicate piece of machinery, all to the sounds of Barbara's singing and Kate's sweet moans of pleasure.

Her hands begin to inch their way down the smoothness of his waist, his hips, as he kisses the curve of her arched throat. She closes her eyes, blocking out all but the feel of him. Her hands flow over him like a liquid coating. They glide down his thighs, then swirl up coming together in their relentless search. But they do not find what they are looking for.

Her hand sinks into the velvet softness between his legs, sinking down deep into him, her fingers now the aggressors, her hands doing the stroking, the kneading, the urging. They try to shape, to build form where there is none. But it is all to no avail.

He rolls over onto his back, pulling himself out of her hands and releases his hold on her. "Ah, shit," he sighs softly as he lies staring into the ceiling. "This happens sometimes." He sighs again, crossing his arms over his forehead. "When I'm with somebody new."

She turns on her side, propped up on one elbow, her other arm draped across his chest with a familiarity that conveys it can't be marred by anything as ordinary as a physical inability. "That's not why I'm here," she whispers, her fingers drawing little circles on the tightness of his shoulder. "I just want to be with you, be close to you."

She looks down at this sad little boy of a man. God, how thankful she is that she is not saddled with an appendage that has a mind of its own. How grateful she is to have a body that works in harmony with itself, and all at once, a rush of power exhilarates her. She is completely aware of every pore, every drop of blood surging through her veins. She has never felt more of a woman.

He yawns without opening his mouth, his nostrils flaring lazily. "I guess I should take you home."

"I'm in no rush." She smiles, cuddling closer, one of her legs swinging over to straddle him as the back of her hand caresses his cheek. "It doesn't matter," she reassures him again, and this time she feels his body begin to relax.

He reaches up and takes her hand. Covering it fully with his, he presses it into his cheek with a firmness that speaks more than words could. His thumb gently strokes her palm, and together, they drift off into a light sleep until, an hour later, she wakes to his mouth traveling down her body, and he gifts her with the treasure that had eluded them both before.

Chapter Sixteen

Six months to the day when the bullet pierced Scott's red bandana headband, the trial of the accused murderer is about to begin. Kate chooses an aisle seat near the middle of the nearly empty courtroom. The Scholfields are all seated in the front row, mother, father, and little brother. But this is hardly a social event, and Kate prefers to keep a low profile. What could she possibly say to them at this difficult moment in their lives?

Clustered in the back of the courtroom are a handful of Scott's friends but not Casey, Bobby, or Brad. As witnesses they are being kept in another room till it is time for their testimonies. It is a tense and silent tableau, reminiscent of the time in Kate's apartment when the drugs were returned to the detectives. But the perimeter of the large room is full of court officers all chatting cordially as they, too, wait.

Hearing that there was a confession was closure enough for Kate. Then the return of the drugs made it complete. She just sits waiting to hear the confessed killer be pronounced guilty as charged. But why are so many court officers here? Do they expect trouble? The trial was to be the final closure on this nightmare, but the anticipation still makes Kate's anxiety increase.

Behind her up the aisle, footsteps hurry as she turns to see D.A. Herb Ruben. His arms are laden with a stack of files and folders, pink and white bits of paper protruding from every angle. In his haste, he drops one off the top of the stack and nearly loses his horn-rimmed glasses while stooping to pick it up. With one finger he pushes the glasses back in place and greets

Kate with a genial, "Hey, Kate. "

"Herb," she whispers. "How's it look?"

"Good. Excellent. Jack going to be around today?"

"He said he'd try to be." Her frown is one of disappointment. "But I just found out we can't sit together."

"Witnesses not allowed in the courtroom prior to testimony," Herb says as he attempts to reorganize the jumbled files in his arms. He gives the stack a little jiggle and rolls his eyes. "This is six months of my life right here. All the late-night meetings with those little punks and their attorneys. One more week of this case and my wife would have divorced me for sure." He chuckles. "After this case, I'm not so sure she won't anyway."

"Will he be here today?"

"H.G.? Yeah, he has to be. It's his right to be present during all stages of the trial."

"After what that low-life did, he has rights? He already confessed."

Herb's attention seems more focused on organizing his paperwork. "I'm sure H.G. is as anxious as anybody to hear the judge's decision on whether or not to permit testimony regarding the alleged confession."

Alleged? The very word threatens Casey, Bobby, and Brad's credibility.

"Herb. You know it all happened like they said it did."

Herb responds with irritation, as if he were speaking to a slow child. "Gained. Under. Duress."

"I know, I know. Jack has explained the legal part of it to me, but when I hear the word alleged, Herb, he bragged about it. There was no duress at that time. All those kids on my corner knew he did it. When is this going to start, anyway? You told me to get here early and I did. I already feel like I've been here forever."

Herb exhales, his cheeks puffing with exasperation. "It doesn't matter what you know or what I know. It's how the judge chooses to view the facts. If he wants to play it safe and eliminate any grounds for future appeals, he'll rule against leaving the confession in. I haven't heard that any of the defendant's friends are willing to directly rat him out. They were probably advised by their attorneys not to. Anyone who did, would then automatically become part of the prosecution's case."

"Jack said this judge is a middle-of-the-roader."

"Could go either way," Herb says with a shrug.

As though unlocked by Kate's impatience, a door to the right of the bench opens, and a tall man in a long, black robe sweeps in, taking his seat behind the high bench. He is right out of Central Casting, a Spencer Tracy look-alike, with steely grey hair and eyes to match. As he takes his seat, all of the court officers end their conversations, and all eyes are now focused on the judge. But no announcement is made. *Isn't someone supposed to say, All stand?* Reality is very different from TV's interpretation of courtroom dramas.

Then, another door at the front of the courtroom opens, and flanked by two armed guards, H.G. O'Conner is led in. Without even a glance at the Scholfields in the front row, he takes a seat at the defense table, opens the paperback book he is carrying, and begins to read like he is preparing for a classroom test.

His shoulder length hair has been cut short and styled around his face to accent his chiseled features, making him look even younger than Kate remembered. He is wearing a navy-blue jacket with a gilded crest embroidered on one breast pocket. A pinstriped shirt, narrow tie, and shiny new penny loafers complete the transformation. He could easily pass for a Kennedy cousin.

Kate's jaw drops. She wants to scream out, "He doesn't look like that."

Herb grins and shakes his head. "I look at him now and even I find it hard to believe he could be capable of murder. They get 'em all cleaned up. Defense always does that with the perps. Doesn't matter what kind of street scum they're representing. Can't talk now, Kate," he says, standing up. With a nod of his head, he indicates the man who has just seated himself next to H.G. "This is going to be one tough lawyer to go up against. Used to be a D.A. Knows all the tricks."

Without anyone saying "Court is now in session" the judge begins to speak. He states, for the record, the victim's name, when and where he died, and the name of the accused. Now, and forever, entered into the dark side of New York City's history.

The judge looks up from the papers he has been reading and pronounces Scott's murder particularly brutal and vicious, saying that it is his opinion that the actions of Casey, Brad, and Bobby were instigated by a moral desire for biblical justice, and adding that he can understand their outrage. Kate is elated.

He then proceeds to throw the confession out, precisely because of that outrage, finding the victim's friends' explanation, minus their violence, lacking in credibility. He says the account of the confession being made under duress is more believable. Every word spoken during the episode in the Moldorfs' apartment is ruled inadmissible. With that bombshell ringing in her ears, Kate slumps back in her seat.

The jury files into the room, and in an instant, all the players are on stage. Herb is at the prosecution's table leafing through his papers, the defense lawyer whispering in his client's ear at the defense table.

The seats are rapidly filling up all around Kate. The O'Conner family: the parents, two little sisters, and what are probably the grandparents, all arrive taking seats behind H.G. Kate turns to see the rows behind her. She gets a somber nod from Bobby's parents and notices more of Scott's friends have taken seats as well. The last few rows are occupied by strangers, mostly elderly, and all with the empty stares of people who fill their voided lives with other people's real-life dramas. She takes one last look around. True to her word, Brad's mother is a no-show.

The judge wants to know if the People are ready.

"We are," Herb responds as he stands to face the jury. "I'm not going to try to do any whitewash here," he tells the twelve men and women. "The victim in this case, Scott Scholfield, was a drug dealer," he openly lets them know, "just marijuana and a little hash. No hard stuff."

Kate wonders how Scott's family must feel hearing that stated in court officially on New York City records now.

"But Scott didn't make as much money as most dealers do," Herb goes on. "He wasn't very good at what he was doing. That probably sounds like a contradiction to you, but you see, he wasn't pushy, if you'll allow the pun." He puts his hands on the railing of the jury box, leans in, and stage whispers,

"Folks, we're not talking about a hardened criminal here. He was a nineteen-year-old, shy, insecure boy who suffered from dyslexia. He had always been a loner, that is, until he began selling drugs. Then he had friends."

Kate remembers her reaction when she heard that shy, insecure line from Casey and the making friends through drug dealing comment. What must the jurors be thinking? Can Herb really pull this off?

"And because friendships were a new luxury to him, this young man treasured them, and ladies and gentlemen, I want you to know that up until the moment of his death, he considered the defendant to be one of those treasured friends."

His voice loud and clear, he goes on, "You should also know that because Scott was so fearful of being arrested, he only sold to people he knew and trusted. That very same, self-protective stance would become a key factor contributing to his untimely death.

"Now, you are probably thinking, shouldn't such self-preservation have kept him from harm?" He pauses, then spins on his heels, his arm shooting out to point an accusing finger at H.G. as he shouts, "He trusted Harold Gordon O'Connor," in a voice so suddenly loud, it makes Kate jump in her seat. H.G., at least outwardly, doesn't appear to flinch.

Herb goes on to relate the details of the premeditated crime and some of H.G.'s friends' involvement. Garth Gaines provided the gun, and the defendant, accompanied by more of his friends, continued to rob the corpse for days. There is no mention of any confession.

Herb also remarks, "You are going to hear from friends of the victim. Some decent, young men who were so outraged by this brutal murder, that they went to an apartment where they knew they would find the defendant, took the drugs that the victim had been murdered for, and gave them over to the cops. "

Kate frowns. The odd Swiss cheese explanation, full of holes, leaving more unanswered questions than hard facts. But, she tells herself, if the jury has any sense at all, they'll follow the dots and understand what really happened.

Herb goes on, "The fifteen-year-old defendant had become a sort of liaison between his younger buddies and his older victim. He took their drug orders back to Scott and then delivered the reefers to them in exchange for free dope. You have to understand that in the pecking order of drug society, the dealer is on top. The defendant was simply his 'boy,' which did not sit well with Harold Gordon O'Connor. He bitterly resented his lowly status. This murder was planned and carried out for more than the stolen drugs. It was going to make the defendant the 'man' on his little patch of turf. So, Harold Gordon O'Connor decided to make a career move, but the only way to climb the drug world's corporate ladder is to eliminate the competition, and the only way to do that was to kill it. Now you could say the defendant was playing the old game, King of the Hill. But he played it for real.

"I want to make it clear this crime was not solely committed for monetary gain." He points at H.G. again. "This O'Connor kid comes from an affluent family. This killing was for something far more seductive. It was also for the desire for prestige, power, and the right to be called The Man by his peers. Those, my friends, are powerful motives at any age and on any economic level.

"And that's about as cold as it can get. H.G. O'Connor carried out his plan to its bloody end. You should know that two whole weeks before the murder, the defendant announced to his buddies that he not only intended to rip off Scott's stash, but that he fully intended to kill Scott and take over the position of neighborhood drug dealer.

"There were no eyewitness to this killing, no convenient rabbi, priest, or nun to make your job easy. So, the People are going to try to put you there to see it unfold for yourself."

"The victim lived alone and had a lifestyle that often kept him up very late at night. Consequently, it was not unusual for the defendant to ring Scott's doorbell at two or three in the morning, and not uncommon for Harold, better known by his peers as H.G., to ask and be granted permission to spend the night in the victim's apartment. That is exactly what happened in the early hours of that late November night. When the doorbell rang at such a late hour, the victim felt no sense of danger. Sitting on the couch in his own living room, watching TV with H.G., someone he considered a friend, Scott Scholfield couldn't have felt safer. He had no way of knowing the guitar case the defendant carried with him contained a loaded rifle that would end his life."

"This H.G. O'Connor is a very patient young man. He sat there watching Scott light up one joint after another, like a cat watching a mouse. He watched Scott's eyelids grow heavier as the drug he was inhaling lulled him down into the deadliest of dream worlds.

"Only when he was sure the victim had been rendered totally helpless, locked in the grip of a deadly drug-induced sleep, did this young man you see sitting here today, all prettied up like a little gentleman, make his move. Make no mistake, the defendant, who had been boasting about his plan to commit a murder for weeks to anyone who would listen, was not in that apartment for a mere robbery.

"You will be told that the victim was shot at very close range, the bullet entering through the right eye, skimming his red bandana headband. But the shooting didn't end there. You will hear testimony from the coroner that two bullets were found in the victim's skull. Two, yet the weapon used in the commission of this crime was a single-shot rifle. That means the shooter needed to take the time to reload before the second bullet could blast into the now dead skull. Yet the coroner will testify that there was only one entry wound, one unusually large gaping hole in that skull. The conclusion, therefore, is that the second bullet was deliberately fired into the hole made by the first.

"Why would the killer do such a thing? In the sliver of a second that it took to fire the first bullet, the shooter watched Scott's nineteen-year-old brain splatter across the window behind his head. Scott was clearly a corpse. Now I ask you, was that right eye being used as target practice?"

All around Kate, the courtroom hangs in breathless silence. In the front row, the victim's mother, Maggie Schofield's lowered head says it all.

Then in a voice, soft as a feather, Herb gives the jury a chilling, final thought.

"Getting high on marijuana was an everyday occurrence for our little Harold here. But the experience of committing a homicide was a brand new and powerful high for this jaded young man. Was the rush so intense when he fired that first bullet that, like the demand of any powerful narcotic, he needed to have more? Did he crave the experience of killing so fiercely that he took the time to reload and pulled the trigger again, shooting the now dead body? If he had brought more than two bullets, would we have found more spent shells in the cavity that once held the victim's brain?"

Herb picks up a piece of paper and starts rattling off the names on it. Garth Gaines, Claude Moldorf, Amy Drexel, Raul Ramirez, Billy Whitley, Josh and Joel Bernstein, Bernie Maisel, Sheila Barnes, with a brief mention of each one's contribution to the plan.

Then he slaps the list onto the table with the sharp snap of a wet towel. "You might be thinking that a lot of these people should be on trial, too, and I would agree with you, but there is only one person you are here to sit in judgement of." His voice drops to a near whisper. "That person is Harold Gordon O'Connor."

Then, as though an off button had been pushed, Herb's physical demeanor wilts before Kate's eyes. As he shuffles back to his table and sits down, the heavy-set man with flaming red hair seated next to the defendant, stands up.

"Is the defense ready?" the judge wants to know.

"We are, your honor." The defense attorney stands silently leafing through his papers for a moment, then he addresses the jury cordially. "Good morning, ladies and gentlemen."

In spite of his bulk, the man seems more soft than muscular. His ash white complexion is painfully heightened by the luminosity of his unmistakably dyed hair. Kate has an immediate flash of him cavorting across one of her storyboards as a giant animated marshmallow.

The image may be ludicrous, but Kate awaits the marshmallow's response with bated breath. What could he possibly say after Herb's devastating description of his client's guilt?

But as the defense lawyer starts to speak, his voice is surprisingly robust and loud. "The district attorney has made some very serious statements here, but I am telling you now that Harold Gordon O'Connor did not commit this heinous act," he bellows.

"Poor Scott Scholfield is certainly dead, and it is a tragedy to see a life end so young. But right now, somewhere out there, his murderer is walking around a free man, because the prosecution has chosen to put all its eggs in the wrong basket. The burden of proving guilt, however, is one hundred percent on the side of the prosecution and they have put the wrong man on trial," he shouts, this time making even members of the jury jump.

Now he points a finger at H.G., but it is not an accusatory gesture. "This young boy here has his whole life ahead of him. After all the so-called evidence," he smirks, "is presented to you, I am confident you will let him have the future that a fine boy like this deserves, by finding him not guilty."

After Herb's dramatic, and in Kate's view, overwhelmingly convincing opening statement, she is overjoyed at the lawyer's meager defense.

Where did they get this guy?

Chapter Seventeen

Out in the hallway Kate finds a pay phone and calls Jack. "The defense," she reports gleefully, "his lawyer, got up there and said H.G. didn't do it. Can you believe it? That's pretty much all he said. Oh yeah, and what a fine young boy he was. I wanted to throw up. That, after Herb went over H.G. like a steamroller. Whatever the O'Connors paid this guy, I bet they're really pissed right now."

"They should be really pleased," Jack says, bursting Kate's positive bubble. "He chose something simple and set it up right from the start."

He further disappoints her by informing her he won't be driving her home like they had planned. "Traffic below Chambers is a fuckin' horror show that time of day. We can meet later up at the West End for a late bite and a drink."

Back in her seat, Kate hears the judge ask, "Is the prosecution ready with its case?"

"We're ready, your honor," Herb answers.

The parade of prosecution witnesses begins with Garth Gaines dressed in a double breasted, grey suit, his blond hair trimmed to ringlets that surround his face like a halo. He more resembles a little prince than the street urchin Kate knows him to be. Another magic makeover.

After establishing Garth's friendship with the defendant, naming his exclusive private school, and making the jury aware he is testifying under immunity, Herb gets right to the meat of Garth's contribution. The gun.

"Yes, I loaned H.G. my father's gun, but I was told it was only for target practice on the roof."

OK, so that's not the whole story, but at least Herb has now put the murder gun in H.G.'s hands. Kate is pleased.

"Alright, now let's go back to the night of the murder," Herb says. "Where were you that night, Garth?"

"I was at Claude's house with H.G."

"Claude Moldorf, another friend of yours who knew Scott Scholfield?"

"Yes."

"Did H.G. use the telephone while he was there?"

"Yes."

"Who was he calling?"

"Scott, but all he kept getting was the answering machine and then he'd hang up. He wanted to know if he could sleep over at Scott's. He did that a lot."

"What happened later that night?"

"I went home about twelve, and I went to sleep."

"And? And then what?" Herb looks exasperated. Garth was to be, after all, his star witness.

"About three in the morning, Claude called me and said they needed the gun right away 'cause Scott was home and he was alone. Scott told H.G. he could sleep over."

"What did you do then?"

"The gun was in my father's closet, so I had to be real quiet getting it. I met Claude and H.G. in my lobby and gave it to them."

"Was the gun in a guitar case when you gave it to them?"

"Yes," Garth answers in a near whisper.

"Did anyone see the exchange?"

"I think the doorman might have."

Kate is shocked. Jack never mentioned questioning any night doorman.

"When did you next see H.G.?"

"The next day."

"Where and when?" Herb persists.

"I saw H.G. and Claude on the street, each carrying a big black plastic bag."

"Did they say anything to you?" Herb presses on.

Garth licks his lips and glances over at H.G. After a short pause, he answers, "H.G. said it was done."

"Did you ask what he meant by 'it was done'?"

"I asked what was in the bags."

Then Garth says they opened one of the bags, and he saw a bunch of glass mason jars full of sinse.

Herb briefly defines sinse for the jury, then reaching out with both hands, picks up two mason jars stuffed with what looks like dead brown leaves. One in each hand, he holds them up asking in a loud voice, "Can you identify these jars as the ones H.G. showed you the day after the murder of Scott Scholfield?"

In a small, child-like voice Garth answers, "…yes."

"After H.G. showed you these drugs, what happened next?"

"H.G. gave me some of the sinse for loaning him the gun, and he gave it back to me in the guitar case. I thought they used the gun to rip him off. Since Scott was a dealer, they knew he wasn't going to call the police on them." Garth claims he only learned Scott was dead when he heard Casey Palmer had found the body.

The testimony is far more damning than Kate had even dared to hope for.

"What precisely did you ask H.G. when he gave you the drugs?"

"I asked what Scott said when he saw the gun."

"And his answer was?"

"Scott didn't say anything. H.G. said Scott was half asleep and pretty stoned."

"When did you next see Casey Palmer, one of Scott's true friends?"

"I was at Claude's later that day, and he pushed his way in with two other guys, Brad Hillrich and Bobby something. I don't know Bobby's last name. They took all the sinse and left."

Kate gasps aloud. She wants to scream out to Herb, no, take that back. Clarify. The jury will think Casey and his friends were there only to steal the drugs for themselves.

Without looking at the witness, Herb asks, "Oh, by the way, on this occasion, did you indicate to anyone present where the rifle was hidden?"

The defense lawyer leaps to his feet, arms flung out as if to stop a Mack truck. "Objection," he shouts. "The only purpose in pursuing this line of testimony is to use it against my client."

Kate thinks, is this guy for real?

Herb gives the lawyer a withered look and reminds him, "That's the whole purpose of this trial, Paul."

Apparently, for some odd reason, the judge agrees with the defense. He rules against Herb and reprimands him for violating the pre-trial hearing.

Herb throws his hands up in mock disgust but leaves it there. "No more questions," he tells the judge. "I'm through with this witness." But walking back to his table, his face reveals he got what he wanted.

The defense lawyer hikes up his trousers and saunters over to the witness box. He smiles. "Good afternoon, Mr. Gaines. How long have you and the defendant been friends?"

Garth looks puzzled. "Um…I guess a couple of years."

"Where were you born, Mr. Gaines?"

Garth asks for a glass of water and downs it quickly, then, looking puzzled, answers, "New York City."

"Do you know where Harold was born?"

"No." Garth looks really puzzled now.

"In what grade is Harold in school?"

"I'm not sure. He's older than me, I think."

"I see," the lawyer says. "What about Casey Palmer? Do you know where he was born?"

"No, I don't know." Garth is scratching his head. "I don't understand," he responds apologetically. "I mean the subject never came up."

Kate doesn't understand either, but unfortunately, the lawyer has managed to get Casey's name linked to Garth's in a vague friendship sort of way. Is this one of the lawyer tricks Herb was referring to?

"You claim to know Harold well enough to loan him a loaded gun, which you had to steal from your father, yet you're not sure of his age, and you don't know where he came from," the lawyer says, clearly pleased with Garth's responses. "So, Mr. Gaines, are we to believe you handed over a gun to a casual acquaintance, no questions asked?"

"No...well, yes, I gave it to him, but he was my friend."

"When did you first hear of the plan to rob Scott Scholfield?"

Garth licks his lips and asks for another glass of water, which he consumes slowly. "I, well...I heard he was robbed when they said Scott Scholfield was dead."

The lawyer walks briskly over to his table and picks up a piece of paper. "I have here the testimony you gave before the Grand Jury six days after the murder. In it you state," he slips on his bifocals and reads, "the first time I heard about the plan to rob Scott was the day before he died." He glares at the witness. "Were you lying then, or are you lying now?"

How could they allow Garth to lie on record? Like the sudden dropping of an elevator, Kate feels a sickening twist in the pit of her stomach.

This time it is Herb who leaps to his feet with an objection. The judge then orders the jury to leave the room while "a point of law is clarified."

With the jury box empty, the defense lawyer immediately requests a mistrial on the basis of Garth's contradictory Grand Jury testimony. Pointing to his client he loudly asserts, "This fella has been prejudiced."

Herb quickly explains, "This particular Grand Jury testimony was given by Garth only to obtain an indictment against Claude Moldorf on the charge of possession of stolen goods, i.e. Scott's jars of marijuana which was," he adds, "dropped when Claude agreed to also testify against H.G. Separate and different testimony for a separate and different case, consequently irrelevant to the defendant in this trial." The judge buys the argument. Request for a mistrial is denied.

But none of this is explained to the jury when they return, and the discrepancy of time and content in Garth's two testimonies is left to fester midair. The only thing proven here is that Garth has a history of lying under oath. The defense lawyer's motion for mistrial might have been denied, but as the trial resumes, Kate is distraught to see he is smiling openly.

"Did Harold ever carry music books in his guitar case?" the lawyer wants to know, suggesting his client might have had an interest in something other than getting high and killing people.

"I don't know. Maybe," Garth answers in a small voice.

After establishing that it was Claude who, on the day after the murder, was the one who literally physically placed the rifle back in Garth's hands, the lawyer asks the young witness, "Would you know how to tell if a gun has been fired?"

His voice cracking, Garth answers, "It would be smoking?" Ignoring the ridiculous answer the lawyer asks, "On that day after the murder, when Claude Moldorf returned the gun to you, was it still in the guitar case?"

"Yes."

"What did the two of you do, then?"

Garth answers, "We got high together," which just hammers one more nail into the coffin of his credibility.

For the next hour, the defense lawyer nitpicks away at Garth's weak memory with such curious questions as, "Was it raining the night you gave them the gun? If you didn't leave the lobby, how can you be sure it wasn't raining?" And, "On the third occasion that you went to the roof to test-fire the rifle, were there two girls present or was it one boy and one girl?" and finally, "Where were your parents on the night Scott Scholfield was murdered?"

Garth's answer to the last question, "They were up at our house on the Cape," turns Kate's attention back to the jury box again.

Having a house on Cape Cod may be of little significance to the bearded academic in the tweed jacket; the two stylishly-dressed, white women; the balding Wall-Streeter; or the twenty- something woman with the make-up and clothes of a fashion model. But how is this display of affluence, of what the haves have, over the have-nots, going to play with the others? The two black grandmotherly women, the middle-aged Hispanic man who looks like he might be someone's superintendent, the old Jewish woman who has Lower East Side written all over her, the very pregnant Puerto Rican woman, and the rumpled old man so feeble he needs assistance from a court officer every time he enters or leaves the jury box.

Fortunately, the lawyer doesn't dwell on the trappings of Garth's silver-spoon life. But the next subject makes Garth even less appealing. It is a detailed record of Garth's drug history, and oddly, Garth seems more at ease answering this block of questions.

He was almost twelve when he smoked his first joint. His drug of choice? "Marijuana." And he freely admits to smoking at least a dozen joints a day, school days being no exception. Yet he offers a resounding no to the question of his ever dropping acid.

Garth responds with an embarrassed smile when asked how he paid for his drug habit.

His answer is, with his generous weekly allowance.

"By the way, did you ever buy marijuana from your buddy, Claude Moldorf?" the lawyer wants to know.

"Only a jay or two once in a while. When I couldn't fine H.G."

The defense lawyer beams. It was clearly the answer he was fishing for. "So, if Claude was dealing drugs, too, it would not be unusual for him to have these mason jars in his apartment as well. Isn't that so, Mr. Gaines?"

This time Herb is bouncing up and down with his objection, insisting that whatever Claude does or doesn't do with his life has no bearing on H.G. O'Connor's trial, and the judge, Kate is happy to see, now agrees with the prosecution.

But the image of Claude Moldorf as a second neighborhood drug dealer now exists as clearly as the smirk on the defense lawyer's face. For sure, this lawyer has a big bag of legal tricks up his sleeve.

The limitations of the judge's pre-trial hearing pop up again, when the defense lawyer asks, "Were your parents present when you spoke to the detectives in the Emergency Room at St. Luke's Hospital?" the lawyer asks, without giving the jury any explanation of the beating circumstance that led him to be in an ER that night. With no adverse judgement from the judge, the defense lawyer pulls off yet another legal sleight of hand.

Trying to view this through the jury's restricted eyes makes Kate feel like she is reading an Agatha Christie mystery with every other page missing.

"Yes, my parents were there," Garth mumbles feebly.

"In the statement that you gave on that occasion, you stated that you reclaimed the rifle from Claude Moldorf's hands, not Harold O'Connor's.

Was that on the day after Scott Scholfield was killed? And did you also say that Claude paid you ten dollars for the loan of the weapon? Do you recall telling the detectives that, Mr. Gaines?"

Kate looks at Herb, expecting an objection, but his head is bowed. He seems more engrossed in what he is writing. Kate has the sinking feeling that he might not have heard the troublesome question.

Garth is looking at Herb, too. When it is clear there is not going to be an objection from the prosecution, Garth mumbles softly, "Yes, I do remember saying that."

"And was that true, Mr. Gaines?"

"Not exactly," he sputters, looking about as close to tears as he could get without bursting out in them.

The lawyer leans so far into the witness box that he is almost nose-to-nose with the withering witness. "Tell us, Mr. Gaines, when did you first admit that your statements were all a pack of lies?"

Kate squirms in her seat, but she tells herself Herb's lack of objections must be perceived as reassuring. The defense's cheap theatrics are probably a common tactic when the defense has no case.

In response to the lawyer's pack of lies statement, Garth says, "I told the district attorney the truth the first time I met him." His answer is spoken so softly that the judge has to ask him to repeat it.

"Young man," the defense lawyer says in a softer tone, "at this present time are you under psychiatric care?"

"I'm in therapy."

"No more questions."

Like he was duplicating the defense lawyer, Herb stands up, adjusts his belt, and saunters over to the witness. "I do have a few more questions for this witness, your honor."

Herb casually drapes his elbow over the railing in front of Garth, setting the tone for a far less threatening dialogue, and Garth looks noticeably relieved.

"You indicated that you told some lies to the detectives while your parents were present," Herb begins. "Will you tell the court exactly when you leveled with your parents?"

"Later that night, I think." His face scrunches up and he scratches his forehead. "I mean…well, sorta the next morning." Even when Garth is telling the truth it comes out sounding like a falsehood.

"From the time you leveled with your parents till now, have you told the truth?"

'Yes.'

Raising his voice an octave higher, Herb almost shouts, "Are you telling the truth today?"

"Yes, I am," Garth asserts, but his directness in these waning moments of his testimony is so out-of-character, it, too, doesn't ring true.

Herb glances down at his notes. "How long did you say you've been smoking grass?"

"Since I was twelve, about three years."

"In all that time, prior to seeing Scott's mason jars up in Claude Moldorf's apartment, did you ever see anyone else store marijuana in that odd way?" Herb asks cleverly, turning Garth's detrimental drug expertise into a plus for the prosecution.

"No, never," Garth answers with the credibility of an expert witness.

Kate is impressed.

That concludes Herb's attempt at damage control.

Released from the hot seat, Garth is out of the witness box and out of the courtroom in a flash, as Herb announces, "The state calls Vivian Gaines."

The jurors noticeably perk up at the appearance of the spoiled, rich, druggie kid's mother. Reacting as one, their heads turn toward the tall, slender woman in the doorway through which Garth has just escaped.

She is impeccably groomed, slim, wearing a black suit and pearl jewelry. She has ash-blond hair, styled in an impossibly perfect pageboy, and the classic cheekbones that exude old wasp money.

In contrast to her son's time on the witness stand, Vivian's testimony is brief. She only corroborates Garth's claim that a call from Claude had been made to the Gaines' residence at 3 a.m. on the morning of the murder. And with that, Herb is through with her. So apparently, is the defense. "No questions," H.G.'s lawyer says without bothering to look up from his papers. As the judge announces that the trial is through for the day, the lawyer puts his arm around his client's shoulder and whispers something in his ear, to which H.G. responds with an enthusiastic nod.

Chapter Eighteen

That night Kate sits across from Jack in the nearly empty West End Bar, using her fork to rearrange the Caesar salad on her plate, while Jack uses his fork to twirl spaghetti on a spoon. He listens to her monologue with little comment as he eats his pasta. Only occasionally does he interject a nod or a huh.

She asks about Garth's doorman. Did he contribute anything? But Jack informs her, "The guy didn't know shit. At 3 a.m., he was probably sound asleep." Jack shrugs off Kate's idea to question the upper floor residents of Garth's building to see if they heard the test shots that were being fired on the roof. "Would be like trying to find a fucking needle in a fucking haystack," is Jack's response, and he reminds her that since the trial has begun, the investigation is over. "You're going to have to live with whatever Herbie's got," he tells her.

Casey spends the night at Bobby's house so Kate goes back to Jack's apartment. She is finally all talked out and exhausted. Without words, he makes love to her, doing it all for her. He asks nothing of her and afterwards she lets herself fall asleep, lets herself melt into his comforting strength. Wrapped within the sweet warm circle of his arms, she falls into the deepest of sleeps.

Just before dawn she wakes Jack to drive her home. With the early rays of morning light, she will be heading back down to the Center Street Courthouse.

Back in her same aisle seat, Kate watches Claude Moldorf take an oath to be truthful. Little Claude looks even more child-like than she had remembered. With his velvet bow tie, shiny patent leather pumps, and mahogany-colored hair, professionally styled of course, he is the quintessential Little Lord Fauntleroy. When he states his age as fourteen and a half, there is an incredulous stir among both spectators and jurors.

Herb opens with the question, "Where was H.G. living when you hung out with him?"

Claude smiles like a little cherub on a valentine. "Nowhere in particular. He used to sleep in the water tower sometimes." Amazingly Herb lets that enigmatic answer slip by without any explanation to the jury, leaving Kate with the unnerving feeling again, that Herb may not be paying attention to what his witnesses are saying.

But the jurors appear to be all ears now. Sleep in a *water tower*? Agatha Christie is turning into Looney Tunes.

"...and he crashed at Scott's place a lot, too," Claude readily offers. "But I suppose if you're talking legal residence, it would be his parents' apartment on Riverside Drive."

Claude's testimony corroborates much of Garth's. "Yes, H.G. did say that he was only going to use the gun to scare Scott when he robbed him."

Did Claude ever hear that murder was part of the plan?

Claude's answer is an emphatic, "Of course not."

"Did H.G. O'Connor ever tell you that he killed Scott Scholfield?"

Claude answers loud and clear, looking directly at H.G. when he says, "Yes, he did," and Kate feels a chill run through her. This little Claude is one cold cookie.

Unlike Garth, Claude is kept on the stand for only a few minutes of cross-examination by H.G.'s lawyer. Most of the questions pertain to Claude's own dabbling in drug dealing.

Claude coolly smiles as he informs the jury, "Everyone sells a jay now and then." When confronted with Garth's testimony that Claude was the one who returned the murder weapon to Garth, he dismisses that bombshell with a simple, "Just doing a favor for a friend." And with that, he, too, is dismissed.

For this pitifully minor contribution, the district attorney's office had, by prior agreement, dropped all charges against Claude. It looks like little Claude Moldorf had cut himself one sweet deal. As he struts out of the courtroom, the name of the next witness is announced. It is Bernie Maisel.

A court officer holds the door open, and Bernie steps into the courtroom. It is larger than he expected, and though the lighting is no different than it was out in the hall, he feels instantly bathed in the brilliance of a white-hot spotlight. Walking up the center aisle, he sees a wave of heads on both sides turning to stare at him. It is that dream he has where he has been pushed onto a brightly lit stage with his whole school looking up at him, and he has just realized that he is naked from the waist down.

Bernie clasps his hands together, pressing them against his hardening genitals as he hurries up to the witness box. On the way he makes a point of locating where H.G. is seated. Now, at least, Bernie knows where not to look.

Seated in the enclosed witness box he feels protected by some kind of magical Star Trek shield. The D.A.'s questions seem to come from a million miles away. "How old are you? Where do you go to school? When did you first smoke grass? How many joints do you smoke in a day?"

Bernie hears the answers coming out of his mouth like a radio of background noise. Then the questions move to an area that requires his complete attention. The subject of questioning shifts to H.G.

"Now, Bernie, tell us what you and H.G. used to do together," the D.A. asks in a non-threatening tone.

Bernie begins to relax a bit. With one finger he pushes his thick, horn-rimmed glasses back up a notch, gives a little shrug of his shoulders, and says, "Hang out. Smoke."

"Smoke dope?"

"Yeah," he mutters, glancing over at his own attorney seated in the front row. His parents had told him they were instructing the attorney to be present when Bernie testified. They made their displeasure of his actions clear to Bernie by telling him, they, themselves, had chosen not to attend the trial because of the public humiliation Bernie had brought to the family name. Bernie couldn't be more pleased to learn of their no-show decision.

Herb then directs Bernie to, in his own words, trace his steps the night of the murder.

Bernie begins by recounting hanging out at Claude's. He says H. G. was there along with others whose names he cannot remember. Claude's parents, he explains, were on Fire Island, having some work done on their summer house.

Unfortunately, Bernie has to admit to accompanying H. G. on the 2 a.m. walk over to Scott's house. "It was all H.G.'s idea to go over there," Bernie is quick to inform the court.

"On that occasion did H.G. have the guitar case with him?" Herb asks.

"Yes."

"Do you know if the rifle was in the guitar case?"

"Yes," he readily volunteers, like his parents told him to do, adding, "I watched him load it and put it in there."

"Was this done up at Claude's with other people present?"

"Yes." Bernie fidgets in his seat. He didn't realize how difficult it would be to rat out H.G. right in front of H.G.

But the district attorney's questions drone on. "What else was H.G. doing with the gun when you were up at Claude's?"

Bernie shifts uneasily in his seat. Even without looking he can feel H.G.'s eyes boring into him, and it makes him feel like a piece of shit. "He was sort of playing with it, you know, just fooling around. Pointing it at people saying, "Bang, you're dead."

"This was a loaded rifle he was pointing at people?" Herb is quick to establish.

"Yes. Everybody was laughing."

"Did H.G. ever point the rifle at you?"

"Yes."

"Were you scared?"

"No. I was high."

Herb picks up the rifle and, balancing it across his outstretched palms, asks, "On that same occasion did you hear H.G. say anything about killing Scott?"

Bernie looks up at the ceiling trying to remember H.G.'s exact words, the way his lawyer had told him it would be to Bernie's best advantage. He takes a deep breath and says, "Not H.G., but I heard Claude say that if H.G. didn't do it that night, he'd never do it."

"Do you know what he meant by 'do it'?"

"I think he was talking about killing Scott."

"Was anything else said about the murder plan?"

"Claude said it would make him rich."

"And when you realized that they were serious about committing the murder, what did you ask H.G. and Claude?"

"I asked them what they were going to get for it."

Bernie's testimony is making Kate very uneasy. Herb's questions are making it sound more like Claude might have pulled the trigger, and she is relieved to hear Herb say, "No more questions."

But she is not relieved for long.

The defense lawyer has questions, too. He asks if Bernie ever had a conversation with Claude about the murder plan when H. G. was not present.

"Yes," Bernie has to admit. "One time we were up on my roof, waiting for H.G. to bring the gun to test fire again, and I asked Claude if he was really going to do it and he said yes."

The lawyer stands smugly nodding and smiling. "Let me get this straight, Bernard. Are you testifying under oath that Claude Moldorf told you he was going to kill Scott Scholfield?"

Bernie presses back in his seat as if to avoid a blow. "When I said 'you' to Claude, I meant a collective you," he clarifies meekly. He wasn't expecting a personal attack. Why would he be? Bernie didn't shoot anybody. He was just the keeper of the keys.

The lawyer nods agreeably and starts to walk back to his client's table, making it look like Bernie saying a collective you got Bernie off the hook.

But no such luck. The lawyer stops dead in his tracks, spins around, and grasps the witness box so forcefully Bernie can feel it shake. He then shouts at Bernie, "So when you asked him, 'Are you going to kill him?' you were referring to both Claude Moldorf and the defendant?"

Bernie can just about choke out, "I guess...sort of."

The lawyer's voice suddenly lightens. Cordial again, he asks, matter-of-factly, "By the way, Bernard, did you ever tell your parents that you had knowledge of an impending crime or make any attempt to warn Scott?"

"No. I mean my parents didn't know Scott, and I only knew him to say hello to once in a while."

"And, during the four days between the actual murder and the discovery of the body, did you hear any discussions about the killing from anyone other than Claude?"

"Yes. I was with Garth and Claude and...um...a couple of other people were there, too. Garth said 'It was done.'"

"What did you take Garth's comment to mean?"

"That they killed him."

"Objection," Herb shouts loudly. "The defense is attempting to put Claude Moldorf and Garth Gaines on trial instead of the defendant."

Bernie sinks deeper into the witness chair. He can feel Claude and Garth's eyes glaring at him from wherever they are right now. It's not Bernie's fault those words came out. Damn lawyer tricked him into saying all that stuff.

As the lawyer picks up a piece of paper and stands studying it for what seems like forever, the bones in Bernie's butt begin to throb against the rock-hard imprisonment of the witness chair. When is this going to be over? On top of everything else, Bernie has to pee so badly. He clasps his hands over his penis and takes a deep breath.

"The police," the lawyer insists on continuing with, "they contacted you or you contacted them?"

In a flash, Bernie relives the water tower door being pulled open with the vision of a gun barrel pointed at him and with all his groin muscle strength he strains to keep from peeing in his pants. "They contacted me," he answers so softly that he is asked, by the judge, to repeat it.

"Did you tell Detective Kuchinsky that Harold O'Connor was a good friend of yours?"

"Yes."

"And did you say to the detective on that occasion, that on the day after the murder, Harold told you that 'they', Bernard, 'they' killed Scott Schofield?"

Bernie just sits there biting the edge of his thumb. He really can't recall his exact words or even which detective he talked to, and all he can manage to choke out is, "I can't remember exactly what I said."

"Mr. Maisel, do you recall telling Detective Kuchinsky that the aforementioned conversation took place when you were alone with Harold, and only later did Garth Gaines show you the rifle and say, 'We used this'?"

"I don't...well, maybe I did, but I had already seen the rifle a lot." Bernie's eyes blink against the onslaught of verbal punches, and he braces himself for the next blow. But to his utter amazement and relief, the lawyer just turns and walks back to his table saying, "Then I guess I was mistaken. I have no more questions for this witness."

For the rest of the day, Herb parades a string of H.G.'s friends across the witness stand. Was it four more kids? Or five? Kate has lost count. They all look like they've been popped out of the same privileged mold. All their pampered lives unfold as one. A microcosm of the American dream gone terribly awry. Each kid has a beguiling, child-like face, and every one of them is a long time, heavy pot smoker. How do they get stoned every day and still manage to look so young and wholesome?

Also, when did marijuana turn into a deadly nightmare? Grass. The very word has such a green harmlessness about it. Like the quaint hash brownies of the sixties, grass seemed like the most innocuous of the mind-expanders. Nothing an enlightened parent of the seventies, like Kate, needed to be concerned about. Even the term mind-expanders had an appealing ring to Kate such a short time ago, Scott's lifetime ago.

Although high in quantity, the combined testimonies of H.G.'s cronies added little credibility to their overall picture. Most of their statements are so brief and similar, that they blur together. All confessed to taking part in the test-firing episodes, explaining that Garth always supplied extra bullets for the single-shot gun. Though all the witnesses testify to hearing about the murder plan, not one admits to being an actual participant in the crime.

Each and every scenario carefully excludes that particular witness from any participation that might be construed as incriminating. The same incident, when reported by different individuals, is reported to have happened at different times, in different locations, and often with different people present. The once etched-in-stone facts are becoming fuzzy around the edges. Can Herb pull off a win with all this Swiss Cheese he's handing the jury? Of course he can, because truth is on the prosecution's side. Good always wins over evil. At least it does in every crime movie Kate has ever seen.

Even so, Kate has noticed the jury seems, at best, bored by all these spoiled, little, rich kids. Some jurors even sit in the jury box with their eyes closed. Their ears, too? Kate hopes not.

One fact is not disputed, however. Every single witness testifies to having seen H.G. and Garth entering or exiting the victim's building throughout the four days between the murder and the discovery of the body. That's got to put the final nail in the H.G. coffin.

Yet it is the final young witness of the day who brings the true horror back to the surface. His testimony is simply that he heard that Scott opened his eyes and looked at the shooter just before the trigger was pulled.

With that, Maggie Schofield, head bowed, gets up and hurries out of the courtroom.

Chapter Nineteen

Day three begins with Casey Palmer's testimony. As his name is called, Kate wraps her arms around herself the way Jack would if he were here. Only after her son is sworn in does she dare look up at the witness stand.

Conservatively dressed in a dark suit with a pencil thin tie and his once-treasured, shoulder-length hair cut to a short bob, he barely resembles the son she knows. He looks more like a candidate for the Young Republicans Club than a product of the Palmer household. Drugs? Not in the life of this young man.

His expression is blank, but his eyes are fixed on H.G. If looks could kill there would be no need to go on with this trial.

Herb begins with Casey's relationship with the deceased.

"He was one of my best friends," Casey tells the court solemnly.

"And your relationship with the defendant?"

"None whatsoever," Casey answers tersely. "Sometimes he would stop by Scott's when I was there, just to pick up small amounts of grass. Him and me, we never spoke."

"Did you ever see Claude Moldorf or Garth Gaines up at Scott's?"

"Never. Scott only let in people he considered friends."

Then Casey is asked to describe what he saw when he found the body—the blood- splattered window he looked through, the TV still playing in front of Scott's lifeless eyes, the hideous state of his friend's decomposed body, and the stench of death that he will never forget.

Herb also asks Casey about his discovery of the jars of stolen dope that he took from the Moldorfs' apartment. The judge disallows any explanation, except for the fact that H.G. was present on that occasion.

Then Casey testifies to packing the thousands of dollars' worth of dope into a suitcase. With no mention of the confession, Casey's words "and then we took it away from them" bears a very strong resemblance to 'and then we ripped them off,' if the jurors choose to see it that way.

Herb makes an attempt at damage control by saying, "What did you do after you left with the drugs?"

"I called the police and told them H.G. killed Scott, and I made arrangements to turn the suitcase over to them."

"No more questions," Herb says, sitting down and leaving the jury to ponder another dark chunk of Swiss cheese.

The first thing the defense lawyer does is to establish that Casey, too, has immunity, which infers that this witness also has something to hide. With a smirk, the lawyer tosses the jury an incredulous look that comes close to a wink of his eye.

"Mr. Palmer, you testified that at the time of the murder you were a full-time student?"

"That's right," Casey answers icily.

"Are we to believe that as a full-time student your schedule allowed you to spend your days hanging out at a drug dealer's apartment? Or did you just cut classes a lot?"

Casey's face flushes with rage, and Kate has all she can do to keep from exploding. Why isn't Herb objecting?

"I don't cut classes," Casey responds a bit too loudly.

But the lawyer's next question, "What kind of drugs do you take, Mr. Palmer?" does bring Herb to his feet and wins him a "Sustained" from the judge, and a "No more questions," from the lawyer.

All Casey's preparations, the endless discussions about trivia, the terrible anxiety over every detail. Should I wear the blue shirt or the white one? Now it is over, at least it is for Casey.

And what did the prosecution win with this testimony? As the jury files out for lunch with only the already-testified drug histories of H.G.'s cronies to guide them, it isn't hard to imagine what their opinion of Casey and his likely drug history, too, probably is.

Bobby and Brad's testimonies come in the afternoon, adding nothing new. Even Kate finds herself closing her eyes occasionally. The jurors, too, at best seem distracted. One examines his fingernails like he is seeing them for the first time, another has her eyes closed, and the rest have blank stares in assorted directions, all look like their thoughts are elsewhere.

Only when Brad uses the words "pulling out" in his description of the discovery of the mason jars at Claude's does the scene liven up. The defense lawyer leaps to his feet again, waving his arms and shouting objection. The words "pulling out" he says, imply that something more occurred.

Something more did occur, Kate thinks. Your client confessed. But she has to sit tight-lipped as the judge once again agrees with the defense. The words pulling out are stricken, the jury ordered to forget them and that concludes Brad's attempted contribution to H.G. O'Connor's just desserts. Without knowledge of the confession, the combined testimony of Scott's three friends hardly puts a dent in the defendant's plea of innocence.

But, Kate tells herself, the expert witnesses will. The first to testify is the ballistics expert.

"How long would the process of reloading this weapon take?" Herb asks, handing the gun to the witness.

The witness holds the rifle horizontally, pivoting slightly from left to right so that everyone in the room gets a clear view of it. The Scholfield family, in the front row, has no way to avoid it.

"For a novice I'd say about a minute," the expert explains, inserting an imaginary bullet along with the real clicking and snapping sounds, as he manipulates the weapon. "Close the bolt again. Lock it. Now you're ready to fire another shot."

"If this gun were fired by someone, could the second shot ever be considered accidental or the act of sudden emotion?"

"With a full minute needed to reload, I'd say definitely not."

"No more questions." For the first time Kate sees Herb end the day's proceedings with a smile on his face.

On the morning of the fourth day, Jack stands bare-chested in front of the bathroom mirror. He pulls the razor down one cheek, leaving a fleshy pink slash cutting through the white foam, but he is not thinking about shaving. He is remembering how, sleeping on her stomach, the sweet smooth curve of her ass had glowed with a pearly whiteness in the morning's early light. Taking, once again, those perfectly rounded little buttocks and cupping them in his two hands, he gently rolled her over. Rolling her into him. Her eyes opened just a crack, and she smiled a sleepy smile at him, reaching up to let him absorb her, to let him suck in every bit of her. The memory makes him smile, too. Sex is always better for Jack in the morning.

But that morning was two days ago. He is also thinking how nice it would have been if he could have woken up next to her this morning.

He's been seeing her for how many months now? Three? Four? No, it's got to be more than that. It started after they picked up the O'Connor mutt, and that was back around the holidays. It's a long time for Jack to still be attracted.

The string of one-night stands he'd had during his marriage, the waitresses, barmaids, nurses, and occasional stews provided him with the sexual relief that his wife, Paula, considered a low priority once their daughter, Jenny, came along. A man's got to have that relief, doesn't he? If a man can't get it from the woman he calls his wife, he has to look elsewhere. It wasn't like anyone was getting hurt. He made sure Paula never had a clue.

Yet Paula has been the one, steady woman in his life for almost twenty years now. When he lived at home with Paula, those nights he was out bouncing, he'd tell her he was working a case. He could always count on Paula being there when he came home. She was the last thing he saw before he went to sleep, no matter if she was sound asleep, and the first thing he saw when he opened his eyes in the morning. He liked having that. He missed having that. Then Kate Palmer came along.

"Great sex," he'd told Randy when he first started screwing Kate, and surprisingly, all these months later it has stayed good.

But the real surprise is that he finds himself enjoying their times together when they aren't in bed. She laughs a lot and makes him laugh, too, and most importantly, she doesn't try to control him. No inquisition if he's ten minutes late. But why should there be? He's not cheating on her. Not even tempted to.

With Kate he finds they talk a lot more, something there was never enough time for with the one-night standers. They talk about things that have nothing to do with police work: Jack's school, his hopes for Jenny's future, and his plans for his own future. She's all for him becoming a teacher. She's a good listener. How refreshing is that? The bimbos he's used to humping only wanted to know if he ever shot anyone. They always looked disappointed when he told them that he never had. In all these months he never once got that question from Kate.

With Kate, he found himself rubbing elbows with assorted long-haired, artsy types, the kind of characters he never thought he'd be caught dead associating with. At first, he hated being dragged to those gallery openings, those backstage parties with show-biz assholes who think they're too good to give Jack the time of day, and those political rallies where he has to watch he doesn't get caught in the way of any camera lenses. You never know whose files those photos could turn up in, one day.

The extraordinary thing was that, in time, Jack actually found himself enjoying the new voyeurism of it all. He was intrigued by people who dyed their hair green, male couples who wore matching wedding rings, and Madison Avenue WASPS who talk in ten-dollar words and have nothing to say. For Detective Jack Kuchinsky who'd seen and done it all, just being able to have new experiences was an experience.

And he got a real kick out of taking her to places that don't exist in the bleeding heart of the cocoon she lives in. He took her to the track, the fights, home games at Yankee Stadium, after hour bars in Harlem, and Social Clubs in the South Bronx neighborhoods she'd never dare to even drive through without his protection. These were places that those shallow, empty suits she was used to dating would be scared shitless to set foot in.

Food was a big part of their relationship, too. On the Lower East Side, he'd take her for pierogis, then to Coogan's cop bar up on 169th for corned beef and cabbage, and pig-out nights at Jo & Jo's in the South Bronx cop bar, where the Italian hot table can't be beat.

Kate brought new, unexpected tastes into Jack's life, too: Gazpacho soup, sushi. Jack never thought he'd see the day when he'd put a raw fish in his mouth. French cheese, snails, and things made of soybeans that didn't taste half bad. It was a far cry from the meat and potato menu of his marriage, though. He's got to admit that nothing will ever rival Paula's pot roast.

Even Kate's kid turned out to be okay once the smoke settled. The kid's problem was, with no father around, he got himself hooked up with the wrong crowd. Jack saw plenty of that up in Harlem, not that he was going to let himself get suckered into any kind of father role here. He's got his own kid to worry about.

Jack likes how Kate is always available, even on short notice, but no, he doesn't want to spend one hundred percent of his free time with her. The way he's got it now, he can have that one, steady woman in his life, like he did when he was with Paula, without the irritation of having to account for all his time away from her. And no, he doesn't need to stray to find a little sexual excitement anymore. He was really beginning to think he'd stumbled onto something special here. And once the perp was locked up, she didn't say boo about the bullshit Scholfield case anymore.

Yeah, they had a good thing going until the trial started, and she's been driving him nuts with it ever since, fuckin' calling him at his office every time there's a recess and boring him with every minute detail over dinner. What does he care what the expression was on Herbie's face when the judge ruled for or against him?

Even when he's in bed with her, she doesn't shut up or stop yapping about the damned trial. It's like this is the trial of the century, like this shooting was such a tragedy.

How does it look, Jack? What do you think, Jack? Why didn't you question the doorman more, the tenant upstairs, downstairs, Howdy-Doody, the man in the moon? Civilians, they always think they know more than the cops do. He sits, listening in silence most of the time, hoping she'll take the hint. She never does.

Jack has certainly seen his share of real tragedies: a mother and father whose little girl has been raped and killed, somebody's son shot because he walked down the wrong street at the wrong time, and a cop gets killed and Jack has to console the grieving widow at the wake.

But the Scholfield death? Just one less drug dealer out there to pollute the few clean kids that are left. A couple more days and this case is history for Jack, and if it's not for Kate, then maybe she's history, too.

He puts the razor back in its case, slaps some cold water on his face, then blots it dry with a wadded towel. He's due in court in an hour. The D.A.'s message was that Jack's first up at bat.

When Jack enters the courtroom, he spots Kate immediately, up front on the aisle. That silky, long blond hair would stand out in any crowd. As he walks by, she turns to look at him, and his fingers reach out to slyly give a lock of her hair a small affectionate tug, to let her know, "It's okay. I'm here now."

He takes the witness stand and swears to tell the truth as he has done so many times before. He unbuttons his jacket and sits down as easily as if he were about to watch a Giants game.

"Detective Kuchinsky," Herb begins in that whiny-wimp voice of his, "will you tell the court, what is the function of a homicide detective?"

Jeeze, he hates when a D.A. pulls this kindergarten crap on him. "To investigate homicides." He has to embarrass himself by answering the obvious.

He's asked to establish some particulars of the crime scene: address, date he was called there, and the fact that there was no sign of forced entry.

Herb hands him a batch of glossy eight by tens and asks, "Are these photographs of the deceased taken at that crime scene?"

With no sign of emotion Jack flips through the dozen or so photos of a rotting carcass that had once been a healthy, young man. No, Herb, they're pictures of my daughter's confirmation. "Yes," he answers, and hands them back. As he does, he glances out at the spectators, making momentary eye contact with the victim's mother.

Her face is almost as drained of life as her son's in the photos. Her eyes are red, but bone dry, as if she'd used up her lifetime quota of tears. Her eyes plead for Jack to take one more look at the photos and tell her he's made a terrible mistake. No, Mrs. Scholfield, it's not your son after all. No question she deserved better than the low-life she got dealt for a son. He feels for the woman, but he can't give her what she wants, her son back.

He looks over at Kate. Her eyes, like the victim's mother, implore him, too.

What do they all want from him? Jack has his own problems, like not being able to see his little girl every day, and figuring out what to do with the rest of his life if he retires, and how to survive the boredom of the job if he doesn't.

And then there's money…There's never enough to cover two households, and now Jenny's orthodontia added to the list of what he has to shell out. Finding a good woman who doesn't always want something from him is also challenging. He was beginning to think Kate Palmer was that woman. Now she's sitting there looking up at him with those gimme-gimme eyes, just like the rest of them.

Herb's attempt to pass the photographs on to the jurors has touched off a slugging match with the defense lawyer, as Jack knew it would. With the jury hustled out of the room, Jack sits back and takes a coffee-less coffee break in the witness box.

"If those photos are admitted, it will be highly prejudicial to my client," the lawyer argues vigorously. "Any human being would have to be affected by what's in those pictures. Casey Palmer testified that when he looked through that window and saw the hideous condition of the body, he'd seen enough. These photographs only illustrate what the medical examiner is going to testify to later. The jury doesn't need this ghoulish embellishment."

Got to hand it to him, the guy's a sharp piece of work, using the words of a prosecution witness to benefit the defendant. But Jack's professional admiration is not shared by all. Out where Casey and a handful of Scott's other friends are seated, a noisily animated flurry is admonished by the judge.

The brief time-out ends with the judge ruling the photographs admissible. Being in black and white makes them, he says, far less inflammatory.

With that, the jurors are brought back in and a beaming Herb, along with the rest of the silent courtroom, has to wait as each juror takes his or her turn to view the pictures of what Jack has spent the last eighteen years of his life viewing. In apartments, back alleys, on rooftops, and in the trunks of abandoned cars. Join the club, folks.

Jack is shown the weapon and identifies it as the rifle he picked up at the Gaines' apartment. When he indicates the three gold letters on the butt, R.R.G., and confirms them as being Garth's father's initials, another muffled rumble stirs from the victim's friends' enclave.

Jack is then asked to describe the circumstances concerning the recovery of the drugs, and he shifts uneasily in his seat. "I received them from a lawyer, Mel Rubinstein, who represented Casey Palmer, Brad Hillrich, and Robert Ardsley," he tells the court. As he hears himself say their names, a hot rush of anger surges through him. Fucking, arrogant, little shits. They made his job a hundred times tougher. The so-called Upper Class? He found out with this case that they're as dirty as any mutt on the street.

Before getting up to cross examine, the defense lawyer takes an inordinate amount of time to listen to something his client is whispering in his ear, and Jack uses the lull to take a hard look at the young defendant. A shithead is a shithead, no matter how they pretty 'em up. What a shame he and Randy didn't have a chance to get this sucker alone. This one would have snapped like a twig.

With a reassuring pat on the mutt defendant's shoulder, the lawyer finally stands up. "Detective Kuchinsky, how many of the victim's mason jars did you recover from Casey Palmer's attorney, Mel Rubinstein? He is a criminal lawyer, I believe, isn't he?"

Oldest lawyer trick in the book: try to make somebody else look more guilty than the lying piece of scum they're defending.

Jack takes a small notebook out of his pocket and flips through it till he finds what he's looking for. "My notes indicate eight."

The lawyer walks over to the evidence table and starts poking around in the individual bags. "One, two, three," he counts out loud, then frowns, "I only see seven jars here," he exclaims as though he'd been personally robbed.

Herb stands up, shoulders dropping in mock irritation. "Come on, Paul," he says under his breath, but loud enough for all to hear, and wearily pulls a small bag out of one of the larger ones. "It was explained in discovery that, while in police custody, one of the jars had been dropped." Herb holds up the bag and jiggles it, the rattle of broken glass verifying his claim.

The lawyer moves on with his questions for Jack. "When you interrogated Bernard Maisel was anyone present?"

"His parents were there."

"Did you take hand-written notes at that time, detective?"

"Yes. Later they were reduced to DD5s," Jack responds professionally, and clarifies DD5s for the civilians are a police report. Jack likes questions where he can give a pat, indisputable answer.

"Can you produce the handwritten notes now?"

Ah, shit, he can't. Fucking Herbie never told him to bring them. He hates it when a D.A. leaves him out on a limb like this. It's the D.A.s' responsibility to see that all his prosecution witnesses are fully prepared, it's not the detective's job. "Those particular notes are in a case folder in my office."

"What was the result of the canvass done at the victim's building?"

"One individual," Jack flips through the notes he did bring, "a Mrs. Wong, I believe, told me she thought she'd heard a shot on the day the victim died." He finds the page. "Yes, Wong."

"I see." The defense lawyer perks up. "But this Mrs. Wong is not on the prosecution's witness list, is she detective?" Before Jack can open his mouth to defend himself, the impression Jack and Herb are trying to hide something is further compounded by, "and after the prosecution paraded its juvenile witnesses before the jury, all claiming that the victim was shot at night, you just stated this new witness heard a shot on the day of the murder. The day, detective? Exactly what time of day did this Mrs. Wong, whom the prosecution has curiously chosen not to produce, tell you she heard the shot?"

This is what Jack hates about the cross. He does his job to the hilt, sometimes putting his own life on the line, then some motherfuckin', shyster lawyer comes along and tries to trip him up, tries to make Jack look like some kind of incompetent fool. And why? Just to get another shithead off the hook. Lawyers? What do they care about justice? What they care about is the fat check that comes along with all the not-guilty verdicts they get.

Herb makes a feeble attempt at damage control, explaining that the Wong information was only hearsay and therefore deemed unacceptable.

Without missing a beat, the lawyer moves on to the rifle. "Was it ever dusted for prints?"

"I don't believe it was." Jack has no choice but to reveal, fully aware his uninformed audience is now probably convinced he is a complete incompetent.

He looks out at Kate. She looks more sad than disappointed, like a little girl who's just been abandoned. He wants to reach out and put his arms around her to tell her he didn't just let her down. He wants to remind her that half the time, dusting for fingerprints doesn't mean shit because they evaporate in a matter of days, hours even, depending on the material and the temperature. He wants to tell her that Mrs. Wong was a half-deaf, old hag who barely knew what day it was. He wants to tell her that all that should matter to her is that her son is alive and kicking. Her son is not even in trouble with the law anymore. Bottom line, your own is all that matters.

That's all that Jack cares about. His daughter, his mom. Maybe Paula, still. If anyone ever tried to fuck with her, yeah, he'd be there for her.

"Specifically, what items, if any were dusted for prints, detective?"

Jack wants to say, "Schmuck, do you have any idea how many homicides have come across my desk since the Scholfield kid was blown away?"

Instead, Jack asks Herb for the report from the crime scene and sits studying the long pink form for a few silent seconds before handing it back. "A couple of drinking glasses, doorknobs, and the glass top on the coffee table."

"That's it?" The lawyer gasps in mock amazement. "Did Harold's fingerprints match any of those taken from the crime scene?"

Cute piece of work, this guy, forcing Jack to concede, "No, not that I recall," when this smug son-of-a-bitch already knows that. It would be irrelevant even if they found the defendant's prints anywhere in the victim's apartment since it has been established that he often went there.

"I have no more questions," the lawyer concedes, returning to the defense table where he listens to some whispered comments from the defendant.

Herb stands up. Reading from the notes he's been taking throughout the cross-examination, he asks, "Detective Kuchinsky, what was the first thing done to that gun after you received it?"

Now it is redemption time for Jack's professional reputation. "It was vouchered, then sent to ballistics, then to the property clerk's office. That's standard procedure." Jack knows that just following orders goes a long way to helping erase the stigma of incompetence.

"At some point did you touch the rifle?" Herb asks.

"Of course," Jack answers with a sigh. How is Jack supposed to have picked up the gun at the Gaines' apartment without touching the damn thing?

"How many people would you estimate touched that weapon?"

"Anywhere from ten to thirty."

"No more questions."

Jack is mortified. No, Herb, there have to be more questions. It's your job to educate the jury. Civilians think fingerprints are etched in granite; they think they last forever. You have to tell them prints rarely read. Don't leave it looking like I fucked up.

Unlike his entrance, Jack exits without even a perfunctory glance Kate's way.

He looks really rattled as he hurries down the aisle. She knows she shouldn't take it personally, but the rebuff does bother her, leaving her feeling let down...let down by his testimony performance as well.

Jack's testimony was certainly the far greater let down. That was not the Jack Kuchinsky she expected to see up there. Or, has she just watched an unscrupulous attorney in action, who molds evidence even from an expert witness like Jack, to benefit his client? Kate is beginning to understand why Jack despises the legal profession so much.

She did know, however, that Jack would not be sitting down beside her after he testified. He'd called last night to tell her that. The jury's seen her sitting there, front and center, from day one. It's got to be clear she's got a personal stake in the outcome of this case. Jack said his fraternizing with her could damage his credibility as a witness. It makes sense, but poor Jack did a pretty good job of damaging that himself.

The prosecution's next witness is the coroner, a petite Indian woman dressed all in black, her dark complexion made even darker by the red dot in the middle of her forehead. She states, in a pleasant British accent, that her department handles approximately three thousand autopsies a year. With that said, she establishes her credentials as an expert in the art of slicing and dicing cadavers. If Kate found herself sitting across from this woman in the subway, she would never have guessed her to be someone who spends her days probing dead flesh from nine to five.

To describe the body, as it was found, the witness slips on her glasses and reads from the Homicide Scene Visit Sheet, "White male. Seated on couch. Feet propped up on coffee table. Arms stretched out along back of couch. Head slightly to one side in a somewhat unnatural position. Body badly bloated. Condition of crepitus visible. Skin on arms, head, and chest turned decidedly black." It is what Casey saw when he looked through that window. Now Kate is seeing it, too, along with David and Maggie Scholfield.

But Herb insists on making his captive audience see more, asking for the findings of the autopsy report, and the witness is given another piece of paper to read from.

"Both eyes open but collapsed and sunken in due to the advanced state of decomposition. All fluid in eyes drained and seeping into brain. Two bullets found free-floating in brain." She looks directly at the jury and explains, "Because of the advanced state of decomposition, the brain had become totally liquefied."

Kate reels from the impact of the picture the coroner's words have painted, but when the witness reads, "Single entry wound of an unusually large size in right eye," a ray of gratitude cuts through the horror. That proves Herb's contention that H.G. purposely reloaded and shot the second bullet into the hole made by the first.

She goes on, "Powder burns around entry wound. Tongue swollen and protruding from mouth. Death occurred four or five days earlier. That is the conclusion of the autopsy report," and she hands the paper back to Herb.

Herb then gives the witness two bits of shiny metal, and she rolls them over in her palm for a moment, closing her eyes and lifting her head, as though the feel of the metal brings back a cherished memory. They are, she says, the bullets that were recovered from the victim's skull.

Bits of metal recovered from a skull? They were recovered from a place that knew joy and laughter, sadness and pain. It was a place where a sense of humor, a love of music, an appreciation of beauty once flourished; where the love of family and friends was kept; where hopes and dreams for the future were safely stored away. Was any of that recovered?

When Herb sits down, to Kate's utter amazement, the defense lawyer stands up. Why would the defense want another word to come out of this witness's mouth? All she can attest to is a description of the monstrosity that his client created.

"Doctor, how many decomposed bodies have you autopsied?" the defense lawyer wants to know.

"Personally? Probably about eighteen hundred," she answers with a sweep of her small hand.

Kate notices there is a gold band on her wedding finger. How does this woman go home after cutting up cadavers all day, and with those same little hands, prepare dinner for her family? How do they eat it?

"Correct me if I'm wrong, but aren't there different kinds of decomposition?" the lawyer asks as if he didn't already know.

"That is correct, sir. A body decomposes fastest in air, in warm temperatures, such as one might find in a flat." She corrects herself, "I mean in an apartment. Water next. Underground last."

The lawyer paces back and forth, his hands locked behind his back, his eyes first on the ceiling, then on the floor, showing everyone that he's really thinking this one out. He asks, "Isn't it true that in this case, the upper half of the body was more decomposed than the bottom half?"

"Yes."

"So then, doctor, you are saying that in examining the lower part of the body that was less decomposed, you would conclude that death occurred, perhaps, a day or two earlier? Not as you stated in your report, four or five days earlier?"

The witness looks like she can't believe what she is hearing. "I don't understand your question, sir." Neither does Kate. Time of death is one of the few homicide facts that is etched in stone.

"My question is very clear," he responds abruptly. "In examining the bottom part of the body, wouldn't you have to conclude a different time of death?"

The expert frowns and shakes her head. "Well, I suppose one might in theory, but parts of the same body cannot die days apart. That is an absolute fact. My evaluations are made after examining the entire body. In this case I found the top part to be at the level of four or five days of decomposition."

"Isn't it true that the top part of the body was close to a radiator? That fact could have accelerated the rate of decomposition, couldn't it, doctor?"

Now the woman looks really irritated. "Yes, but in my professional opinion, as I have already stated…"

He interrupts, "And this unnatural position which you reported the body to be in. Are you suggesting it was moved by someone?"

"I said the head appeared in a somewhat unnatural position."

"Were you the medical examiner who was called to the Scholfield apartment when the body was discovered?"

"No, I was not. I did the autopsy later."

"Then are we to conclude that all your testimony regarding the condition of the body at the crime scene is second hand?"

The witness leans forward, her nostrils flaring ever so slightly. "Sir, as you well know, in my capacity as a supervisor, I am qualified to quote from official reports."

"Would you tell the court what crepitus is?"

The witness nods in compliance. Being asked to explain a medical term breaks the tension. "It is a condition created by the building up of gas under the skin during decomposition causing the skin to become paper thin and bubbly. It produces a crackly, popping sound when touched. The deceased had developed this condition."

144

Kate's eyes are once again drawn to where Maggie is sitting. Even from the back she can see that the woman is trembling.

"Isn't it a fact that crepitus, as well as liquidation of the brain, are conditions that are ordinarily only found after a body has been dead for eight or nine days?"

What is he doing? First, he wants her to say Scott was dead one or two days, now he's got it up to more than a week. Why is Herb permitting this lunacy to go on?

"Ordinarily, yes," the witness yields, "but not in cases of gunshot wounds. The hole created by the bullet lets air directly into the brain. That immediately speeds up all phases of decomposition."

"Is it possible another doctor might have a different opinion?" He persists like the pit-bull he's shown himself to be.

With a sigh and a glance at her watch, the witness concedes. "Doctors can, sometimes, disagree." And with that, the list of expert witnesses comes to an end.

Chapter Twenty

It is almost 10 a.m., and in just a few minutes, the defense of H.G. O'Connor will begin. In the hallway outside the courtroom, amidst the morning's pedestrian rush of lawyers, court officers, and plain-clothed cops on their way to other trials, Kate stands talking to Herb.

"I'm kind of worried about the judge," she tells Herb, keeping her voice low. The O'Connor family is standing only a few yards away, waiting for the courtroom to open again. "He has ruled a lot in H.G.'s favor." What she really wants to know is why Herb isn't objecting more.

Herb, with his arms, as usual, full of pink paper files, gives her a little shrug. "That's the way he is, this judge. He's a big advocate of defendant's rights. But don't be misled by his rulings. I was talking to him in chambers yesterday. This kid has really gotten to him."

"What do you mean gotten to him?" a panicked Kate wants to know. "Please don't tell me the judge is sympathetic to H.G."

"He's got a teenage son, too. Kid's picture is on his desk. Nice, clean-cut kid. He said the kids he's seeing in this trial, even the defendant, look a lot like the friends his son brings home. Same private schools, expensive haircuts, talk about country houses. Money knows money."

"You're not telling me he's taken a liking to these kids?" she asks with horror.

"Quite the contrary. You got to understand, this judge sits up there day after day, seeing poor, mostly ghetto kids, come before him for robbery, murder, dope dealing, rape, whatever. He can be objective 'cause there's nothing for him to identify with. But here, he's seeing affluent kids from so-called good homes, accused of committing the same heinous crimes as the ghetto kids. With this bunch, the way they look, the lifestyles they're describing, he told me it's like watching his own world on trial."

"He said that. Does that mean, at sentencing, he'll be harder on H.G. or more lenient?" Herb's sharing of the judge's anxiety only heightens Kate's. She folds her arms across her chest, sorry that she'd stopped to talk to Herb at all.

He shrugs again and smiles inappropriately. "Eh, who knows."

Enough handling Herb with kid gloves. She pays her taxes that pay Herb's salary. "Listen, Herb, when you're in his chambers having these private conversations, can't you talk to him off the record? Make him understand that even though the confession isn't admitted it still exists. He knows H.G. did it, for God sakes. Everybody knows H.G. did it."

Herb's face flushes red. "Kate, I got a lot on my mind this morning," he snaps curtly. He leafs through one of his files, pulls out a paper, and makes her wait while he peruses it for a few seconds. Then he looks up and grants her an empty smile. "In a case where there is such obvious guilt, it's a lot more prudent for a judge to rule more often in favor of the defendant. Less chance for an appeal that way." He motions toward the people beginning to file into the courtroom. "We're going to start now." His smile warms up. "Act two."

She crushes the empty coffee cup in her hand, drops it in the trash can, and follows Herb into the courtroom. How quickly coming to this dreary public place has become like a job, her daily routine. A part of her wants to stand up and scream, "Let me out of here." But her detention is self-imposed and obligatory. After what H.G. put her son, and her through, how could she sit in her office, drawing little cartoon characters when the trial is going on? How could she miss experiencing the moment of H.G.'s just comeuppance?

Until that guilty verdict is read aloud, Kate, her son, along with the two lawyers, the O'Connor family, and the judge and jury are as much prisoners here as H.G. is.

Before the jury is brought in, the defense lawyer is on his feet again, making yet another attempt at having the charges dropped. His rationale for letting

H.G. walk? He claims, "The prosecution has not presented a strong enough case."

Where has this guy been all week?

On the murder charge the judge disagrees. "The People have met their burden here," but on the robbery charge he pauses and nods his head. "I'm not convinced. I might consider dropping that charge."

Kate wonders if this one of those less chance for an appeal moves Herb said this judge is prone to make.

Herb vehemently opposes dropping anything. But Kate doesn't understand why. Drop the bullshit robbery charge and give the defense his puny victory. Convicting the defendant for murder is all that really matters.

Now, all of a sudden, the defense lawyer says he wants the robbery charge left in, saying if he can't have both charges dropped, then he wants both left standing because, "The jury may be willing to believe my client agreed to participate in a robbery because he did not think anyone was going to get hurt. If the sole charge standing is Murder Two, then they would be backed into a corner, forced to convict on the greater charge in order to punish for the lesser."

Kate strains to follow his reasoning but this is all beginning to sound like a gobbledygook game. Has everyone forgotten the word justice?

Apparently, the judge is fluent in gobbledygook. He nods like he thinks the lawyer has just said something brilliant. Then he looks down from his bench as though he were about to bestow a blessing on the two adversaries and declares, "This is not a simple case."

It is to Kate, and it was certainly simple when they started.

The judge goes on, "I want to be sure the jury understands this case on a fair and equal basis." Then he offers the option of a third charge. He suggests splitting the murder charge in two. The first, Intentional Murder premeditated, and the second, Felony Murder a homicide, occurring during the course of another crime such as robbery. "In the event the jury fails to find the defendant guilty of either murder charge," the judge says, "I can then send them back to deliberate on a third charge, Robbery."

"I can live with that," Herb tells the judge.

But the defense lawyer can't. "What if they decide the robbery happened days after the murder?" he speculates.

"Jesus, Paul, you know that would be a larceny charge. You can't commit robbery on a corpse," Herb says.

"Alright then, how about this," the defense lawyer persists, concession clearly not a word in his vocabulary. "Let's say my client had no intention of killing anyone, but because of the drugs in his body, he shoots the victim and then robs him as an afterthought. I could go for a manslaughter charge."

Is this due process? Sounds more like they're playing "Let's Make A Deal" with Scott's death, rewriting the history of the crime to accommodate the desires of both legal sides.

The judge, brow knit, lips pursed, eyes off to one side, is actually pondering this crap. Kate has the unnerving feeling that she is watching three men breaking the law. But these men are the law.

After nearly an hour of wrangling with every possible scenario, except the one that actually occurred, they return to square one. The two original charges of Murder Two and Robbery are left standing. With that settled, the jury files in and the defense calls someone named Julia Annenberg as their first witness.

She is a small, doll-like woman in her late thirties, dressed in a grey polka-dot shirtdress. As she steps into the witness box, her diamond earrings, like two twinkling stars, catch the light on both sides of her pretty face. When she raises her hand to tell the truth, her ring finger reveals a considerably larger sparkler. She states her occupation is a housewife, smiles and corrects herself with, "I mean homemaker."

"You're currently married?" the defense lawyer asks with a cordiality he has not displayed before.

"Yes. My husband John is a pediatrician at Lenox Hill hospital."

"And you have children?"

"One. Daniel. He's two and a half." She turns to the jury and adds with a little laugh, "Almost over the terrible twos," causing some smiling reactions from the female jurors.

Herb immediately objects. Kate wonders if her pep talk might have had an effect on him after all.

Herb tells the judge, "Mrs. Annenberg's family life has no relevance to this case."

But the lawyer insists it does, claiming it will show the defendant's state of mind on the day of the murder, and again, he gets what he wants. The line of questioning is allowed to continue, and the witness presses her hand against her stomach and beams as she offers without being asked, "I just found out that Daniel will be getting a little brother for Christmas."

Kate looks over at the jury. The two older black women and the Jewish grandmother are all openly smiling. Whoever Julia Annenberg is, she is certainly coming off favorably with them.

The lawyer finally gets down to business. "Mrs. Annenberg, what is your relationship to the defendant?"

The witness smiles fondly at H.G. "I'm Harold's cousin," she says, looking like she is about to blow him a kiss.

"No offense, but you seem much older than Harold."

She laughs. "I am. Although my father and Harold's father are brothers, there are almost twenty years between them. I've always been more like an aunt to Harold."

"Did Harold ever live with you and Dr. Annenberg?"

"Yes. The summer before last, he spent two months with us. He was having a few problems with his dad at the time. Nothing serious," she's quick to clarify. "Being a pediatrician, John sees it all the time. He calls it adolescent testing. Growing pains. Harold's parents, John and I, and the caseworker, all agreed that a change of environment might be good for Harold. Get him out of the city for a while, to Dobbs Ferry. That's where we live in Westchester. It's a much more relaxed setting. A place where a young boy can feel safe on the street."

A caseworker? The perfect wife/mother just revealed a chink in her dear Harold's armor. A kid who needs to be assigned a caseworker is in a lot more trouble than just growing pains.

"After that summer, how often did you see Harold?"

"About every other week, but we often had long talks on the telephone," she responds pleasantly.

"Can you recall the last time you saw Harold before that Thanksgiving holiday?"

"Yes. The day before the holiday he came to see me."

"In Dobbs Ferry?"

"Yes. He took the train up."

"Do you remember what time of day he arrived?"

"Absolutely, because I made lunch for him as soon as he got there. It was around noon," the witness says looking straight at the jury.

Kate begins to feel those little birds fluttering in her chest again. Noon in Dobbs Ferry on the same day Scott was later killed? H.G. was doing a lot of traveling, back and forth, that day.

"I remember it was unusually warm, more like a spring day. So after lunch, we went for a walk down by the river. Our house is right on the Hudson. The view is magnificent," she offers like anybody gives a damn. "We took little Daniel with us. Harold is so good with children."

"Where did you go after your walk?"

"Back to my house. I fixed some tea and we sat and talked till almost four. Then I drove him to the station, and he caught the four-ten back to the city."

Oh, shit. The woman has the time screwed up. By four, countless people, including Casey, had seen H.G. in the neighborhood.

Yet, head bowed, Herb is as usual, totally engrossed in his note taking.

"When you took Harold to the train, did he tell you where he was going and what his plans for the evening were?" the defense lawyer asks as if Harold was going to tell her he was on his way to commit a murder.

"Yes, he did," she answers pleasantly. "He was going back to Manhattan to pick up a change of clothing. Harold was feeling a bit anxious about the upcoming holiday. The plan was for him to catch the next train back to Dobbs Ferry and stay with John and me for the long Thanksgiving weekend." She shakes her head wistfully. "You know how stressful family get-togethers can be for a teenager. Harold has always been a very sensitive boy."

This time Herb does object, and with a passion that Kate has not seen him display before. His arms shoot up like someone has just told him to stick

151

'em up. His voice shrieks, like fingernails on a blackboard. He is demanding the word sensitive be stricken from the records. "This is pure conjecture on the part of the witness," he argues.

He wins this one. This time it is Herb who sits down sporting a Cheshire cat grin.

But where is his victory? Twelve people just heard what appears to be a nice lady, describe the young, frail, and certainly clean-cut looking defendant as sensitive. The word is stricken, but the image it left behind is indelible. Herb might have scored a technical knockout but even when the defense loses he manages to come up a winner.

The witness's cordial manner makes it clear she wasn't at all intimidated by Herb's bombastic outburst. She picks up her description of the O'Connor's Thanksgiving holiday gathering right where she left off. "Since it was our year to host the dinner with Peg and Roger, Harold's parents, it just made sense for him to stay with us." Her smile couldn't be more sincere when she adds, "We so enjoy having him."

"After you saw Harold board the four-ten train back to the city, when did you see him next?"

"A few hours later. Early evening. He stayed with us through the long holiday weekend."

Like a lightning bolt hit her suddenly, it dawns on Kate. This woman isn't confused about the time at all. This woman knows exactly what she is doing. She is blatantly lying.

Kate is spellbound by what she is watching. A woman who has sworn to tell the truth in a court of law, her hand on a Bible, looking straight at the jurors and cool as a cucumber, testifying to times and facts that could not have happened. Kate holds her breath, half expecting a court officer to step up and slap the cuffs on the witness for perjury, and half expecting a bolt of lightning to come down and strike the woman as she sits in the witness chair. Kate is fully expecting Herb to do something.

But nothing happens to her. Herb doesn't even object to lies going into the court records. In a manner so relaxed that she might be telling little Daniel a bedtime-story, the witness just continues relating her account of the night her sensitive cousin committed a brutal, cold-blooded, and premeditated murder.

"Ordinarily, 11 p.m. is late for me," the Dobbs Ferry cousin goes on, successfully slipping in the time again. She has obviously been well coached. "But I sensed Harold needed a little company so I made some tea, and we talked till almost three in the morning. Then I went to bed, and Harold turned on the TV in the den." She smiles again. "He kept the sound low, of course."

The farce continues with, "I can't say exactly what time he dozed off, but when I got up to feed Daniel, that was a little past six the next morning, Harold was sound asleep on the sofa in the den. I know 'cause he left the TV on, and I went in there to shut it off. But I didn't disturb him. I believe he slept till about ten in the morning."

In the back of the courtroom a murmur, like the moan of a wounded animal in the woods, interrupts the testimony and the judge has to, once again, admonish a cluster of Scott's friends.

Fueled by the woman's audacity, Kate feels her heart pounding out of her chest. She wants to stand up and start screaming, "Liar. Liar. Liar." But all she can do is grit her teeth, sit silently, and in her head, plead to the jurors to see through this witness's pathetic sham. All eyes, and a handful of juror's smiles are riveted on the amicable woman. Were their roles reversed, even for the best of causes, Kate would be choking if she tried to tell those lies under oath. Kate would be betrayed by her own conscience, her eyes would blink too much, her face would twitch, her mouth would become drier than any desert. God, how she wants to stand up and shout out the truth to those misguided, smiling jurors.

The defense lawyer is smiling, too. "When Harold got up that Thursday morning, where did he go?"

"Nowhere. He stayed in the house most of the day practicing his guitar."

The fucking woman is even covering his ass on the guitar case.

"As it turned out, Harold ended up staying with us all the rest of that week, then he went home to see his friends."

None of his friends saw him that week; that was when the police were looking for him. Dobbs Ferry, so, that was where he was hiding out. Kate feels like her head is going to explode.

"When did you next see Harold?" the perennially-smiling lawyer asks.

"A month later in the police station."

"Mrs. Annenberg, are you familiar with the Amtrak train schedules between Dobbs Ferry and Manhattan?"

"Very familiar, but I have to tell you, there aren't many late-night trains. I mean trains after midnight, and if you did manage to get one, when you got to midtown Manhattan, you would still have to wait for a subway or bus to go to Harold's Upper West Side home."

"Then, in your opinion, would it have been possible for Harold to leave your house after you went to bed at three, travel to Manhattan by train and subway, commit a murder, and then return to your house for you to find him asleep at 6 a.m. the next morning?"

Thankfully Herb is on his feet, immediately objecting, saying the witness's personal opinion is irrelevant, and the judge agrees this time, though not soon enough to stop the witness from blurting out, "Absolutely not."

"No more questions," the lawyer says, looking out at the O'Connor family with a broad smile and an affirmative nod, while Julia Annenberg is left to sit in a few minutes of uncomfortable silence as Herb rummages through his files.

Apparently, Herb didn't find what he was looking for, because he finally puts his papers down and walks over to the witness box empty-handed. He begins with the question, "How close are you to your cousin?"

"Very close." Does this woman ever stop smiling?

"Do you love him very much?"

"Yes, I do." Smile, smile, radiant smile.

"Enough to do anything for him?"

Kate is on the edge of her seat now. Go for it, Herb.

"Yes," she says so softly she is asked twice to repeat her answer.

Herb leans into the witness box and looks at her real hard. "You wouldn't lie for him though."

"No," she answers a bit curtly.

"Did you have any conversations with the defense lawyer prior to testifying here today?"

"Yes, of course," she admits with an implied tone of "What a stupid question that is."

"How many?"

She looks off to the side for a moment. "Let's see. We spoke on the phone two or three times. I saw the lawyer, Mr. Schaffer, at the police station, and I believe there were two more occasions."

"During your first meeting with the defendant's lawyer, Mrs. Annenberg, did you discuss the particulars of your testimony?"

She looks puzzled. "Well, I told Mr. Schaffer that Harold was with me in Dobbs Ferry the night someone committed that awful murder."

"Do you remember seeing your cousin exactly ten days before Thanksgiving?"

"No. Not exactly ten. It could have been a week."

"How about eight days before. Or nine?'

The woman's eyes narrow. "I didn't keep track of every time I saw him."

"Yet you have no trouble recollecting seeing him on that one particular Thursday," Herb blasts out at her, his hands slamming down on the witness box.

The witness lifts her chin and answers coolly, "No problem. It was, after all, Thanksgiving."

For a few silent moments, the two antagonists are left to square off in fierce, unblinking eye contact. Then someone in the room coughs, and with that Herb turns, and with his back to the witness, he informs her that he has, "No more questions."

No, Herb, you have many more questions. Kate wants to shout out. If this woman is not lying, make her prove her story. Demand she produce a dated train ticket, a corroborating witness. Demand an explanation of why the sensitive boy needed a caseworker. Request an explanation of why, if he was so innocent, did he hide from the police for a month. Demand she produce something, Herb. *Do to her what H.G.'s lawyer did to your witnesses.*

But Herb's golden window of opportunity has already shut. The Annenberg woman has descended into the grateful arms of the O'Connors, and the defense lawyer is already standing up. Buttoning his jacket, he tells the court, "The defense rests," and with that final statement, he lets everyone know that H.G. O'Connor will not be taking the stand in his own defense.

Chapter Twenty-One

The defense is first at summing up. Stroking his chin, as though he had a beard, H.G.'s lawyer tells the jury "I've been watching the twelve of you, and if there is one thing that has impressed me, it is your constant attentiveness."

Kate wonders what twelve people this man has been watching. More than once she has wondered if some of them were even awake.

"Is Harold guilty of this heinous crime?" he shouts at them, then stage whispers his answer to his own question, "No, he is not. I believe that when you begin to sift through the myriad of falsehoods that the prosecution has presented here, you will have no alternative but to find, for this young defendant, that the People have not proven their case beyond a reasonable doubt."

"What did the prosecution give you as witnesses? A bunch of lying little potheads, that's what. The Gaines kid sat right here and admitted he is a liar. Compare that to what the defense gave you. You saw with your own eyes, Mrs. Annenberg's integrity. It all but radiated from the woman," he flaunts, elevating his one and only witness to sainthood. "She testified under oath where Harold was at the very moment someone fired that lethal bullet into Scott Scholfield. Harold was miles away, having tea with Mrs. Annenberg in Dobbs Ferry. That is a sworn fact."

"Compare her testimony to the garbage the prosecutor paraded before you. Remember that Mrs. Annenberg was crystal clear about her facts. Times. Places. Dates. How does her testimony stack up against the performance of all those juveniles, most of whom were testifying under immunity? Huh, need I say more?"

Apparently, he does, because he spends the next hour itemizing every minute discrepancy in every one of their testimonies. And, unfortunately, there were indeed many discrepancies. "Yes, the prosecution put a lot of kids up there who claimed, in one way or another, that Harold did it. A lot. But when it comes to witnesses, ladies and gentlemen, it's not quantity that counts. It is quality, and that's a fact you can take to the bank. How dare a bunch of druggies come here and try to destroy this innocent young man."

He smiles and rubs his hands together gleefully. "Now the crime scene. A wealth of inconsistencies exist here, too. To start with, and I'm quoting the precise words the coroner used in her official report the, 'body was found in an unnatural position.' This victim was a big guy. Over six feet. Look at the defendant. Does he look capable of moving so much dead weight?"

"Then we have the fingerprints, or rather, the lack of. Detective Kuchinsky testified that Harold's prints were not, not found on either the gun or anything in the victim's apartment. A place, if you chose to believe those juvenile witnesses, Harold is 'supposed' to have frequented often. Was he always wearing gloves when he went there?"

Kate folds her arms across her chest and smolders. Prints not found only because the cops didn't bother to look for them.

"Now we have Palmer, the ringleader who snatched the drugs from Claude Moldorf. And by the way, we were never told how they came to be in Moldorf's possession. Palmer's description of his discovery of the corpse is a pretty hair-raising story."

Kate's son is suddenly in the defense's cross hairs, and she feels that unpleasant knot in her stomach tighten again.

"I ask you," the lawyer continues, "if you were put in Palmer's shoes, got up to your friend's front door and thought he might be in some kind of trouble, what would you do? Go get the superintendent to let you in? Call 911? If you were a kid, call your parents maybe? How about calling the police? Palmer had a lot of options."

Kate's fists have rolled into two tight balls. Casey did call the police.

"But what did Palmer choose to do? Risk his life climbing up and down a rickety fire escape, three stories above the ground, for what? To peek in the window, he tells us. Why was he reluctant to deal with the authorities or even his own parents? If he really did smell this 'odor of death,' wasn't it his responsibility to call someone?

"You must understand that there is an entire family that will be impacted by the outcome of this trial." With a sweep of his arm he indicates the O'Connor compound, and Rosemary O'Connor begins to dab her eyes with a tissue as all heads turn her way.

"What we have here, folks, is a hundred percent frame up. Textbook case, if I ever saw one. You see this handsome young man seated before you. He had everything going for him. He was outgoing, popular. And what is the crux of the state's case against him? A gang of druggie misfits who had nothing going for them. This bunch of jealous losers envied Harold. You sat there as Harold's peers did and saw how confusingly these low-lifes presented themselves. You heard them admit to drug taking and drug dealing. Throw them all together, and you won't find one moral fiber in the lot."

He slips his hands in his pockets. "I want to thank you for listening," he says like they had any choice once they were plucked out of the jury pool. "I won't have an opportunity to talk to you again. This is it for me. This is it for Harold. If there was anything I said or did that you found offensive, I hope you won't hold it against Harold. You have been given the awesome responsibility of passing judgment on a fellow man. But, my friends, on the basis of the inconsistencies and confusing testimony presented to you, I am confident you will come back and tell the People, 'Don't you dare ask us to convict Harold Gordon O'Connor.'"

He walks back to his table. Standing behind his client he rests his hands on H.G.'s shoulders. "I am confident that you will find this young man not guilty because he is not guilty." He gives his client's shoulders a last bolstering squeeze. "This boy's whole life is now in your hands," he tells the jurors. Then, he just sits down.

To the accompaniment of a few scattered coughs, Herb stands up and walks over to the jury box. Kate feels like she is watching one of Jack's prize fights, and she sits holding her breath for round two. She has, as Jack would say, "bet the farm" on Herb who is now looking like the underdog.

She tells herself, Herb might be the underdog in the contest of presentation and personality, but real life trials don't hinge on the quality of the D.A.'s performance, do they? Every scrap of evidence, backed up by an overwhelming number of witnesses, is on the prosecution's side. Stack that against what the defense presented. It's finally the time when only the facts will be considered. Hope you enjoy prison life, H.G.

Herb begins by reiterating one of the most relevant facts. "The defendant was the only member of his young clique to have had access to Scott Scholfield's apartment. You heard testimony that he often slept over, slept on the victim's couch." He pauses, then in the style of his opponent, shouts, "The very same couch he left the victim to die on."

Yes, Herb, yes. Kate silently applauds.

"About the discrepancies," Herb candidly admits. "True. Some of the dates and times vary a bit. These are scared young kids, trying to remember exact details of something that happened six months ago. Six months is a long time in a fourteen-year old's life. But each one has given us another piece of the puzzle, and when you put it all together, the salient details all add up; they dovetail into an obvious conviction. The end result is a complete picture of premeditated murder, committed unequivocally, by the defendant acting alone.

"The defense has suggested that the defendant was framed. By whom? Garth Gaines? You witnessed his unsure demeanor, his nervousness, and heard about his dependency on drugs. Yes, Garth did lie at first out of fear. His first instinct was to try and minimize his own role in the crime, the loaning of his father's rifle to the defendant for, he thought, target practice. But he quickly saw he could not lie his way out of it. What we have in Garth is a child who was easily manipulated by a crafty H.G. O'Connor. But Garth was not smart enough to manipulate the system. Frankly, I don't think Garth is a very bright kid. This is a person who does not have control of his own life, no less the ability to conceive a plan to take someone else's life. Can you, in your wildest dreams, see him or Bernie, or any of that crew having their druggie little heads together enough to conspire against the defendant? It's

160

too ludicrous to even consider.

"Now you might be thinking Claude Moldorf is the one who could be clever enough. He certainly is the brightest of the bunch, but where is his motive? Money? I think not. You heard how all these kids came from affluent families. How many times did they testify that their ample allowances afforded them all the marijuana they could ever want. No, no motive of greed can be attributed here."

Kate wonders what Herb's motive is. Can he really win this case by bad-mouthing all his witnesses? He must think so.

"The defense has suggested jealousy, envy. What was there to envy about the defendant? He was as much a druggie, to use the defense's own words, as the rest of them. Think back. Not once did you hear any one of these kids express animosity toward the defendant. They were truly his friends, and I suspect most of them still are. Make no mistake, they didn't testify against their buddy because they thought it was the right thing to do. No, not one of these kids, not even cocky little Claude, agreed to rat on their friend until their backs were up against the wall. It came down to testify against H.G. or go down with him." He tosses his notes onto the table with the same disdain he has just cast on the character of his witnesses. "In my opening statement I said there were no heroes here.

"Yes, I agree with you," he says like he has just read the combined jurors' minds. "In this case, the moral guilt casts a long shadow over all those juvenile witnesses who sat before you and freely admitted to having prior knowledge this murder was going to take place. Freely admitted they did nothing to stop it or try to warn the victim."

"Scott Scholfield was out there selling dope to kids. There's no getting around that. You have a right to feel contempt for every one of the individuals in this case. I certainly do. In a moral sense, they are all guilty of something. But I enjoin you, as did the defense," and he holds up one finger, "you are here to only sit in judgment of the defendant."

"Six months ago, H.G. O'Connor had no qualms about being in your shoes. He sat in judgment of the victim, but ladies and gentlemen, he was hardly exercising his civil responsibility when he bestowed the death penalty on poor Scott and elected himself executioner."

"The People are charging the defendant with premeditation in carrying out that 'execution' because this shooting cannot, in any way, be considered to have happened during the course of the robbery." He walks over and picks up the rifle. "Indisputable proof of the defendant's use of a single shot rifle. Expert testimony told you that, in order to shoot a second bullet, it would take a full minute to reload. He had to choose, choose, to fire that second bullet into a body he had just killed."

"Now let's see how long that is," he says as he stands in silence, looking down at his wristwatch. The tiny hand seeming to take an interminable length of time to tick away one revolution. When it does, he looks at the jury and tells them, "Ample time for the shooter to reconsider his actions if the first shot had been accidental, wouldn't you say?"

Kate agrees wholeheartedly. The jury can't help but agree, too. Go for it, Herb.

He puts the rifle back on the evidence table. "I'm going to take you back to that moment when, in the middle of the night, H.G. arrived at the victim's front door. What do you think Scott might have said when he saw the guitar case? Maybe, 'You came here to play me a tune, pal?' Maybe, at that hour, Scott was too stoned to even notice the guitar case. He likely offered H.G. a joint, saying something like, 'One toke'a this primo weed and you'll be blown away'." The uncomfortably contrived dialogue makes Kate cringe. Can Herb really pull this off? He has to.

Kate looks over at the jurors. A few have their eyes closed again. Some gaze up at the ceiling, some down at their shoes. They clearly didn't come here for fiction.

But, Kate notices, H.G. is suddenly all ears. For the first time, he has turned sideways in his chair, leaning forward to catch Herb's every gesture. He seems glued to Herb's every word now. The little bastard looks like he is actually enjoying this part.

Then Herb reaches the point in his "story" where Scott begins to nod out. "With each drag of the reefer Scott's eyes stay closed a little longer, until finally the moment comes when they no longer open. His heart still beats, his chest still rises and falls, but from that moment on, for all intents and purposes, life ended for nineteen-year-old, Scott Scholfield."

"H.G. O'Connor knows, first hand, how thoroughly this drug can insulate a brain from any outside stimulus. He knows the dope has taken away Scott's awareness of anything, any sound or movement. Scott is now in a place H.G. has been to many times before.

"H.G. walks over and opens the guitar case, mindless of the sharp clicks and snaps it makes when opened. He knows that nothing, nothing in this lifetime, can rouse his intended victim anymore."

Kate shakes her head. Didn't Herb say pretty much the same thing in his opening statement?

Herb continues his rendition of reenactment. "Did H.G. O'Connor stand there with the weapon in his hand, savoring the deliciousness of his domination over Scott's helpless body? That tells us this shooter left no margin for error. Ladies and gentlemen, I'd put money on it. "

"In order for the bullet to enter at the angle it did, the shooter had to be down on one knee. And massive powder burns on the corpse tell us he had to position the barrel only inches from his target, the victim's sleeping brain. H.G. knew the drug had his victim tied tighter than any ropes ever could. With the rifle butt likely resting on his shoulder, he had the luxury of time to look through the sight and choose, choose, the exact spot he wanted to penetrate. Did he take the time to aim at other fatal targets, the victim's nose, mouth, temple, or heart. We know now the choice he made was Scott's right eye.

"Did his thumb stroke the cold metal trigger as he lined up the little black cross with the dead center of his friend's closed eye? Did he playfully say, 'Bang, you're dead,' as it was testified he had done when he playfully pointed the same loaded weapon at his other friends?"

With his victim helplessly unconscious, he had all the time in the world to play.

Herb walks over to his table, picks up a pitcher and pours himself a glass of water. He, too, has the luxury of time. All around her, Kate feels the room holding its collective breath. My God, Herb is actually pulling off this dramatization.

"Yes, ladies and gentlemen, he had all the time in the world to play with his victim who he knew was going to be out for hours. Did he try to take aim from a couple of different angles? Only the defendant can answer that for you. And only the defendant knows if, when he did pull the trigger, when he saw the first bullet rip through that sleeping brain...only he knows if the eyes blinked open for a terrified fragment of a second and actually looked at him?

"Had they opened, they must have bulged with unimaginable horror." And for a few torturous seconds of silence, Herb paces back and forth in front of H.G. O'Connor's twelve peers, letting everyone ponder the unthinkable picture he's verbally painted for them.

"What we do know, for a fact, is that when a body is hit with a bullet at such close range, it will jerk forward, then, succumbing to gravity, slump back again. So much for the unnatural position of the head. It's simply a matter of physics. This natural phenomenon is what the defense is now trying to pawn off on you as proof of some kind of conspiracy theory."

Herb shakes his head. "I ask you, what position is natural for a body shot twice at close range? In the split second of that first shot, this young man sitting before you, saw Scott's pale complexion splatter with blood and brain matter. The shooter watched that crimson ooze pour down Scott's cheek, over the shoulder, down the chest like a red waterfall. He watched his friend weep tears of his own blood."

Kate listens intently, but notices Maggie Scholfield spring from her seat and hurry out of the courtroom. Oh God, enough Herb.

But it's not enough for Herb. Without missing a beat, he launches into the second bullet. "The victim was clearly dead, so why shoot again? In my opening statement, I told you why. This wholesome-looking kid, his Royal Preppiness here, had only one goal in life. He lived to get high. But after so many years of turning-on, he'd gotten pretty jaded. The highs weren't so high anymore, that is, until he saw his bullet tear open a living skull. In the early hours of that November morning, the defendant unexpectedly found his ultimate high, and he was instantly hooked. But the deed was done, and the rush of adrenaline was already slipping away from him. Shooting into flesh was such a powerful narcotic that he had to have more. That, my friends, was the point of the second shot. An instant replay of a hideous high, if you will.

"He still had the gun in his hands, and we know he had a second bullet in his pocket." Herb cocks his head to one side, and with palms and shoulders up, makes a gesture of, "Why not shoot the corpse again?

"The eye, now oozing a mass of grey brain matter along with the red blood, was his target. Two bullets were found in the brain. That, ladies and gentlemen, is a fact we know for sure. But, remember, the coroner testified that there was only one entry hole. That second bullet had to be carefully aimed into the hole made by the first, and that's about as cold and deliberate as a murder can get, folks. My God, this monster was using a mutilated corpse for target practice.

"Perhaps the only reason a third bullet wasn't found floating in the victim's brain is because the defendant only brought two with him. A detail only he can verify."

"But notice he chose not to take the stand in his own defense. This Harold O'Connor is no Garth Gaines or Bernie Maisel. He chose to play it safe. No way was he going to put himself in a position where a prosecutor's questions might trip him up."

"You've seen him here day after day, stoically listening, along with all of you, to the tragedy he knows he inflicted on the Scholfield family. The victim's mother, father, and little brother will all carry that pain for the rest of their lives. Does this character, sitting here, cool as a cucumber, care? Throughout some of the most grisly testimony I have ever heard, does he look like he is sorry? Remorse? Not a sign of it.

"No, he didn't take the stand, but his own words, relayed to you by one of his former confidants, are perhaps the most damning evidence against him. 'I shot him in the head while he was watching TV,' is what one of his buddies testified the defendant bragged to him. His own words. There truly is justice in that."

Herb straightens up, adjusting the front of his jacket with one hand, smoothing back his hair with the other. "Ladies and gentlemen of the jury, that's your whole case right there."

Kate is both drained and exhilarated. Herb's done it. He made them be there, made them see it happen. No one could have remained unmoved.

"In closing, I want to say something about the victim here. Scott was one of society's rare rehabilitation success stories. After years of criminal activity selling drugs, he was about to turn his life around." He holds out his palms, maneuvering them to juggle his words. "He was looking forward to making a new, clean start, with a decent life his family could be proud of. He had plans to go back to school to study photography. He was going to have Thanksgiving dinner with his folks. Family. Friends. Future. All that was on one side of the scales. The other side? Drug-dealing and his friendship with the defendant. In those early hours of that cold November night, H.G. O'Connor tipped the scales his way. "

Shoulders back, chest out, Herb's slight frame suddenly appears to Kate to be broader, even taller.

"With all that you have heard and seen, I am certain you will not hesitate to come to the conclusion that Harold Gordon O'Connor is guilty of the premeditated murder of Scott Scholfield." He walks over to his table, takes one of the mason jars out of a bag and holds it up for all to see, the glass catching a ray of sunlight that flashes out penetrating the neon-lit courtroom like a lighthouse beam. Then he sets the jar down on the railing in front of the jurors and stands there, his finger tapping the lid. The light emanates from the jar penetrating the jury box like a white, hot spear with Herb saying softly, "A human life has got to be worth more than this."

As Herb sits down, the mason jar, left on the railing, looms larger than life. With its contents, once the incentive for Scott's murder, it is now all that is left to plead for his justice.

Chapter Twenty-Two

I t has been three days since the judge charged the jury. Charged, a word that used to only mean something Kate did at Bloomingdale's.

The minute the jury deliberation room door shuts behind the last juror, the spectators stand up. Kate hurries over to Herb who is gathering up the evidence, the mason jars, the gun, and loading it all into a shopping cart.

She meant to compliment him on his closing, but can't help but immediately blurt out, "How long do you think this will take, Herb?" How long could it take after a week of them constantly hearing proof that H.G. did do it?

Herb just shrugs as he stands gathering up his papers. "In murder cases, they usually stay out for at least one overnight. An airtight case doesn't guarantee a quick verdict, even if there is total agreement from the beginning. Juries don't think fast verdicts make them look responsible." He chuckles. "They'll probably spend most of the time reading newspapers and playing cards."

Kate isn't amused.

She watches as the O'Connors stand up, embracing H.G. before he is led away to wait elsewhere. Hugs and handshakes all around. Then they all rush over to the man who had defended their son, a check in the grandfather's outstretched hand.

It was a scene that left Kate feeling uncomfortably privy to someone else's personal business, like opening a bathroom door and finding it to be occupied.

Arrest. Trial. Conviction. One, two, three. That's how Kate thought it would go when Jack had called her with the news that they got H.G. "I got a nice Christmas present for you and your son," he'd told her. Now, six months later, with her leave of absence from work in its second week, this damned nightmare is still overwhelming her life. Yet this close to the end, how could she think of leaving? In order to achieve peace of closure, she needs to hear every last word that will put H.G. O'Connor away for good.

She thought Jack felt the same way. He's been there from day one, sharing the horror, the frustrations, and the rage at what H.G. had done. Jack shares Kate's passion for justice, too. She's sure of that.

Also, since the arrest, Jack has shared the good parts of Kate's life, too...her son, her friends, and her interests. He's told her that he loves her. In the dark, his face hovering over hers, he softly breathed the words into his kisses. "You're my woman now. You know I've fallen in love with you."

Her eyes closed, she would respond, "I love you, too, Jack," and she does, at those very special, very private moments.

Okay, so those exchanges of love only happen when they are in bed together. Always in the dark, always in a whisper. Still, those three most magical of all words have been exchanged. Doesn't that mean a connection, a bond of trust and respect now joins these two people? The words "I love you" certainly mean that to Kate.

Without even thinking about it, she feels a sameness with Jack now, flowing freely, comfortably between them. Their needs and desires blending as smoothly as their bodies do. And because she is so passionate about this case, because she so desperately needs a just conclusion, she feels that he must understand that, because he feels the same way. He had listened so attentively to all her prior accounts of the trial. So, she is naturally eager to replay every last word of Herb's moving summation.

She goes to Jack's apartment that night, sits down on the bed and begins her replay of Herb's summation when Jack stuns her.

"Enough already with every mother fuckin' word outta Herbie's mouth," he snaps at her in a tone she's never heard him use before. "I'm in bed now. I'm relaxin'. Bad enough I gotta deal with this bullshit on the job. Do me a favor, hon, just tell me when the verdict comes in."

He's been like a father to Casey and become a friend to David and Maggie. Kate is in bed with him almost every night, and all this boils down to his seeing the case as nothing but a job, and a bullshit one at that. Those words may not have totally shattered the sweet "I love you" moments, but they certainly put a dent in Kate's side of it.

She doesn't let him know how much his unexpected outburst, his hostile tone, had disturbed her, but that night is the first time they don't make love. That night Kate only has sex with Jack Kuchinsky.

He is sound asleep when she gets up to get dressed later that night, and she doesn't wake him to take her home like she always does. This time, she lets herself out and cabs it home. Before midnight, she is back in her own apartment, curled up in her own bed, and glad to be there alone.

That was three days ago. Since then, she has only communicated with Jack by phone, too tired to come to his place tonight. Too drained, maybe tomorrow night, sweetheart, she'd tell him. And it was true. She was tired and drained.

And each time they talked, he'd ask her, "How'd it go today?" now actually sounding like he wanted to know. The old Jack was back the very next day, like the uncomfortable evening never happened. But Kate never brought it up. Now she makes a point of keeping her daily courtroom report sound bites quite short. The benign subjects of the weather, the daily ball scores, and what they both had for lunch dominate her conversations with Detective Kuchinsky. This is no time for Kate to have a dispute with the man in her life.

Chapter Twenty-Three

Since deliberations began, the buzzer that signals a readback of testimony has sounded so often, it seems the jurors are asking to have the entire trial played back. Wasn't anyone listening, or are they just confused by all the names?

And each time the jury returns to hear the readback, court officers bring H.G. back in as well. His arrival is always followed by his mother rushing up to the railing that separates them and bestowing a token of affection on him. Gum, candy bars, cigarettes. Seated at his table with his back to the spectators, Kate observes that he accepts each and every one of his mother's gifts, handed to him by his lawyer, without ever even turning to acknowledge the giver. It is a small thing, but Kate notices it, and she hopes the jurors have noticed it, too.

Now, on the afternoon of the third day of deliberations, only a handful of spectators have chosen to remain. They read newspapers, do crossword puzzles, lie along the benches with open magazines over their faces. Jackets and sweaters are strewn across the warm, stuffy room. Discarded newspapers dot the empty seats, gum wrappers and wads of Kleenex litter the floor. In these waning days, the courtroom more resembles a late-night, bus depot than a hall of justice.

But with the passage of time, Kate has begun to notice a disturbing shift in the attitudes of the two opposing camps. The O'Connors no longer huddle in hushed conversations with their lawyer. Instead, they talk amongst themselves, openly now, and often audibly. Since yesterday, more than once, a flurry of soft laughter has even burst from them. Rosemary O'Connor is rarely seen wiping her eyes anymore, and they've all replaced the somber blacks, browns, and greys they wore throughout the trial with brighter colored garb.

The infamous Julia Annenberg showed up this morning wearing hot pink and sporting a tote bag emblazoned with the message I Was Made for Dancing. Kate takes that gesture alone as a collective thumbing of the O'Connor noses.

As the long hours of deliberation slowly pass, like the passengers and crew of a cruise ship, the few spectators left and the court officers have grown familiar with one another. They chat about things other than the trial, some now calling each other by name.

It is late afternoon and Kate is passing the time talking to one of the bailiffs. A hefty Italian, displaying the trappings of his profession from his belt, handcuffs, a holstered gun, and an impressive set of keys dangle from his waistline. "So, I guess you hear a lot of stories here," Kate asks not really interested if he does.

He laughs. "In here, you hear it all. Usually it just rolls off me, but this one," he shakes his head, "not one of those kids has any conception of right and wrong. That attorney pegged 'em right. Buncha lying little potheads." He shakes his head again, "There's dope everywhere today. My little girl, she's only four, but I sit here listening to these punks, and it's got me scared. This is the kind of world my daughter's gonna grow up in." With a hand on each hip, he hikes up his belt, causing both a stomach that is no stranger to pasta and a bunch of keys to jiggle. "Maybe it's time I start looking for a place outside'a the city."

Kate looks up at the clock, shifting her empty coffee cup from one hand to the other. "What is taking them so long? What she means, but doesn't want to put into words, is could somebody in there actually think H.G. didn't do it?

Before the bailiff can respond, the buzzer rings again and moments later Kate is back in her seat listening to the judge read the jurors' latest note. It is, "We have reached a verdict."

Casey, Bobby, and Brad all bolt from their seats, and with high fives all around, dash out of the courtroom to where more of Scott's friends have been waiting out in the hall. On the other side of the aisle, the O'Connors look like they've just been fast-frozen on the edges of their seats.

Kate sighs with audible relief. Remote as it might have been, the threat of a hung jury is now past.

But before the verdict can be read, all the principals must be in place. Herb never left. H.G. is immediately ushered back in, but the last member of the essential trilogy, the defense lawyer, is nowhere to be seen. A court officer, replying to Kate's impatience, tells her that the defense lawyer is out of the building. He is rumored to be having a late lunch somewhere in nearby Chinatown. The whole courtroom will have to wait until he puts his chopsticks down. It is over and still it goes on.

Verdict, the word is out. Like water flowing into an empty glass, strangers begin pouring through the door. Word of a decision must have rumbled through the halls. Men and women in dark, no-nonsense suits begin lining the back wall and the sides of the courtroom. They quickly fill the perimeter, their symmetry only broken by the sharp corners of their leather attaché cases jutting out at odd angles. The court officers stand patiently at attention. And Herb, like any good host, greets the arrival of each fellow lawyer with an amicable wave, a nod, or, a thumbs up.

All at once there is a festive spirit in the air. The legal newcomers are a noisy lot. Chatting about one another's cases, other appeals, other verdicts. They cackle and rub their hands together in gleeful anticipation.

Why are these people all here? Kate wonders? Is it because they care that a young life was so brutally taken? Is it because they want to see justice prevail?

No. They are here to bask in the glow of another colleague's victory. This pack of legal vultures has flown in to see a teammate score, to savor with him, along with Kate, the sweet taste of the kill.

All around Kate, the empty benches have begun to fill, some with spectators, but others with an alarming number of Casey's friends. Tense young bodies all arrive flushed and breathless. A lot of hasty phone calls must have been made.

With their arrival, Kate feels the air around her stretch, grossly expand. Like the stretching of a giant rubber band, if something doesn't happen soon, it will snap. Kate will snap.

Apparently, those in authority feel the mounting tension, too. Suddenly everywhere Kate looks she sees a uniformed officer, all with noticeable guns on their hips. But the escalating police presence is not reassuring to her. What do they think is going to happen? The more the room fills with cops, the more threatened Kate feels. The more alone. She feels like she is standing in front of the elevator door again with Casey's words "I gotta go. Brad knows who did it," ringing in her ears. She feels helpless again.

When the defense lawyer finally arrives, forty-six minutes late by Kate's wristwatch, he strides quickly up the aisle and through the gate that separates the players from the audience, leaving it clanging and banging behind him. As he plops down next to his client, the door to the deliberation room opens.

No court officer shouts cease deliberations this time, and for the first time, a burst of laughter and applause from the room precedes the jurors' entrance back into the courtroom. As they file in, the men all have their jackets and ties back on, all ready to go home. Freshly applied lipstick is apparent on some of the women, and a few jurors are smiling. The decision made in that room may imprison H.G. for the rest of his life, but it has just freed the twelve people that made it.

From his high bench the judge leans forward on his black-robed elbows and addresses the mere mortals before him. "You are about to witness one of the most important aspects of our democratic society. Both sides care very much about the outcome of this trial. Only one side is going to be satisfied with your verdict." His eyes take the time to scan what seems like every face in the jury box. "Control will be maintained in this courtroom." Then he asks the jury, "Have you reached a verdict?" striking Kate as a pretty stupid question when he just read aloud the jury's note saying they had.

The juror in the first seat of the first row stands up. "We have, your honor," he says, clutching a small piece of paper as though he might forget what the verdict was.

H.G. is ordered to rise and face the jury. He is ashen grey, and Kate is startled by how frail and even sickly he looks. He stands there sucking away at his lower lip, head bowed, his body noticeably shaking. Eyes closed, palms together against his chest, he appears to be praying.

"On the charge of second-degree murder, how do you find the defendant, Harold Gordon O'Connor?"

"We find the defendant not guilty."

Both sides of the spectators gasp as one. But it's not over, Kate tells herself. Second degree murder is only the intentional murder charge. Surely, they have decided to take the third choice and say he killed Scott during a robbery.

"And on the charge of felony murder, how do you find the defendant?"

"Not guilty."

No. No. Not, not guilty. Kate is instantly trapped in the eye of a raging human storm. This can't be happening, her lips silently mouth. But all she can do is sit there staring in horrified disbelief as the audible rage of the victim's friends collides with the jubilation of the O'Connor's family joy. The jurors "not guilty" on the robbery charge alone is barely heard above the uproar.

Tears are rolling down H.G.'s beaming face as his mother rushes up to embrace him, caressing his cheeks, stroking his hair and kissing him, while the Scholfield family hurries out of the stunned courtroom.

The words "You made a mistake, you fucking fools. Go back and get it right" ricochet, without a voice, inside Kate's head while all around her, Scott's friends are going crazy. Animated arms fly in the air, feet kick at the benches. Frantic screams of "He did it. He is a murderer," fill the air as all the uniformed officers start to move in like a threatening tidal wave. All this commotion is to the accompaniment of the judge's rhythmic pounding of his gavel.

Kate struggles to break through the iron grip of bewilderment. She has to physically force her stunned body to stand up, but as she does, she is terrified to see her son, his eyes blazing, his mouth screaming obscenities, bolt from his seat. Bobby and Brad, all of them along with him, all headed to the front of the court, as an army of police with their nightsticks extended, rush toward them.

Kate's arms instinctively flail out to her son, and she begins to shove her way through the sudden chaos. Just like Rosemary O'Connor, Kate's only thought is to get to her son. But with every step she takes toward him, the cops edge him farther away from her, away from the front of the courtroom where H.G. is being shielded by a tight circle of cops.

"Casey," she tries to shout above the commotion, "We have to get out of here." But there are too many people swarming around her. They jostle each other like they are all blind, no one seeming to know where to go, what to do.

Kate feels her body in motion, but it is going nowhere. Ahead of her, she sees Casey and Bobby being forced toward the door to the hall by court officers, one with his gun extended. "Oh God, don't shoot them," she yells, desperate to make her plea be heard above the clamor.

Then she spots Brad angrily arguing with one of the court officers. Fortunately, the officer is one she befriended during the trial. She pushes her way to them, grabbing Brad's arm and telling the officer, "It's okay, he's with me." That's when she sees where H.G. is huddled behind the bench being guarded by an army of cops. Ahead of her, a larger-than-life Casey is being forced through the open doorway. He spins around and spits on the courtroom floor shouting, "That's what I think of your justice," and then, in an instant, he is gone, pushed out into the hall where Kate can no longer see him.

She is frantic now. Panic swells in her chest, and with a burst of sudden strength that comes out of nowhere, she forces herself and Brad through the press of bodies and out into the hall after Casey. "We've got to get to Case and Bobby," she tells a dazed Brad.

"Casey," Kate shouts over the crowd, "Casey," but it is hopeless. There is too much rage, too much of the O'Connors' loud joy, fueling the rage. And over it all, the judge's relentless gavel continues to pound. The clashing emotions escalate to a deafening crescendo until, suddenly, a very different sound cuts through it all.

A piercing gasp halts the insanity, and Kate turns back to see H.G.'s grandfather drop to his knees. In the slow-motion dance of the dying, the old man's hands clutch at his chest, his head falls backward, his back arches against the powerful pull of death, and in one desperate quest for life-giving air his mouth opens astonishingly wide.

"Heart attack," a court officer shouts. "Get a medic!" Instantly the stricken man becomes the focal point of everyone's attention.

Court officers rush to his side, locking arms to hold the surge of onlookers back. "Give him air. Give him room." Like pallbearers carrying a coffin, they hoist him up from the floor and lay him out on one of the benches. Someone yells, "He's hyperventilating. Where the hell is that medic?"

From her spot in the hall, Kate can just make out the hunched back of one of the cops rhythmically rising and falling over the dying man, as unseen hands must be pressing down on a breathless chest. Arms are reaching in, as a tie is tossed in the air, and shirt buttons, like tiny missiles, shoot up out of the confusion.

Suddenly, all Kate can think of is how much she wants to see the old man die. Here and now, those fools on the jury will see how H.G. takes yet another life. This death will be the justice that will settle the score. For one breathless moment she claws at any fragment of rationale for her ungodly thought.

"No," Kate says to herself, appalled that she was even capable of thinking such a thing. With the realization that she was wrong in hoping for the old man's demise, the golden gift of retribution is snatched away from her. The sweet taste of that unexpected flash of vengeance is gone, as quickly as it had appeared. The old man is already sitting up, pale and looking older, but very much alive. The impact of what she has just wished on this innocent soul comes crashing down on her. For a moment she feels she is no better than H.G.

"We've got to get to Case and Bobby," she tells Brad. "We've got to get you all out of here."

As she hurries Brad out of the courtroom and into the hallway, the last words she hears are the judge's as he thanks the jurors for fulfilling their "civic responsibilities." In response to that final indignity, Kate attempts to slam the courtroom door behind her, but its heavy weight denies her even that sliver of retaliation.

Out in the corridor it is even more chaotic. Uniformed police are everywhere. Cops and court officers are using their nightsticks like swords, separating Scott's friends into clusters of twos and threes, forming cordons around the small groups as they herd them down the wide hallway.

Casey and Bobby are flailing and bucking like wild horses in a futile attempt to escape their corral. They spin on their heels, tears streaming down their faces, eyes darting wildly, as they look for a way out. In the horror of this sudden purgatory, the cops are always, always, edging Casey just beyond Kate's reach. "Case, Case," she keeps calling.

Then reality dawns on her. The cops are not pushing Casey away from her, they're pushing Casey away from H.G. She hears herself scream out to no one and to everyone, "You're protecting a murderer."

A hand comes down on her forearm, the grasp firm but not hostile. "We don't always like what we have to do, miss," a white-haired court officer tells her calmly.

"Shouldn'ta turned out this way. It's a shame," comes from the cop next to him.

At the bank of elevators, the cops have Casey, Bobby, and Brad pinned to the wall. Casey is seething, "Fuck that judge. Fuck the system."

Bobby's eyes shoot from one cop to another. "We gave him to you. Gave him to you, and you dumped him right back in our laps." He smashes his fist into the elevator's closed door with words that terrify Kate. "You fuckin' assholes, now we're gonna have to take care of it."

"The punk deserves everything he gets," one officer chillingly encourages.

"Our hands are tied now, kid," another chimes in.

The words pierce Kate's heart like the icy finger of death, and she franticly pounds the elevator's down button.

As the door opens, nightsticks aggressively urge the boys into the elevator's safety along with a thankful Kate. Then she is startled to hear the rattling and clinking of glass behind her.

It's Herb pushing that damned shopping cart full of the evidence as if he were on his way to the check-out counter. But the rifle butt protruding from one of the bags proclaims he's been to the supermarket from hell.

Once inside the elevator, Kate is all over Herb. "How could you let this happen? You said you had so much evidence. He can't get away with this. You've got to do something."

Casey, Brad, and Bobby kick and punch at the elevator walls, muttering obscenities and moaning like wounded animals. At first they seem oblivious to Herb's presence in their elevator.

But the man Kate believes responsible for this ultimate miscarriage of justice, District Attorney Herb Ruben, is now, at least for the time it takes the elevator to reach the lobby, her captive. "There must be something, Herb. An appeal? You can do that, can't you?"

Herb looks as dazed as everyone else, standing there aimlessly tidying up the bags of mason jars in his cart, as if neatness might score one last point for the prosecution. He shakes his head in disbelief. "Maybe I am in the wrong job. There's just no way, no way with what we had. All those witnesses. Is it possible the jury was so disgusted by those druggie kids, that they just didn't care?" he asks, like Kate knows the answer.

The elevator door opens and Herb wheels the cart out into the lobby. "Only guilty verdicts can be appealed," he tells Kate over his shoulder, still shaking his head in disbelief. "They just handed the kid a lollypop."

"You handed it to him, Herbie." Brad smolders behind his back.

"You fuckin' blew it." Bobby agrees.

"Oh, man, Herb. What did you do?" Casey moans.

Herb stops abruptly, stiffening as though the boys just stuck a knife in him. He turns on his heels and yells back, "You little creeps blew it. Why didn't you take care of it when you had the chance?" Then his body deflates along with his voice. His last words to Kate are, "I was so sure on this one. Maybe my wife is right. Maybe the legal profession isn't my calling. When I was working my way through law school as a shoe salesman, I thought being a prosecutor would be, would be…would be…," and he trudges off into the exiting crowd. The last indignity of his defeat was having to navigate a shopping cart through the lobby's rush-hour traffic. "Excuse me, pardon me, can I get through, please?" His words trail off as he is sucked up into the swarming crowd.

Casey looks like a ticking time bomb. "I'm going to tell those twelve assholes what they did," he seethes. "They're not gonna walk away from this so easy." He looks back at the elevators and shakes his fists. "They gotta come down here sometime."

"Please, no, Case. You'll only make things worse," she pleads.

But her choice of words seems to have done that. He looks at his mother as if she were a crazy person. "Worse?"

What if Casey sees the O'Connors come out in the state he is in? She won't see her son be led away in handcuffs. But she is tumbling down a dark chute, now. Plummeting into the nightmare of nightmares. God knows what Casey will do if he sees any of those jurors, If he sees H.G walk out free as a bird.

She grabs both of Casey's arms, pressing them to his sides with all her strength. Holding on to him for dear life, she tells him as calmly as she can manage, "We are going home now."

He answers her with a violent shrug of his shoulders that frees him, and he storms out of the lobby with Brad and Bobby trailing behind him.

When Kate catches up with them out on the street, she finds that the madness that overwhelmed her in the courtroom and in the hallway is still enveloping the boys; only out here, there are no authorities to keep it in check. There is only Kate.

Her son is kicking the tires of a parked car, shouting, "I'm gonna tell those fuckin' jurors that they're going to have to live with what they did. The dude told me, he fuckin' told me he did it."

Bobby pounds a car's hood, victimizing the unlucky vehicle with his fists. "We were such idiots."

Brad holds his head like it is going to explode. "We played by the rules, we told the truth, that's what did it, telling the fucking truth. If we had lied...All we had to do was lie like they did... Ah, shit. Ah, shit," and he falls forward onto the battered car, his last words along with his face, buried in the crook of his arm.

Kate is relieved to spot a pay phone only a few steps away. She fumbles for change, and with the sound of the boys' rage in the background, she quickly dials Jack's office number.

"Detective Kuchinsky. What can I do for you?"

A wave of relief that she is not handling this alone anymore washes over her. "They let him go, Jack," she blurts out, cutting off his discouraged, "Ah, fuck."

"We're out on the street and Casey, Brad, and Bobby, they're going crazy. Talking about confronting the jurors."

"You can't let them do that," Jack responds angrily. "They'll be arrested, for sure, Kate."

"Oh, Jack, they're so out of control. I don't know what to do. I gotta get them away from here. H.G. could be coming out any min…"

"No worries about that. Court officers got him out another door by now. Grab a cab, get those kids home."

"Jack, Casey's not listening to me."

"Now you listen to me, Kate," Jack says, his calmness letting her know that he is listening to her. "Nothing's gonna happen to your son. Put him on the phone."

She holds out the receiver. "Case, Case. Please talk to Jack, please."

"What can he do now?" he snarls, but he does snatch the receiver from Kate's hand saying, "Yeah, what?" to Jack.

"We gotta talk, buddy. This is a bad thing that happened."

"Talk 'bout what, Jack? It's over, man. They let the scumbag off."

"Hear me out, Casey. Your mother is pretty upset. I want you to get her home. Now. Okay? You do that for me? Look, I know you're all angry, you gotta right to be, but you don't need any more shit happening tonight."

"Jack, how could they-"

Jack cuts him off with, "This is not the time or the place, guy. I'll sign out early. We can all have a couple of beers. You, me, Bobby, Brad, and your mom, if you want to. Meet me up at the West End's Jazz Bar 'bout ten. We can talk about it then."

"What good is talking going to do now? He beat it, Jack."

Casey shakes his head, but Kate can hear in his voice, see it in the slope of his shoulders, that he is giving in.

"Ten o'clock." Casey reluctantly agrees, but just as he hangs up, one of the jurors exits the courthouse and hurries by. Casey's eyes grow wild again. Shaking his fists in the air, he yells at the man's back, with Brad and Bobby chiming in, "You put a murderer back on the street. Dickhead. I hope he kills your fuckin' kid someday."

Outside the West End Bar, a blackboard announces:

THE JAZZ ROOM
Proudly Presents
CHARLIE MANN and THE BLUE NOTE TRIO
Tonight's Sets: 12:00 and 2:00

At ten o'clock in the evening, the small, dimly lit Jazz Room is quiet and almost empty. Two black musicians enjoy a pre-set drink in one booth. In another, next to a small stage on which a bass, a set of drums, and a piano await their players, Kate sits alone, staring into a glass of wine.

Two hours before showtime, the raucous sounds of the jukebox and the boisterous laughter from Columbia's college crowd in the West End Bar's big front room barely filter into the tiny Jazz Room. Kate loves jazz, but tonight she is not here for the music.

She looks up from her glass just as Jack walks in, waving to one of the musicians who greets him with a friendly "Yo, Jocko. How's my main man?"

Then she sees he is not alone.

Behind Jack, a forty-something, Middle Eastern man with salt and pepper hair and an open shirt revealing a pretentious collection of gold chains, stops to light a cigarette. "Morty," she says to the jerk, "This is a surprise."

"How ya doin', beautiful lady?" The man grins, taking Kate's hand and bowing to kiss it with a flourish.

Hasn't Jack told him what happened? The boys will be here any minute. Tonight is supposed to be just us. It was supposed to be a very personal meeting.

"Jack said he was going out for a couple of beers." Morty flashes another one of his phony smiles. "How could I refuse joining him when he said he was going to meet you?"

She turns and silently scowls at Jack as he slides into the booth next to her. How could he have brought an outsider along tonight of all nights? And of all people, Jack had to invite his obnoxious friend, Morty.

Jack, too, takes her hand. Giving her fingers an "I'm here now," squeeze. "Hey, girl. How ya doin'?" he asks with a sincerity that touches her heart. "Where the guys?" he wants to know.

Kate's frost melts. "Casey and Brad stopped by the Scholfields," she tells him, returning the hand squeeze. "They should be here any minute. Bobby's in the West End's kitchen. He had to work tonight, but he'll join us on his break." She sighs. "I'm pretty drained. Guess we all are." How can she be angry at Jack when he looks into her eyes that way? "Jack, I really appreciate you talking to the boys tonight."

Morty offers the news that, "The Yankees won today," but no one responds.

"I tell ya the truth, babe, I'm not sure what I can say to them," Jack confesses, as Brad and Casey walk in. A moment later Bobby, in a long white apron, pushes through the kitchen's swinging doors.

With handshakes and introductions to Morty, "My buddy from way back," the boys pull up chairs.

Casey, leaning so far forward he is almost in Jack's lap, asks, "What's our next move?" he questions with such fervor, Jack's got to come up with an answer.

But Jack hasn't got one. "Not guilty is absolute. It's over, Casey."

Bobby falls back in his seat, his two fists coming down hard on the table. "But they made a mistake."

"I told you nobody would care about Scotto but us," Brad mutters bitterly. "Look what they gave us for a D.A. A fuckin' bargain basement Herbie."

Pressed close to her in the booth, Kate feels Jack's body stiffen. He says, "I grant you Herb Ruben's no Perry Mason, but you have to understand, when the People get handed a chunk of Swiss cheese, nine outta ten times, the perp walks. I'll be honest with you, I'm not at all surprised."

But Kate is surprised by Jack. Wasn't this meeting his idea? Isn't it to give the boys some hope along with consolation? She was sure she could count on Jack to come up with some legal loophole that might reverse the verdict.

Morty hands out foamy beers. "Lighten up, guys. I've brought us each a cold one," Morty says, grinning widely as he hands out the drinks.

So far, the only solace Jack seems to want to extend is the warm press of his thigh against Kate's in the crowded booth.

The tension now gone from Jack's body, he leans ever so slightly closer to Kate. His shoulder, his upper arm, melt into her, and as he rubs her ankle with his bare foot, she becomes increasingly uncomfortable. With the boys sitting across from her, with their eyes on Kate and Jack, and with the shock of today's events weighing so heavily on everyone, except Morty, Jack's clandestine show of affection, one which she would ordinarily respond to with a loving look or even a small public kiss, is not welcome tonight. It only makes her wish he would stop, and she discreetly slides her leg away from his foot.

"What if you find new evidence?" Bobby asks hopefully, just as Morty returns again with a pitcher of beer and a refill on Kate's wine.

"Wouldn't matter if we did," Jack informs Bobby, then he looks up at Morty with an out of place smile. "Thanks, buddy." He lifts his glass in a mock toast. "Just what the doctor ordered." His attention turns back to Bobby and the smile quickly fades. "You guys gotta understand, this mutt can go out and scream from the rooftops that he killed your friend, and we couldn't lay a hand on him now. Not for the murder. Only with a guilty verdict can new evidence reopen a case. You heard of double jeopardy? Well, now you are experiencing it." He picks up his glass of beer, holding it out as he makes his point. "Look, I don't like it any more than you do."

Brad is methodically lighting one match after another, blowing them out and tossing their little carcasses into the ashtray in front of him. "America the beautiful," he mutters. "Home of the free and the brave. And home of people who get away with murder."

"You got it, bro." Jack agrees. "Twelve empty suits sit up there, spend taxpayer's money listening to expert witnesses, ballistics reports, and coroners' reports. Indisputable hard evidence. And then the liberal shitheads just can't bring themselves to convict. I see it all the time. Never mind that the defendant's some kind of low-life piece of shit. They'd rather put a rapist back on the street, a child molester, whatever. Why? Because most people are weaklings. Cowards. Afraid they'll spend the rest of their lives feeling guilty for locking someone up. They have mush for consciences. And balls? Huh? Forget it." His eyes narrow. "You know what I say to myself? I say John Q. Public deserves what he gets." He takes a sip of his beer and wipes the foam from his lips. "Number One, that's who I look out for. I got a gun. Nobody's gonna fuck with me."

"Hey, guys, the Yankees won today," Morty announces again. Is he really trying to change the subject? No one responds.

Since that fateful November night, most of Kate's attention and energy has been centered on protecting her son, his friends, and herself. She tried to comfort the Scholfields as well. But with the pressure, the bitter realities, and the final disillusionment she has had to endure, she now realizes what Jack has had to deal with for most of his working life. This time it is Kate's leg that presses up against his. This time it is he who does not respond.

Morty stands up and, with a wink and a toss of his head, he indicates the pretty, blond waitress cleaning off tables on the other side of the room. "Got a little business to attend to." He hikes up his belt and smooths back his hair. "Be back in a few." No one, not even Jack, acknowledges his leaving.

Suddenly it dawns on Kate. Why hasn't anybody mentioned the obvious? "Nobody's said anything about perjury," she exclaims like she has finally solved the case.

"Yes, yes," the boys eagerly jump in. "That lying defense lady. All those kids who contradicted themselves."

"You got to prove perjury, and I want to tell you that it's almost impossible to do." Jack wet blankets the idea. "Most of the time, and certainly in this case, it all boils down to one person's word against another. Truth has very little to do with it."

"But the prosecution had so many witnesses stacked up against that one woman," Kate vehemently protests as though winning her argument will win back the lost case.

"The prosecution had all juveniles," Jack reminds her, "This case was lost because twelve people chose to believe the one and only adult witness, who, by the way, appeared a hell of a lot more credible than that flaky bunch of doped-up kids. They all admitted to being druggies. Did you really think people never lie on the witness stand? How do you think a lot of cases are won? Goes both ways, you know."

Kate is frowning. Her son was one of those juvenile witnesses. "What are you talking about? Herb had plenty of adult witnesses. The ballistics guy. The coroner. Garth's mother. You, for God's sake."

"Garth's mother didn't add shit to the case. It was a waste of time putting her up there," Jack snaps back, but just as quickly, smiles. Covering her hand with his, he makes his apology one she can feel rather than hear. "You got to look at what the D.A. was given to work with. The core of this case was the testimonies of kids who got up there and freely admitted they took drugs." He looks over at the boys, "I'm sorry but that includes you guys, too. On top of that, you had some kids actually admitting to lying, stealing, and in the case of the Moldorf kid, admitting to selling drugs as well. The defense was quick to point out that each one of these kids altered the facts just enough to save his own precious ass. Jurors aren't that stupid."

"But the prosecution did get all the important stuff right," Casey persists, "like how H.G. told them he was planning a murder, that they saw him test the gun, and how some of them saw him go into Scott's building that night."

Jack shakes his head. "You don't understand. It's the trivial shit, the minor contradictions that taint a witness's credibility. Doesn't matter if the detail doesn't have relevance to the actual commission of the crime. Say somebody was wearing blue when previous testimony said he was wearing green. Say you thought you saw three people in a car when somebody else testified to only seeing two. Jurors remember stupid crap like that. It takes days to pick over it. In this case, the cousin's story stood alone. There was no one to contradict her. After she testified, she made him tea, nobody got up there and said it was coffee. But all those inconsistencies in the testimonies of the prosecution's witnesses? Far too many kids were put on the stand."

Strength in numbers? Kate had been so sure of that. "But what else could

Herb do when they each knew an important fact that in the end, all meshed together to show his guilt?" she pleads.

"Could have gone with just Garth. He had the most to say," Jack suggests. "Or Bernie maybe. Moldorf was a total loss." He shrugs. "It's all Monday morning quarterbacking now. Only reason this kid got nailed in the first place is because he bragged about what he did. That's how a lot of homicides are closed. People have big mouths. They rat themselves out."

Brad looks like he is going to explode. "We had him. We had him right in our hands."

Casey nods grimly. "We screwed up."

Jack's eyes narrow in a nasty squint Kate's never seen before. "Damn right you did, kid. All three of you amateur detectives. Your actions were a big part of what blew this case." The words come gushing out like steam that has been building up for a long time, and now that it's coming out, it can't be stopped.

But she has to stop Jack. The boys don't need to hear this tonight, even if there is truth to what he is saying. She firmly cups his wrist with her hand. Her touch doesn't shut him up, but his suddenly softened tone tells her that her intervention has made a difference.

"Don't think I'm laying this all on you boys. The blame in this one is across the board. Herb could have presented a better case. And the investigative work? Well, no detective is going to work his ass off on the homicide of a drug dealer."

"I knew it," Brad sneers smugly. "I told you we couldn't trust the cops. A drug dealer, that's all he ever was to you." His jabbing finger pokes at the air between him and Jack. Jack opens his mouth to protest, but Brad holds up his hand. "Now you're telling me it all boils down to who gets killed? Fuck, man. I'm surprised you didn't give H.G. a medal. Bet if he was some little black dude, you cops would 'a made sure he was convicted." Kate feels Jack's body, next to her, tense up again.

"Don't lump me in with the rest of them, kid," Jack explodes, his anger colliding with Brad's indignation like two fists colliding head-on.

Feeling imprisoned in that crowded booth, now openly in conflict, all Kate wants to do is grab her son and get the hell home.

Jack calms down as fast as he flared up. "But you're absolutely right, buddy," he surprisingly concedes to Brad. "With a black defendant in an urban court in this country, there is an automatic presumption of guilt. I grant you it is a tragic inequity, but that is still the way the white, middle-class laws of the land function."

Brad answers bitterly, "White is right, huh, buddy?"

"You're a smart kid, Brad. You know that's not what I'm sayin'," Jack responds softly. "There has never been real equality. Rich has always had it over poor. Probably always will. And color? I hate to have to admit it, but you damn well know white still has it over black. Except when a cop gets shot. Doesn't matter if the cop is black, white, or polka dot. The police put as much effort as they can into catching and convicting the mutt who pulled the trigger. I'm not saying that's fair, it's simply a fact of life." Jack downs the last of his beer and folds his arms across his chest. He looks hard at each of the boys for a moment, then says, "Everybody looks out for his own. What do you think you guys were doin' when your buddy got killed?"

Kate sees Brad's belligerence fade before her eyes, and Casey and Bobby recede back into their seats. A ripple of reluctant nodding signifies Jack is the winner of that round.

"What you guys have to realize," Jack goes on riding his winning streak, "is that, in this case, the victim's life was on trial every bit as much as the defendant was. Hard evidence? It doesn't mean shit unless it is overwhelmingly damning, which is pretty rare. Evidence will always take second place to a jury's personal preference in witnesses. They pick and choose for reasons of decency, of morality, their own conception of morality.

"They like some witnesses, don't like others, and that goes for how they feel about defendants and victims, too. An elderly person, a family member, even a pretty girl, as long as she isn't the slutty type, can please a jury. Witnesses like that, can get up there and perjure their asses off, and a jury will buy it. You saw that happen here. And impartial?" He grunts a humorless laugh. "No such a thing.

"As for this case, you think twelve upstanding citizens are going to feel sympathy for someone they've been told makes big money selling dope to kids? I don't think so."

He looks at Kate and asks, "Was that a jury of his peers? Did anyone on that jury look like a peer of the defendant? And while we're at it, did you notice that jury was pretty heavily blue-collar? Those kids flaunting their affluence, their country homes, their private schools, didn't win any brownie points there either."

Kate nods an, "I was afraid of that."

"So, now I know," Casey says somberly, his brow furrowed angrily. "Tell it like it happened and lose. Lie your ass off and win. Should'a clued me in, Jack. If I'da known I would have given them an Academy Award winning performance. They'll never get over on me again."

Hearing his words, Kate feels a chill run through her. She is watching a piece of her son's beautiful, young life die right in front of her. How can she leave him feeling the system he believed in doesn't work? How can she not, when she feels the same way?

Bobby and Brad nod in agreement, Brad vowing, "I'da never thought of lying under oath before, but now you can bet I would, too."

"Look, my job is supposed to end with the collar," Jack tells the boys. "I shouldn't give a shit what happens next. I don't let myself get personally involved, but this verdict is hard for me to swallow, too. I put a lot of time in this case and the mutt got cut loose. Walked away laughing. Laughing at me, at you guys, at Kate, at the victim's family. No doubt about it, the system failed badly this time. *But it's over now.* Fait accompli. So, I put it behind me. Yeah, you all were much more personally involved, but it's time you put it behind you, too."

Casey slouches down in his seat. "Okay, without the death penalty in New York, the most the little fuck would have gotten is life in prison. They'd give him three meals a day and all the TV he wanted, but at least I'd know he was rotting the rest of his motherfucking life away in a 10 by 10 cell. Now? Now nothing is resolved. Not for Scotto. Not for any of us. When that guy stood up and said "not guilty" it was like he threw gasoline on a fire." Casey leans forward, his lowered voice drawing everyone into his dark confidence.

CHAPTER TWENTY-THREE

"When word gets out that H.G.'s back on the street, shit is going to happen."

"Damn right it is," Bobby and Brad chime in, and Kate's heart sinks.

Casey's hands fly up. "Not from me," he assures everyone, and Kate breathes a hair easier. "But if I pass him on the street I'm gonna have to SAY something. How could I not?"

Brad nods. "Lotta dudes out there are real pissed at what happened to Scotto. There are people who are not going to leave it at just tellin' him off."

"Somebody's gonna get a piece of him," Bobby adds.

Jack polishes off the last of his beer and signals to the waiter for a refill. "I'd be surprised if the family doesn't high tail it out of the neighborhood as fast as they can."

"I hope you're right," Kate responds.

Casey directs his remarks to Jack. "If anything happens to H.G. now, I'm gonna be the first one you guys come lookin' for. Me, Bobby, and Brad. The way I see it now, a system that lets a murderer off just 'cause he yelled 'frame up', that's a system that would have no problem convicting me for something I didn't do. Am I right, Jack?"

Jack pauses; then says softly, "That could happen, kid," and Kate feels a knife plunge into her heart.

Brad looks tired, and a decade older. "I got a grandfather down in Georgia. A sweet, old Uncle Remus who just sits by the pond all day angling for catfish. My mom thinks it would be a good idea for me to drop a line in the water next to him, for a while."

Casey says, "Maybe it's time for me to visit dad in L.A. for more than a long weekend."

Why isn't Jack assuring the boys, assuring Kate, that nothing will happen to them because he will protect them? Sitting next to this man she's been sleeping with for the past six months, sitting so close that the heat of his body flows into hers, she suddenly feels a cold emptiness, like nobody is sitting next to her.

Bobby stands up. "I don't have a 'safe house' to crash in. I'm going to have to tough it out here, but from now on, I'll keep my fingers crossed and keep lookin' over my shoulder when I'm out on the street." He adjusts his apron and reaches over to shake Jack's hand. "Got to get back to work. Thanks for coming, man. Thanks for whatever."

As Bobby heads back to the kitchen, Morty returns. Grinning from ear to ear he lays a hand on Jack's shoulder. "Hey, big guy. I'm gonna split." With a wink, he indicates the blond waitress again. "The little lady says she can get off early, so we're going to go someplace for a quiet drink, if you get my drift."

Jack smiles up at him. "Go for it, buddy." Kate nods a goodbye without looking up at him, meaning "Just go, Morty."

Casey stands up. "Mr. and Mrs. Scholfield are going to have to live with seeing the guy who killed their son walking down the street all la-di-da free. I don't know how they're ever gonna deal with that."

Kate doesn't know how she's going to deal with it either.

Casey zips up his jacket. "H.G. turned all our lives upside down. He might of just killed one person, but he made us all victims the minute we looked through that window and saw Scott turned into something out of a horror movie. Brad, if he goes to Georgia, he'll lose his Columbia scholarship. My mom. Scotto's family. All those kids that hung out on the corner, them, too. Someday, it's going to hit 'em, ya know, that they knew what H.G. was gonna do, and they didn't tell anybody. They're gonna have to live with what they didn't do the way Brad, Bobby, and me have to live with losing the confession because of what we did do. We're all victims now, left behind in H.G.'s wake. And H.G.? All he had to pay for was probably the best high of his life with a broken arm and six months at Rikers. Even the threat of more jail time is behind him now. One good rush, that's all Scott's life was worth. Some joke, huh? In the end the killer is the only one that walks away from this with no strings attached."

Chapter Twenty-Four

With her body language, Kate lets Jack know she wants out of the booth, too. She wants to go home with her son.

Jack's hand cups her shoulder. "Relax, they're big boys," he says, signaling the waitress for refills. "Stay with me for a while. It's better you leave them alone right now."

She sighs wearily. "I guess." Kate leans her elbows on the table and lets her forehead drop onto her clasped hands. "Jack, he's so bitter. They all are." She turns and looks at Jack through the mist that has glazed over her eyes. "I feel so responsible."

"You? Why?"

"Because they trusted me, listened to me. Even Brad, with that big, black chip on his shoulder. They played by the rules, because I kept telling them it was all going to turn out okay, as long as they did the right thing. I promised them justice. What do I say to them now?"

His knuckles graze her cheek tenderly, but his words, "You tell them to get the fuck over it," stun her with their sharpness and her lips part like a startled bird.

"JA-ck."

"I don't mean to jump all over you, hon," he says softly, making amends by acknowledging that is precisely what he just did. "When I told the boys they got to put this behind them, that goes for you, too. You're a good mother, Kate. You stood by your son during a real tough time in his life, and he's never going to forget that. But it's history now." He smiles and adds, "As I remember, you stuck by him when I wished you weren't there."

She can't help smiling back. "We didn't exactly have a cordial first meeting, did we?" She presses her body closer to his, her foot locking around his ankle with a familiarity that says she feels more than friendship for this man. "I've never told you before, but you must know how much it's meant to me, to Case, to have you…"

He interrupts, sealing her lips with his finger. "My pleasure, sweetie."

The waitress brings fresh drinks, and Kate sits quietly, looking into the dark wine for a moment, then she asks, "Do people really get away with murder this easily?"

"An awful lot do. You'd be shocked."

She tries to laugh, but it comes out sounding more like a groan. "I'd be shocked to find I still could be shocked. No, that's not true. I shocked myself after the verdict today." Her finger traces the furrows of initials carved into the wooden tabletop. She frowns and takes another sip of wine. "I had some really disturbing and surprising feelings. I was making my way through the crowd leaving court when the boys were all going wild. In the middle of all the madness, this guy who was with the O'Connors, who may have been H.G.'s grandfather, suddenly had a heart attack right there in the courtroom and collapsed on the floor. My first reaction was to feel… to feel glad, Jack. Glad. I actually wanted to see the poor man die, like that was going to right the wrong in some way."

"In light of what just happened that reaction is pretty understandable," Jack tells her with a smile. "You're only human, Kate."

"But something else happened on the way home that troubles me, too. I had to get the boys away from there any way I could, but it was rush hour and I couldn't get a cab. So, we all piled into the nearest subway. The train was already packed, of course, and we all had to stand. Then, at 34th Street, all these Puerto Ricans from the garment district pushed their way on. All of a sudden, I found myself pressed into the crowd like a sardine. I couldn't reach out to hold on to anything, but I was locked in so tight by all these bodies that there was no way I was going fall down, and I got more packed in at each stop. Everyone was jabbering away in Spanish and broken English. Laughing, calling out to friends at the other end of the car. I got separated from the boys, and that panicked me. I was afraid they might try to get off and go back to the courthouse looking for H.G. and those stupid jurors.

"At the next stop, even more Hispanics piled in. Everywhere I looked, I saw and heard Hispanics. Their bodies were shoved up against me so tight, it was getting hard to breathe, and becoming unbearably hot. I mean, nobody tried to touch me or anything like that. It was just the opposite. They looked right through me like I didn't exist. They were just a bunch of people, happy to be through with a long day of hard work, but all these people were in good spirits, laughing a lot, and making jokes about how uncomfortable it was in that crowed train. It forced me to endure their good-natured tolerance. I was trapped in the middle of them. I was their prisoner for a half dozen stops and, all of a sudden, I found myself hating Puerto Ricans. Not just the ones in the train, but all Puerto Ricans. Every Puerto Rican in the city. I stood there thinking, they don't care what I've just been through, don't care how my son and his friends were suffering. They don't care about what happened to Scott. I loathed them for being able to laugh when the boys and I were…"

"Kate you're not a closet bigot. I know you."

"Jack, I don't hate Puerto Ricans, I don't hate any group of people. Well, maybe the Nazis and the Ku Klux Klan, but that's okay. Everybody hates them."

"'Cause they're hateful low-lifes." He agrees with a laugh.

"But those people on the train, I don't hate them. I just wanted them to share my sorrow, my disillusionment with the system I had believed in. How crazy is that?"

"You didn't just come out of the egg. You're a bright girl, Katie," he tells her.

Katie? That's what her ex-husband calls her. The last thing Kate needs in her life right now is another Charlie Palmer.

"I think I was blaming those people in the subway for not being mind readers. I've never felt anything like that biased rage before. It scared me. I don't want this verdict to change me."

"Welcome to the club, kiddo. It won't change you. It just means you're as human as the rest of us mortals." He takes both her hands in his like a father might, his touch comforting her more than his words. "When you've had a bitter disappointment, a disillusionment, it's only natural for your anger to lash out in frustration at the first available scapegoat. You just found out the world according to Kate isn't the world you've been living in." He smiles. "You bleeding-heart liberals gotta come up for air more often. "

She takes a sip of her wine. "This experience has not brought out the best in me, Jack. I don't know who to blame anymore. First it was only H.G., then the family that raised him to be someone who could do that. Now, there's the jury that let him off, and the judge, for ruling on his side so much. I blame the lawyer for twisting the truth, and poor, pathetic Herb for not winning. Of course, there's the system, too, and I gotta say it, the boys contributed to the confusion." What she doesn't say is she blames Jack, too, for not taking those damned fingerprints. "We didn't get justice, we got fucked over," she concludes, startling herself with language Jack would use.

"You're one of the lucky ones, Kate. Your kid has never been in real trouble. It was only natural for you to have faith in the system. You never had to deal with the system before." Jack continues. "I want to tell you something. If there's enough for an indictment, ninety-nine percent of the time the perp's guilty. And most of the time, the shithead walks 'cause we live in an ass-backwards society where the rights of the defendant always take precedent."

She shakes her head wearily. "How does any criminal ever get convicted of anything? Do you know what the judge told the jury? He said that if they were torn equally, equally, between guilt and not guilty, then they had to find him not guilty. Jesus, talk about bending over backwards."

Jack looks pleased, like a teacher whose pupil's thick head has finally gotten it. "Now you're seeing it from where I've been sittin' for the last fifteen years."

"I feel so violated. I truly believed the system was there to protect families like mine and the boys. What the fuck do I believe in now?" she demands to know from this man who is, after all, a representative of the system that betrayed her. He damn well owes her an answer on this one.

But all he does is look at her with a blank stare, making her wonder if he was even listening.

She rubs her eyes. "I never thought I'd hear myself say this, but that system where the defendant is guilty until proven innocent makes a lot more sense to me now. Isn't that how the Brits view it?"

"They call it the Inquisitorial System," he immediately responds, the academic question seeming to have brought him back to life.

"Our way, I'll bet for every one man we save from being unjustly convicted, we let an army of H.G.s walk out the door." She feels a hot rage rise up in her like a pot about to boil over. "Even if that happened, occasionally finding an innocent man guilty, I mean, wouldn't it be a worthwhile sacrifice to keeping all those other guilty defendants off the street? Equal, justice for all, clearly doesn't work." She shakes her head. "Those words didn't just come out of my mouth, did they?"

He grins knowingly. "You just got religion, hon. Always happens when shit hits home. We make it legal for them to go out and kill again. Repeat offenders they call 'em," he says, looking smugly amused. "Mutts learn fast. It's only John Q. Public that never seems to get it straight."

"Casey was right when he said that H.G. left all of us victims. Even Garth, Claude, and Bernie don't know it yet. It wouldn't matter if a bolt of lightning were to come down and wipe out H.G. now; it's all after the fact. Those kids looked up to H.G., thought he was so cool, and then they saw him get away with murder? Okay, so none of them will probably go out and kill anyone, but what kind of adults are they going to grow up to be?"

"Society pays a heavy price when it doesn't get its pound of flesh." Jack gives a lock of her hair a little affectionate tug, like he did in court. "Fuck those druggie kids and the victim, Scholfield. He was nothing to you, Kate."

He was one of her son's best friends. His parents are Kate's friends. Where has this man been for the last six months? And those druggie kids? They're the future for Jack as well as for Kate.

She opens her mouth to protest, but his hand flies up to silence her, "Christ Almighty," he bellows at her again. "You got to stop fuckin' interrupting me every damn minute."

His outburst is so unexpected, she feels like she has just been slapped across the face. Instinctively she shrinks back in the booth, her body no longer making contact with his. Who is this man?

He sighs wearily, his tenderness returning, but it is too late to make amends this time. "You cut into my line of thought," he says inappropriately. "What was I saying? Oh yeah, I know… you've been through a lot of shit, and I want you to know I'm here for you," he pledges like a true Indian-giver. "Family members dying, children disappearing, God forbid. Those things happen and people survive tragedies like that. They move on. My dad passed away last year." He clears his throat and takes a sip of his beer. "Bottom line is, you didn't lose a loved one. This will pass, and I suspect it will happen a lot faster than you think."

He's right when he says Scott wasn't a loved one. He wasn't her son. Jack may have a no-frills, cut-to-the core way of saying things, but his words come from the heart. He wouldn't be here tonight if he didn't care. But what was that business about being interrupted all the time?

It was nothing, Kate tells herself. Jack's got to be just as stressed out as she is. She doesn't need to doubt him, too. Not now. Not when she feels like the bottom has dropped out of her life. "I know this will pass, Jack. And I know you're right. I wasn't as close to Scott as I am to some of Casey's other friends. But something else has been lost. Trust. I used to really like all those kids that hung out on the corner. Those murderous kids. How do I learn to trust again?"

Three musicians have mounted the tiny stage and begun to tune their instruments. The drums and cymbals clang with a dull, thumping beat. The saxophone roller-coasters its awakening wail. Deep, melodious groans of a base begin to waft through the room, and all around Kate and Jack, the booths and tables fill up with laughing, chatty couples.

Jack looks at his watch. "Almost twelve. Set's going to start. How do you learn to trust again? You'll find a way," he wraps up brusquely. "You should remember there is something you didn't lose. You've still got your son."

She hears herself respond with a wimpy, "What do I do if I run into those smirking O'Connor's? Or, God forbid, him?"

"I don't think you have to worry about that piece of shit showing up in the neighborhood," he assures her, based on his past experiences with criminals who get to walk free. He reaches for the check. "And his family? You pass garbage on the street every day. Just ignore 'em. Simple as pie." Looking deep into her eyes, as if he were taking aim at her soul, he whispers, "Let's get out of here."

She leans into him, brushing his cheek with her lips. "Not tonight, sweetheart," she whispers back, hoping her show of affection takes the edge off her unwillingness to be with him. "I don't want to leave Case alone tonight. And for the next few weeks, I want to be there for him." She leans over and kisses Jack again. "After that, it'll be our summer. I hope you understand."

"I do," he says, sounding like he means it. "My daughter comes first with me, too."

Jack watches her walk out of the bar. Cute kid. Even in her depressed state she manages to swing that little ass. Too bad she's leaving. By this time in the evening, all he wants to do is kick back, have a couple of drinks and some laughs, and have his woman by his side. All around him in other booths, at other tables, guys are doing just that with their girls. Jack pays his dues; he puts his time in on the job, and takes care of his family like a man should. Isn't he owed one lousy, little fragment of relaxation?

He polishes off the last of his beer and signals the waitress for a refill.

It's been a long, grueling day, then having to add on this depressing get-together with the boys to appease Kate, and now finding out he's going back to that room he rents alone is even more depressing. What the hell, might as well hang out here and enjoy a little music for a while. The day has disturbed him, and he is too keyed up to go home to an empty bed.

Home? Why does the word make his stomach tense up? Home is hardly that shoebox he uses to grab a few hours' sleep between tours, to shower, store his clothes and books, and to bring a woman for sex. It makes him feel like a fucking nomad, living in that hole in the wall.

Home is the chintz curtains Paula made for the family room, the smell of grass he has just mowed. Home is Jenny's schoolbooks on the kitchen table.

He does like the way Kate Palmer sticks by her son, though. He meant it when he told her he thought she was a good mother. Even when she was being a pain in the butt by getting in the way of his investigation, he had to give her credit for being at her son's side. It's what he thought dad would do so long ago...

> *...It was on a Sunday, in late July, and eleven-year-old Jackie Kuchinsky waits in the alley behind the laundromat where mom works. It is a nauseatingly hot day, and the sweat is pouring down Jackie's chest, back, and forehead. It is the morning of his eleventh birthday. His older cousin, Joey, said there was nothing to worry about, but his knees are knocking together anyway. They started doing that the minute Joey made Jack go into Mom's purse to pilfer her keys. Joey had it all figured out. With the laundromat closed on Sunday, mom wouldn't even notice the keys missing, and she wouldn't be aware of their going into the closed store to "look around." Joey had assured him, "It ain't stealin' when you find money people dropped on the floor, stupid. Nobody's even gonna know we was there." Joey'd promised to be in and out in a flash, but as Jackie stands waiting under the broiling hot sun it seems like Joey's been in there forever. Jackie's hands are in his pockets, his eyes glued to the toes of his shoes. He has no recourse but to wait because he can't leave without those keys. And then, he feels it. A man's hand slamming down on his shoulder and crashing along with it, Jackie Kuchinsky's whole world.*

"You got yourself in big trouble kid," a man's gruff voice reprimands. "We're going to have to take you down to the station house. Your old man's not going to be happy when he hears about this."

But it would be a tortuously long time before Jackie would know just how unhappy his father would be. Sitting it out alone, hour after hour on that hard police station bench, while Joey managed to duck out the laundromat's front door and avoid capture, Jackie is left to watch the scary cops come and go with guns and handcuffs dangling from their belts. They angrily eye him as they walk by. He's so frozen with fear, he can't even ask permission to go to the bathroom. Waiting out the long hours with such a pressure in his groin, he feels like he will explode. As the clock on the wall strikes midnight, it puts an end to his 11th birthday, along with the birthday cake and the gifts he will never see. At one minute past twelve, dad walks through the door and right past Jackie, like he was invisible. Dad just strides up to the desk, signs some papers like to get a dog out of the pound, and drives Jackie home without saying a word to his son…

Yeah, Kate's kid won't forget she was there when he needed her. A kid doesn't forget something like that. Kate asked if he understood why she wants to spend the next few weeks with her son. He does. He'd give anything to see his little girl across the breakfast table again, to watch TV with her when he comes home from work, to tell her to turn down her stereo, and to see her stuff all over the place. He doesn't have those luxuries anymore. Kate does.

Yes, Jack understands why Kate left tonight. But she's all he's got right now. She, and the job, and school. Tonight, would have been his twentieth wedding anniversary. Jack needed Kate tonight, too.

Chapter Twenty-Five

C asey's departure turned out to have a favorable impact on Kate's summer with Jack. Since she was alone in her apartment, Jack would be free to sleep over at her place for a change. Making love in Jack's small, dismal room quickly became a thing of the past. After he'd put in an eight to twelve-hour shift, she could let him stop by to sit in her kitchen with her, midnight snacking on scrambled eggs and cream cheese. Jack in his underwear and Kate in her nightgown or wearing nothing at all.

First it had been Kate and Jack and the case, then it was Kate, Casey, Jack and the trial. Now it is just Kate and Jack. How Detective Kuchinsky would fit into this new life of hers was something she had not yet considered. She needs some time to catch her breath.

The hazy July sun sifts through Kate's living room windows, offering little more than a muted glow, but the shimmering whiteness of the walls Jack has just painted for her illuminate everything around them.

"Jack, these walls are like glass," she raves. "You did such a professional job. I really appreciate this."

She does. What she didn't appreciate was the attitude that had precipitated his generous offer to repaint her apartment. He started harping on this painting thing as soon as Casey left for the coast. Maybe his irritation over the imperfections on her walls was because Jack was now spending so much more time at Kate's place.

Time and time again he'd stand in the middle of the living room, hands on hips, surveying her ceiling, tsk-tsking, "How can you live like this, hon?" Kate found herself the target of his rough-edged candor that had, at first, seemed so refreshingly charming.

With her walls so heavily laden with artwork and memorabilia, Kate saw the minor imperfections of time as barely discernable. There were a few hairline cracks, a bit of peeling in one corner of one ceiling, and a finish mellowed to an off-white buff by a decade of sunlight. None of that bothered Kate. How can she live like that? Quite well, thank you.

But it bothered Jack immensely. He pointed out every flaw to her until this weekend when he learned he wouldn't be spending his usual Saturday with his daughter because her grandmother was in town.

Toting drop clothes, paint buckets, brushes, and a big bottle of vodka, he showed up on Kate's doorstep and simply announced he was going to take care of it for her.

Yet now that it's done, now that the nauseating smell of wet paint in hot July is gone, the screeching sander unplugged and back in its box, and the vodka bottle is empty, thanks to the Bloody Marys that fueled Jack's perfectionist frenzy as he polished and smoothed every minuscule lump and bump on the walls, Kate is happy with the results. True, she would have been satisfied with a far less flawless job if it meant far less of the sander's continuous loud wail. That glass-like finish didn't come easy.

Attitude aside, Jack did work like a dog trying to please her. "Thank you, Jack. You were right. It really does look so much better," she feels obligated to keep repeating.

He is down on one knee, sloshing a paintbrush around in a can of paint thinner. "My dad had his own paint business," he tells her. "I worked with him before I came on the job. He taught me everything he knew." He wraps the brush in tin foil, slips it into his duffle bag and walks over to where a batch of framed art and canvases have been stacked up against the sofa. "So, at least you're not livin' like a pig anymore." He looks at his watch. "I've still got an hour before my tour starts. Show me where you want these pictures put up."

She makes sure her smile is pleasant when she tells him, "Jack, honey, I can do that later." Decorating her apartment is something Kate enjoys doing alone. And, by the way, she wasn't living like a pig.

He picks up a canvas, an abstract Kate painted in splashes of color and stands holding it. "I don't want you fuckin' up my walls after I worked my ass off cleanin' them up," he says as matter-of-factly as if he were asking for another Bloody Mary refill. Then he looks down at the canvas, "Where do you want me to hang this abortion?"

Okay, number one, they are not his walls. Number two, she would prefer he keep his prosaic opinions on art to himself, and number three fucking is beginning to wear very thin as his all-purpose adjective/adverb. This is a guy who is considering an academic career?

As for hammering a few nails in the wall, Kate is perfectly capable of that no-brainer. She would have preferred it if Jack had noticed how capable she is. Rewiring lamps, doing small plumbing jobs, Kate Palmer has made herself into a pretty good husband. She is about to tell him that she is certainly competent enough to hammer a fucking nail into the fucking wall without creating a fucking crater in his fucking plaster job, when he laughs in that melt-your-heart way he has, and stops her reprimand dead in its tracks.

Flipping the canvas around, he squints at it and laughs again, "Fuckin' thing looks like I used it to clean my brushes off." His words are still provocative, but the tenderness of his tone melts the layer of ice that had just formed around her heart.

"JA-ck." She lightens up, her fists smacking her hips in mock indignation. "I painted that." She takes the canvas from him and tosses it on the couch. Standing very close to him and smiling up into his captivating eyes, she cocks her head with a flirtatious suggestion of mischief. "You have a whole hour?" she asks, unbuttoning the top button on her blouse. "I bet we can think of something more interesting than hanging pictures."

An hour later, she stands in the foyer, kissing him goodbye, his trench coat encompassing her naked body like a warm security blanket. When the door shuts behind him she slips on a robe and turns on some music: Bruce Springsteen. She gets out the hammer and nails, and begins to hang the memorabilia of her life back on her walls.

As the weeks roll by, an irritating side of Jack emerges. But the relationship doesn't sour. It thrives with this newfound togetherness.

In these lazy days of summer, with the weight and worries of the case, the trial, a distant memory as the snows of January, Kate finds hanging out with Jack all summer is far more fun than she'd expected.

They giggled through the summer's selection of slice and dice horror movies, strolled hand in hand through the park's greenery, visited the zoo, and spent hot, sultry nights cooling off in outdoor cafés where margaritas and Mexican food, she was pleased to discover, were a mutual favorite.

Best of all was walking the snow-white sands of Jones Beach together, to the jetty and back, playfully splashing each other along the ocean's foamy rim. They laughed about everything, and nothing at all. Beach days always ended with a feast of steamed mussels, washed down with the tangy sweetness of Chez, Jack's special Strawberry Daiquiris.

He often surprised her with little displays of affection. He insisted on chauffeuring her around whenever his work schedule permitted. "Don't want my woman taking that shithole in the ground." He played Mr. Fixit in her apartment. She didn't have the heart to tell him not to. And in bed, he always saw to it that he pleased her first.

Once, when they were walking in Riverside Park, he suddenly hoisted himself up into the blossoms of a cherry tree and plucked a spray of buds. While caressing her cheek with the sweet-smelling petals and tucking them behind her ear, he told her, "You're beautiful, you know." In his diamond-in-the-rough style, she was beginning to think Jack Kuchinsky was the most romantic man she'd ever met.

It was her pleasure to return the affectionate deeds. She sewed on his buttons, gave him back rubs after a long night of tracking down the bad guys. On nights they ate in, she cooked his favorites, rice pudding from scratch, and something she never, in her wildest dreams, thought would come out of her kitchen, a pot roast. It pleased her to please him.

But as they got deeper into the summer's sweltering dog days, a selfish side of Jack began elbowing its way into their relationship. The nights he slept over, the window had to be left wide open, regardless of the night's chill, and Kate's favorite quilt was replaced by sheets tucked in military-tight, making it difficult to even turn over in the middle of the night. Then there was the

TV remote, which by the end of July, she was certain had been surgically attached to Jack's hand.

By August, Jack said it was up to Kate to think of things they could do. Nights she didn't come up with anything were sure to be spent in front of the TV. Then one day, near the end of the summer, he announced he had a surprise for her, assuring her she was going to love it. "Does a bear shit in the woods?" he asked.

She thought she was finally going to meet his daughter. An introduction that had been noticeable, to Kate, by its absence. He enticed her with the surprise for days and she became excited by his excitement until she found out the surprise was a drive out to New Jersey for a rousing afternoon of miniature golf.

She spent the entire boring day tapping that stupid little ball through windmills, under bridges, around Chinese pagodas, and watched as Jack thoroughly enjoyed every point he scored over her. On the drive home he confided that, after he retired, he hoped to become proficient at real golf, along with ballroom dancing and learning to play bridge. A sudden image of a white-haired old man in plaid pants, a yellow alligator shirt, and a dopey, little hat perched on his head flashed across Kate's mind. Where did that streetwise detective with the flip side of sociology and Chinese calligraphy go?

In the six months between the arrest and the start of the trial, her relationship with Jack gave Kate a safe haven, a cocoon in which she could restore herself. Even with his rough edges, he sometimes kissed her with gum in his mouth, and thought Miro canvases were painted by a preschooler, his presence in her life made it possible for her to feel safe and begin to trust again.

The protection of his cop world gave her time to rejuvenate without having to look over her shoulder all the time. By August, the old, self-sufficient Kate was back, and Jack Kuchinsky was simply a man she was dating. Those anxious weeks of the trial have become, as Jack predicted they would, a lot of yesterdays ago. The stress, the terrible fears of last fall when it first happened, were filed way in a dark corner of her memory bank, along with the need to have a detective for protection.

Eight months into whatever she was having with Jack, they still exchange I love yous, though still only in bed, the subject of meeting his daughter or any family members has never come up, not from him nor from Kate.

She does care for Jack, who stood by her during such a tough time in her life. He must care for her because he is still here, but she has deliberately avoided giving much thought to how Jack fits into her future. Casey will be back home in a few weeks, and Kate is simply having a summer romance with a man named Jack.

Jack next month? Next year? Who knows? More and more, as odd as it may sound, she finds herself longing for the days when they had the case to share.

Chapter Twenty-Six

On a morning in late August, Jack turns over in his bed, stretching, yawning, and chilling his lungs with a big swallow of delicious air-conditioning. Then he squints at the time, 10 a.m. Shit. He sits up and scowls. He has to pick Kate up in less than an hour. If she drags him to one more of those suffocating, hot museums he's going to puke. Thank God those phony-baloney galleries she loves so much are closed this month. A bunch of limp-wristed airheads throw garbage on the wall and call it art. Who the fuck do they think they're kidding?

Not Jack. He knows a real picture when he sees one. In all the galleries she's dragged him to, he has only seen one, once. What was that guy's name again? Hopper, yeah, Edward Hopper. The night she took him to that "retrospective," as she called it, Jack felt he finally saw some art. That picture of the diner really got to him. He'd stood looking at it for a long time, feeling it in his bones. He went to get a refill of the watered-down wine, then came right back to it. The loneliness, the *aloneness*, the fuckin' guy caught it all. Jack should know. He experienced it between the midnight to 8 a.m. shifts when he first started walking the beat, and again last year when he moved into that dingy two by four. Those diners in the early hours, just before dawn, before people with real lives came in for their morning coffee. Jack spent a lifetime in them. This guy Hopper must have, too. He must have seen some shit in his life, like Jack has. He died in the sixties, Kate said. What a shame. The guy knew how to draw, had real talent, and like Rembrandt and da Vinci, he bought the farm far too early.

Yeah, that diner picture really hit home with him. He's been meaning to tell Paula about it. Tomorrow after his lunch with her, maybe he'll walk Paula over there to see it. Kate will be at work, she'll never know.

Sharing something with Paula? Even though he spent two decades with her, sharing something is a new experience. He can't remember it ever being just him and Paula. Seems like they were always a threesome: him, Paula, and the baby; him, Paula, and their little girl; him, a teenage Jenny, and Paula.

He was working for dad when they first hooked up. They met when dad was hired to paint Paula's parents' home in Queens. Funny, thinking back now, he really can't remember how it all started between them, but before he knew it, with the blessings of both his parents and hers, he'd slipped a ring on her finger. A perfect match, they all said. And then before he knew it, there was a baby in the picture.

Not that he had to marry her. Nice girls like Paula didn't get knocked up in those days. But even in that short period of time before Jenny came along, he can't remember when he and Paula ever had enough time for each other.

He'd joined the department that same year for the security and benefits, bought a house out of the city, and spent every spare minute fixing it up.

Paula had her first miscarriage only a few months into the marriage, followed by a second, followed by Jenny. That first year passed in the blink of an eye. No, there was never enough time for Jack and Paula to just hang out, like they're doing now.

The first time he'd met her for lunch, when was it? A month ago? Six weeks, maybe? With the separation, she always makes a point of being out of the house when he comes to see Jenny. She goes to the mall or to a neighbor's. It's hard to believe he didn't actually lay eyes on his own wife for almost a year. Not since that night when he pulled out of the driveway with the trunk full of his books and the back seat full of his clothes.

Getting together now was Paula's idea. In mid-August she'd called as usual, to talk about Jenny, but for the first time, she didn't complain. That's when she'd expressed a desire to see him. What was even more surprising was the smile he heard in her voice when she mentioned that. She wanted a face-to-face in place of a phone call.

Since Paula was now coming into the city twice a week for real-estate classes, she suggested a downtown restaurant. It made sense. He'd told Kate right away, of course. He was only meeting Paula to discuss Jenny.

Kate didn't blink an eye. She even also said it was better for parents to talk face to face. One thing you had to give Kate Palmer, she was not the jealous type.

That first lunch with Paula was nothing like what he'd expected. He certainly wasn't prepared for how fabulous Paula looked. She'd dropped twenty pounds and changed her hair, which was now lighter and longer.

She wore the blue linen suit he'd given her the last Christmas they were together, and the little gold heart he'd given her on their first wedding anniversary. She looked more like the girl she was when he'd first met her, but with a womanliness now that made her damn sexy as hell.

He'd forgotten what a stunning woman Paula could be. It made him feel proud to be seen with her. He decided right then and there he'd have to sit Kate down and have a talk with her about her wardrobe, about those ragged jeans, the ones with the holes in the knees. Jeez, he hates to be seen in public with her dressed like that.

The first meeting with Paula was upbeat and amicable. Jack made plans with her to meet again the next time she was in the city, to talk about Jenny, of course.

This time they lunched outside in the quiet backyard of a small cafe. It was easy to order since they liked the same foods and snacked from each other's plates, as they always used to. It was also easy to talk—a name, a single word, invoking a whole amusing episode from their past, mutual laughter about mutual memories. He'd forgotten how much history there was between them and forgotten how much of it had been good.

That time he didn't tell Kate about his meeting with Paula. Nor has he told her about the subsequent meetings; first once a week, now it's up to twice a week. They get together for lunch, for coffee, for a drink, for a short walk in the park. Whatever he can fit into their schedules. Jenny was still away at camp and the real estate classes had ended so Paula has made her time totally Jack's now.

There is a provocative newness about this woman he slept next to for so many years, this woman who is the mother of his child. He finds a surge of excitement now proceeds each of his meetings with her. Why should he tell Kate? Meetings with Paula are Jack's business, family business.

Now, each time they meet, they end up talking less about Jenny and more about themselves. Their new interests, their hopes and dreams for the future are both surprisingly similar. Along with Paula's new career goals, her attitude has done a one-eighty. She's so up now. She is happy as a pig in shit about the idea of selling houses. He has no doubt she'll do well at it. A woman this charming can't help but be successful at anything she touches, and he told her that. Times have changed. He doesn't need her to be home taking care of a baby anymore, and he no longer feels a working wife would be an indictment of his manhood. Kate, after all, is a working woman and that hasn't made Jack uncomfortable one bit.

Without the distraction of a child around, Paula really listens when Jack talks to her. She makes him feel like he can tell her anything and she'll be on his side. It takes a real woman to make a man feel like that. It turns out that Paula did know about Jack's affairs, and chose not to say a word. It takes a real woman to do that, too.

Still, Paula doesn't know about Kate, and Jack has no intention of telling her. Why rock the boat? What he does with Kate Palmer has nothing to do with what he does with Paula.

This morning he deliberately takes his time showering and getting dressed, then snaps on the TV and sits staring at, but not listening to, some inane talk show. So what if he's a few minutes late in picking up Kate? She can cool her heels for a while. She always makes him wait for her. If he let her, this mother fuckin' woman would put a strangle hold on every free minute he has. Whatever she's got planned for today, you can be sure it's not going to be Jack's idea of fun.

He lingers for a bit in the coolness of his air-conditioned room, thinking about how it's going to be roasting out there today. But it is not just the thought of enduring another dog day of August that is making him feel like he is being suffocated.

Now it is Labor Day weekend. It doesn't matter that the weather is still sultry hot. Doesn't matter if the fuckin' heat wave continues on until the end of September like it sometimes does. To Jack, this weekend means the summer is officially over. So, too, are some things in Jack's life.

He waits in front of the restaurant, sweating like a pig, but not because of the oppressive heat. As usual Kate chose the place, unfortunately Japanese again. God, he hates eating raw fish and that seaweed shit. And as usual, she is keeping him waiting again.

With his hands in his pockets, he shifts uneasily from foot to foot. There'll be some crying, of course, he's prepared for that, but beyond tears, she is a real question mark. Kate could fall apart or fly into a rage. That's why he decided to tell her in a public place. She's too much of an unknown to take a chance on her possibly sticking a knife in him while he sleeps.

Ten long minutes later she hops out of a cab wearing those same ragged pants he hates so much. They're the ones with the holes in the knees. He never did get around to telling her how he felt about that. You'd think she'd put on something sharp to go out to a restaurant. Guess she thinks it's cute to dress like a kid. How embarrassing. It makes Jack feel like it looks like he is dating his daughter. The woman makes good money, too. It's not like she couldn't afford a nice pair of slacks, like the kind Paula wears when they meet for lunch.

Breathless and gushing with apologies, she rushes up to him. She mentions something about how she didn't realize how late it was, and how she had to wait *forever* for a cab—the usual shit. But then she goes and slips her arm in his, snuggling up as though they were lying in bed together and, smiling in that coquettish way she has, gives him a little peck on the cheek. He's got to admit she can be adorable.

"I'm starved," she bubbles as if she didn't have a care in the world, "and I know it's a little early, but I'm dying for some Saki."

He didn't come to this brunch with an appetite, and her up attitude only makes him feel like more of a heel. But what the hell, even if his purpose had been different, he wouldn't have been able to stomach this uncooked Japanese crap anyway.

They're seated at a table so small he feels like he is sitting in her lap. Under it, his knees graze hers. At another time that would have been a turn on. "How the fuck are they gonna fit two plates on this Mickey Mouse dime?" he says, looking around the room. "Maybe they got a booth."

"This is fine, Jack. It's cozy." She nudges his knee with hers to prove her point.

The point she makes is that when they go out, she always has to call the shots. He's glad she reminded him of that. It makes what he has to do a little easier.

"I'll have a Saki," she tells the waiter. She glances down the menu. "Ooooh. They have age tofu, my favorite. Let's split one for an appetizer," she says like he is supposed to know what that garbage is. Then she insists on putting him down in front of the waiter by enlightening Jack, like he's not classy enough to know that it's, "Tofu fried in a spicy sauce. You'll love it."

"Get whatever you want." He looks up at the waiter. "Just bring me a small salad with Italian dressing and a rum coke."

"Italian dressing and a rum coke?" she taunts with another bubble of laughter. "Look around you, my dear. This place is called *Nippon West*."

"Actually, I prefer Chinese," he says, taken aback by how serious he hears himself sound.

"Jack, why didn't you say something? We could have gone to Empire Szechuan." She sounds genuinely surprised, genuinely sorry.

She has always tried to please him. He's got to give her that. She lets him pop in any time after a long tour, two or three in the morning, still welcoming him with a kiss. She gives him back rubs when he's bone tired, and she always laughs at his jokes. When he stays over he gets breakfast, sometimes in bed, with homemade hash browns. And once when he mentioned he thought pajamas were sexy, they became the mainstay of Kate's nocturnal wardrobe. Katie Palmer is a good woman, no argument from Jack.

I never got that kind of service from Paula, although in all fairness, Paula did have a baby to look after, and of course, a child always has to come first.

The drinks arrive and Jack quickly downs about a third of his. The rum's sweet warmth instantly fortifies his gut. The edge softens and he drapes one arm over the back of his chair as he settles back in his seat. "What's new with your son?"

She frowns. "You're polishing that drink off pretty fast."

"What am I, having brunch with the AA patrol?" He can't help himself from snapping. What else is a man supposed to do when a woman tries to control him like that? Kate really covered up that side of her for a long time. He quickly reminds himself why he is here and reaches over to give her hand a little apologetic squeeze.

She looks at him kind of funny, like if she were standing up, she would be backing away from him. He squeezes her hand again, and adds a little smile. "So talk to me."

It works. She slips her hand out of his but her tone, her expression, tells him all is forgiven. "Case showed me a letter he got from Bernie Maisel. The Maisels moved out of the neighborhood right after the trial."

"Whatever." Who the fuck cares about those little shitheads. Not Jack, that's for sure, but he wants to keep the conversation upbeat so, though he's not interested at all, he asks, "What did the letter say?" This woman takes forever to get a story out, but she did pique Jack's interest a bit. And the mention of Bernie takes Jack back to a time when he and Kate shared something together.

Sure, it was a bullshit case from day one. Somebody wasted a drug dealer. So what. But the sociological implications had been intriguing—spoiled, privileged kids running amuck, using the system to their own advantage and actually coming out ahead, actually winning. That was a pretty unique experience, even for a jaded detective like Jack. Could it be a possible theme for his dissertation? Maybe. Even the victim had an unusual twist. A dope dealer who came from an affluent family, and who was not only white, but a wimp with the women. "Don't keep me in suspense; what did Bernie shmuck-head have to say?"

"Well." She leans forward on her elbows. "It's not so much what he had to say, but that he wrote to Casey at all, and *now*, almost three months later." Kate lifts the tiny Saki cup to her lips and takes a sip, dragging the story out a little longer. Her nose wrinkles up. "I always forget how strong this stuff is, but I do love it." She giggles in that girlish way she sometimes has. She takes another sip, and smiles in the way she does when she wants him to do her.

Jack is tempted to tell her, you're polishing that drink off pretty fast, but he resists. Got to keep this meeting civil.

"The letter," she goes on, "it was this long, rambling thing about how he was never really involved in any of what went down. He said he never considered H.G. a friend either. The same shit he tried to lay on us from the beginning. Isn't that bizarre? Does this kid actually expect Casey to write him back saying all is forgiven?"

"Maybe. Who knows. Who cares. Was that it?" he asks, feeling cheated. She piqued his interest for nothing.

"He made a big deal about how he hasn't communicated with H.G. since the trial. He went on for a whole page of that. But he did throw in one tidbit that will interest you. It seems like he has stayed in touch with Claude because he said Claude had been accepted at Amherst. Can you believe that? A school like Amherst. They're supposed to only pick the cream of the crop, and they accepted both Claude and Bernie."

"Claude will probably end up on Wall Street." Jack sighs.

She straightens up in her seat and scowls. "I wouldn't be so flippant if I was you. You just might find yourself cross-examined by that little creep someday."

"I'll be long gone from this job before that could happen." Bernie, Claude, H.G. Names Jack'd already filed away in an old case folder. He's forgetting them faster than she can bring them up.

And he will be. The once unthinkable consideration of pursuing a teaching career has, thanks to the encouragement of both Kate and Paula, become a foreseeable future goal.

She is silent for a moment. Holding the Saki cup with both hands, she takes a sip, then another, then carefully sets it down in front of her. In a dead serious tone, she informs him, "I need to talk to you about something."

Her somber tone makes him internally squirm. What the fuck is this all about? They are here because he needs to talk to her about something. Jack doesn't like getting hit from left field like this.

"It's about Friday night, Jack. I know we always do something that night since Saturday is your Jenny-night. That is, if overtime doesn't screw it up." She takes a deep breath and another sip of the Saki. "Look, Jack, we've never talked about this, but well, I know you never asked me to, but I always leave Fridays open 'cause…I just assume…and well, I've also gotten into this thing of not making any plans for myself without consulting you first. But this Friday coming up, I have other plans."

And she called Bernie's letter rambling? He has to try to interrupt this one and questions Kate, "What are you trying to say? You want to get together Friday or not?"

She reaches across the table, covering his hand with both of hers. "An old friend called me and said he's going to be in town Friday," she sheepishly reveals. "He's not an old boyfriend. Jim has never been anything but a friend. A good friend. I haven't seen him in ages, and I'd like to…To catch up, you know. He wants to take me to dinner and my first reaction was to check with you. Then I started thinking…well, I just went ahead and made plans to see him without talking to you first, Jack. I hope you're not upset."

He answers her question with a shrug. Upset? Hardly, in light of the reason he is having brunch with her today. But he does notice she didn't say anything about introducing him to this "old friend". Another one of her not-so-subtle inferences that Jack isn't good enough for that crowd of empty-suits she is used to hanging out with.

"So exactly what are you trying to tell me?" he asks, fully aware of the edge of irritation in his voice.

"Look, Jack, I'm used to being on my own," she looks like she is going to cry.

Jesus, before he even has a chance to say his piece, she's already starting shit with him.

She insists on going on. "It was one hundred percent me getting into this thing of not making plans without checking with you first, but lately, it's starting to make me feel sort of…well, a little…"

She looks like she is trying like hell not to say whatever it is she wants to say. Then she sighs and lets it out. "A little claustrophobic. Don't get me wrong, please." Her eyes, brimming with tears, widen with sincerity. "I love doing things with you, it's just that lately, I feel my time is kind of being taken for granted." She holds up her hands, not that he had any intension of interrupting her. How could he when he is having such a hard time following whatever the fuck she is trying to say. "Jack, I'm not blaming you for anything, I just need a little more space in our relationship. Do you understand what I'm feeling about us?"

He doesn't have a clue. Everything is such a big deal with this woman. She always reads something into what anybody says or doesn't say. She's the kind of woman you got to walk on eggs with. It's become exhausting being with her.

Her near-tears look is suddenly wiped away with a smile. Her eyes are twinkling in that cute, flirtatious way that once attracted him so much. What a brat she can be. "I'll make it up to you," she promises seductively. "We'll do something extra special Sunday night."

"No, we won't," he blurts out, so abruptly that her whole body jerks backward as though his words had physically smashed into her. Damn. He didn't mean to get into it that way.

The waiter arrives with the refills Jack had earlier signaled for. Perfect timing. He takes a fast swig to fortify himself for the speech for which he has not yet found the right words. It's play-it-by-ear time, buddy. "Kate, I don't know how to say this to you except straight out 'cause that's the kinda guy I am."

This is not a stupid woman, she's got her antenna up now, and the look in her eyes has abruptly changed. In the same way he's done a million times before, he's looking into the eyes of a victim, only this time Jack's not the detective. This time Jack is the perpetrator.

He hurt Paula and Jenny by walking out on them. Now he's got this woman sitting here in front of him just waiting for him to hurt her, too. *God, he doesn't want to hurt any more people.* But the poor kid is trapped. She sees the punch coming and she can't even duck. The feeling of his knees touching hers under the tiny table only makes him feel like he is violating her even more. Yet he doesn't dare break the physical bond for fear his pulling away would only further magnify his rejection of her.

He reaches across the table and takes her hand, compressing the smooth soft fingers that he once loved to feel stroking him. He wants to convey he means no harm. "It's not your fault, babe. It's me. Hundred percent me. You're a good woman, Katie. They don't come any better," he tells her, hearing his words come out with a raspy unnaturalness, "but it's just not happening between us. Not anymore."

She deftly slides her hand out of his grasp and pulls the Saki cup close to her as she settles back in her seat and takes a long, deep breath. Except for an infinitesimal narrowing of the eyes, there is no expression on her face. She just sits staring at him, making him wait it out for a few seconds of ear-shattering silence. All he wants to do is get up and get out of there, but he is trapped now, too, and obliged to finish what he has started.

Her lips withdraw in a nasty pink line and her fingernails begin to tap the side of her Saki cup with a nerve-racking, dull rhythm. He takes a drink of his rum coke and shifts uncomfortably in his seat. He is no longer looking into the eyes of a victim.

"Not happening? Not happening?" she parrots. "Where did that come from? 'Hey, man, it's not happenin',' she sing-songs contemptuously. "What do you think this is, the God damn sixties?"

She's right. Damn, damn. His choice of words did come out sounding pitifully inane. Superficial at best. He didn't even begin to convey his true feelings of regret, and that he does care for her. He cares about her, but she's just not right for him. Fuck, she looks really angry. It is the same look mom had when she caught twelve-year-old Jackie in the closet with eleven-year-old, Shirley Koufakis.

Although the thought of invoking this woman's wrath has been giving him nightmares for days, now a part of him hopes, prays, he has done just that. The nastier she becomes, the less he will feel like a total shit.

He sighs, closing his eyes for a moment, and tapping his forehead as he struggles to find some gentle way to do this, but there really isn't any. He looks her straight in the eye and gives it to her no frills, direct and honest. "Katie, there are things I want to do with my life, and I tell ya, I just can't see myself doing those things with you. I'm not talking about the big things. The career move to teaching, you'd be great there. Fantastic. It's the inconsequential things that kill it for me. I want to take up golf someday. You make jokes about how boring you think the game is. I want to travel, go to Las Vegas, maybe the Grand Canyon. I never had time to enjoy myself like that. I can't see myself in those places with you. You dream of seeing places like Borneo and Tibet. When we go down to Atlantic City, you're more interested in watching the people than playing the slots." He shakes his head angrily at his choice of examples. "It's not golf. It's not Atlantic City. It's just that I can't see myself sharing that many things with you."

There, it's out. No matter how she takes it, he already feels a hundred times better. The weight has lifted. She can go off like a cannon now, for all he cares.

But she doesn't. "I didn't expect this today, you know," she says real calm and without anger. He almost thinks he detects a small smile.

"I know you didn't, hon."

Now her mouth does turn up in a little smile. "I never could see myself taking up bridge or ballroom dancing either," and with a sigh of resignation she adds, "It was inevitable that we would be having this conversation someday." But then the hurt returns to her eyes and she says, "I'd just prefer to be sitting where you are, rather than where I am."

God, how he wants to put his arms around her. To hold and comfort her, to protect her from the pain he is inflicting on her. But the fucking table is in the way. "We had some good times together. I'm not denying that, Katie, but you deserve a guy who will really appreciate you. You're a pretty woman. You'll have plenty of guys knocking on your door."

She sits up straight and suddenly appears amazingly tall. In her eyes a fresh spark of anger extinguishes any trace of the victim. This is not somebody he would want to find himself in a dark alley with, right now.

"I always had plenty of guys knocking on my door," she informs him tersely. Her eyes, are even more narrow now, and she cocks her head to one side asking, "Did that lunch you had with your wife have anything to do with

217

this?"

"Not really," he mutters, feeling his face flush, but how can he answer that truthfully? He musters up every scrap of sincerity he has and tells her, "If you ever need anything, Katie, if anyone ever tries to fuck with you, I want you to know you can always call me. I mean that." And God knows, he does mean that.

She smiles benevolently, the way a mother smiles at a naive child. "I'm a big girl, Jack. I can take care of myself, but I do appreciate you telling me that. And I know you mean it." She pauses, her eyes never letting go of his. Then with absolutely no emotion, she asks, "Are you going back to your wife?"

He shrugs an "I don't know" and picks up the menu. "Let's order. What was that thing you wanted to split?"

Chapter Twenty-Seven

It is October and autumn has finally come, but as Jack drives along the Long Island Expressway with his car windows rolled up tight and his windbreaker zipper pulled up snugly under his chin, he doesn't feel at all chilled by the damp nip in the air. The weather is of no consequence to him this afternoon. He's making another shift in his life. The trunk of his car is filled with his books, and the backseat is loaded with his wardrobe. The next exit on the expressway is his.

Minutes later with the golden, guttural strains of Bruce Springsteen flowing out of his car radio, he turns into the cul-de-sac and pulls up in front of his house. He listens to Bruce melodiously assuring him, "Still at the end of every hard-earned day people find some reason to believe," then turns off the motor and gets out of the car.

He looks at his watch, 2 p.m. Another hour before Jenny is back from school. He smiles remembering Kate's suggestion of what he could do with a whole hour. Paula's home, her car is in the driveway. He knew she would be home. Her advanced real estate class lets out early on Wednesdays. That's why he asked his lieutenant for a personal day today.

He stands there surveying his property. The hedges need trimming badly, the bayberry bushes are crying out for a pruning, the shutters haven't been painted since he left, and the screening on the front door looks like it needs to be replaced. It feels good to be home.

Kate opens the window, inhaling the crisp breeze that blows in off the Hudson River. Its cold sharpness invigorates her. Autumn is her favorite time of year.

Why do some people view autumn as a time of dying? Perhaps it's because the green leaves of summer turn themselves into a brown, yellow, and red carpet at the foot of the trees that previously gave them that green life. Yes, they leave behind barren branches like skeletons against the sky, but what a misunderstood metamorphosis autumn is.

They call spring a time of rebirth and write poems and songs about it because those same skeletal branches beat the snowy odds of winter by blooming with little green buds. Yet Kate finds nothing exhilarating about the slow, creeping onset of springtime. Apart from the momentary thrill of that first sprig of green poking itself through the frost, the oh-so-slow opening of that tiny bud sifts through the winter's greyness at an extraordinarily boring pace.

But the onset of autumn is quite a different kind of blooming. It's a full orchestra on arrival. It is the season Kate can always count on to burst into her life with a dramatic clash of colorful cymbals. She goes to sleep in a city smothering under a hot, sticky haze, and wakes up to a bluer than blue horizon that only a chilly autumn breeze can sweep in, the ritual of that first cold slap across her face immediately freeing her from the lethargy of summer.

Overnight the monochromatic green river's edge bursts into a blazing palate of hot reds, brilliant yellows and oranges no citrus tree could ever dream of bearing. And, like the color of the trees with the onset of autumn, Kate, too, feels a change in herself. Big, bulky sweaters, high leather boots, and long flowing coats with silken scarves to catch the gusty winds, replace the sandals and shorts required to survive the mugginess of a Manhattan summer. Autumn in New York has always been Kate's time of rebirth.

Maybe that's why the conversations she'd had with Jack Kuchinsky after the trial have been so much on her mind lately, especially the one about life being a balance of positives and negatives, ultimately resulting in what Jack called, "just conclusions".

She thinks about how the search to finding anything "just" in the experience of Scott's tragic death and H.G.'s acquittal, had seemed so futile. She contemplates how she felt so defeated and had been too exhausted to even try to find a milligram of justice in it all.

However, Kuchinsky, dear man that he is, provided her with a summer in limbo. He gave her lazy days at the beach, and languid walks in the park. He caressed her and whispered sweet nothings in her ear. He allowed her the wonderful illusion that she had a man by her side, who would protect her from all the shit this last year had thrown at her. She will be forever grateful to Jack Kuchinsky.

Now with the beautiful blazing of autumn colors all around her, the sweet nothingness of last summer is as muted a memory as the horror of that last Thanksgiving. But there remains within her the need to somehow find a just way to resolve all that happened. Then last night at a concert, sitting next to the new man in her life, Oliver, it came to her.

The air in the Lincoln Center Concert Hall was charged with the power of Tchaikovsky's Symphony No. 5. Oliver's hand held hers, and she was completely engrossed in the music when all of a sudden, the solution fell into her head. Of course, that is what she must do, that is what she was meant to do.

There is a world of Kate Palmers out there. A world of other Scholfields and O'Connors who need to know what happened, so it doesn't happen to them. If she can make even one family take a closer look at their teenager's life, then she has done something worthwhile.

As soon as she got home from the concert she sat down at the typewriter, her hands poised above the keys like a pianist about to perform. The bold black letters stared up at her, challenging her, daring her to pound them, the words flying out of her fingers as though someone else was guiding her to write....

... CHAPTER 1

Detective Jack Kuchinsky pushes open the glass door that separates his two worlds. On it the words NEW YORK CITY POLICE DEPT. 24th PRECINCT.

As he begins to climb the worn linoleum steps...

Epilogue

Jack Kuchinsky: Jack lived with his wife and daughter in their suburban home until his daughter left for college, and then he left for good. In the following years, he completed his own studies, earning a master's degree and a Ph.D. in Sociology. He retired from the police department and now teaches at Manhattan's John Jay College of Criminal Justice.

After a few years of relationship bouncing, Jack settled down with an African American woman, fifteen years his junior. She is a nurse at Harlem hospital, whom he met while interviewing a victim there. Now married, he lives with her and their three-year-old son, Steven, in a Riverdale, New York co-op. Aside from the age difference, in every other aspect, Jack's second marriage is a carbon copy of his first.

Kate Palmer: After her book, which she wrote as fiction, was made into a TV movie, Kate quit her job at the ad agency and devoted her full attention to writing. She is currently working on her third novel. All of her stories deal with the impact that parental values have on their teenage children and carry an anti-drug message.

Kate never remarried. She still lives in the same, big, rambling West Side apartment, and enjoys living there alone. Most of her friends, as well as most of the men she dates, are a decade or more younger than she is. All are, in some way, connected to the arts.

She and Jack Kuchinsky have stayed in touch over the years, but they have never been lovers again. It is usually, though not always, Jack who instigates their meetings for lunch, coffee, or an occasional walk in the park.

<u>Casey Palmer</u>: Casey graduated from U.C.L.A., but his continued and escalating use of marijuana during his California years plummeted him down a spiral of lethargy, and eventually into a dependence on cocaine.

After years of making excuses for him, "He's just having a hard time getting over Scott's death," or "It's just his artistic temperament," Kate finally faced up to her son's addictions. With the support of Charlie Palmer, she told Casey they would not communicate with him until he demonstrated an honest desire to turn his life around. After being estranged from his family for six months, Casey got himself into a rehabilitation program and remains drug free to this day.

He now lives in a loft in Soho where he pursues a successful career as a sculptor. He sees his mother on a regular basis. He never married but is in a long-term relationship with a woman several years older than himself.

<u>H.G. O'Connor</u>: After the trial, H.G. completed his high school education at a New England boarding school. He returned to New York City to attend NYU but dropped out after one year to join an upstate communal cult where he and his girlfriend, Amy, still live today. They and their two children are vegans and raise almost all of their food on the commune which they share with nineteen other families. They engage in group sex with other members of the cult and are not sure who fathered Amy's current pregnancy.

<u>Claude Moldorf</u>: Claude went on to graduate from Amherst in the top ten of his class. He majored in International Banking, and upon graduation, landed a job with a leading Wall Street firm. Today, with a salary in the high six figures, he owns a duplex on Madison Avenue and a summer house in the Hamptons. Claude has never married and is rarely seen in the company of a woman. He is currently involved in a sexual relationship with a Hispanic bike messenger, eight years his junior.

<u>Garth Gaines</u>: Garth still lives with his parents in their West End Avenue apartment. After graduating from NYU, the same university where his father still teaches sociology, Garth went on to Graduate School where he

is currently studying microbiology. He has never held a job and has not considered his future beyond school. He does not date and has few friends. He did not maintain his relationship with Claude Moldorf, H.G. O'Connor, or any of the others after the trial. He spends all his spare time studying or traveling abroad with his parents.

<u>Bernie Maisel</u>: Immediately after the trial, Bernie and his parents moved to suburban New Jersey. After graduating from Amhurst College where he studied criminology, Bernie went into law enforcement, getting a job as a New Jersey State Trooper. He remains in that job today. Since becoming a police officer, he has become involved in three shootings, one of which resulted in the death of the perp. All three incidents were declared line-of-duty, and Bernie was fully cleared of any and all charges. Today he, his wife, and new baby live just down the street from his parents.

<u>Brad Hillrich</u>: After spending nearly a year with his grandfather in Georgia "watching the grass grow," Brad, his mother, and little brother all moved to New Mexico where, through his mother's insistence, they joined an ashram. Brad never returned to New York and did not continue his formal education. Today he still lives, works, and meditates at the same ashram.

Through his letters, he continues to maintain a relationship with Casey who, during the time he was struggling with his cocaine addiction, visited Brad and spent a clean month with him at the ashram. Brad has not seen or heard from Bobby Ardsley since he left New York.

<u>Bobby Ardsley</u>: For the first few years after the trial, Bobby worked in the kitchens of several restaurants on the Upper West Side. He never did encounter H.G. in the neighborhood or anywhere else. His fear that an attack by someone else on H.G. was not only imminent, but might be blamed on him, proved to be unfounded.

Bobby's escalating interest in the martial arts led him to spend more and more time in Chinatown, where he eventually became involved with members of an Asian gang. Today he lives on New York City's Mott Street with his Thai girlfriend. It is unclear how he supports himself. He and Casey have remained friends.

Herb Ruben: Herb continued to practice law for three more years as a New York City prosecutor, losing some cases and winning some. He was offered a job teaching Trial Law at his old alma mater, Queens College, and though it meant a considerable pay cut, he took it. He still teaches there today. His wife did eventually divorce him, and he is now remarried to a female police officer. He has no children by either marriage.

David and Maggie Scholfield: The Scholfields still have the same apartment across the street from Kate Palmer. Soon after the trial, they sent their only remaining child away to prep school in England, and then sent him on to complete his education at Cambridge. He is currently a pre-med student in Boston.

David continues to have a successful career as a TV producer. He spends most of his time in Detroit, where he manages one of the affiliates, only returning to New York City for holidays and occasional weekends. Maggie remains in Manhattan. She spends most of her time volunteering to care for AIDS babies at Harlem's Hale House.

The O'Connors: H.G.'s parents moved out of the city almost immediately after the trial and left no forwarding address.

Charlie Palmer: While driving home after a night of vodka martinis, Charlie was involved in a minor fender bender on the Los Angeles Freeway. When he got out of his car to inspect the damage, he was struck and instantly killed by a passing motorist.

Randy Watts: Randy is still a detective with the New York City Police Department. He and Jack Kuchinsky have remained friends.

About the Author

Pat Jenkins is a Long Islander who started out as a photographic model and is the last living Armstrong Girl of renowned calendar artist Rolf Armstrong, a contemporary of George Petty and Alberto Vargas fame. She is featured in the coffee table book *The Great American Pin-Up* written by Louis Meisel.

She longed to escape her middle American life and experience the remote corners of the world, so she traveled to all seven continents, visiting the Antarctic, Indian Tibet, Easter Island, The Australian Outback, Tasmania, Greenland, Northern Kenya, Siberia, and more, where she frequently stayed with native families. Travel to many of these locations, at that time, was rare.

Pat did not start out with the dream of writing as the goal of her unusual travel choices, but once, on her first excursion out of the US, when her foot touched down on Iceland's inky-black, volcanic soil, she knew she had to share these journeys. Thus, a career as a Travel Journalist emerged out of Iceland's volcanic ashes. Her first article, "When Children Meet Unexpected Warmth In Such a Cold Place," was published in the *New York Times*. For many years, she worked freelance and on assignment with the *New York Daily News*, *New York Post*, and other periodicals.

Graduating from the University of Life, Pat Jenkins now resides in New

York City where, in leaner days, she once drove a yellow cab.

AUTHOR WEBSITE:

https://www.patjjenkins.com/

Also by Pat Jenkins

Throughout my writing career, I have been published in a wide range of journalistic outlets, including the *New York Times, Long Island Newsday, New York Post, Daily News, New York Magazine, Sojourn Magazine, Vogue, House & Gardens,* and *The Polish Daily News.*

"SUMMER ON THE CITY" (July 7, 1975) *New York Magazine*
  "A selective guide to seeing , enjoying, receiving, and learning about New York City on absolutely no dollars a day..."
  Read the article HERE

"BEAUTIFUL BONAIRE" for the New York Post (February 7, 1984) *NY Daily News*
  "In crystal clear water up to my waist, tropical fish, looking like they've swum out of a Walt Disney cartoon, gently nibble at my fingers... Only four jet hours from New York brought me 60 miles off the coast of Venezuela to the island of Bonaire."
  Read the article HERE

"DOWN THE MISSISSIPPI TO THE GULF OF MEXICO" for the *New York Post* (February 26, 1985) *Daily News*
  "Strangers only days ago, now they embrace. Walters and busboys with gentle Jamaican smiles shake our hands and join in a rousing rendition of Auld Lang Syne... Many of us exchange addresses and pledge to meet again."
  Read the article HERE

"THIS MARGARITA HITS THE SPOT" for the *New York Post* (December 17, 1985)
  Margarita Island, located 60 miles off of the South American coast consistently has sunny, breezy days, making it hard for visitors to leave.
  Read the article HERE

"BARBADOS IS A BARGIN IN SPRING AND SUMMER" for the *New York Post*'s Travel and Resorts section. (April 8, 1986)

"Sure, like everybody else in the Caribbean, they've got golden beaches, crystal-clear water, swaying palms, and non-stop sunshine. So what's different about Barbados? How about underground caves, a flower forest, wild monkeys, flying fish, goat racing, a haunted churchyard, fire-eaters, and limbo dancers."

Read the article HERE

"CAMEL TREKS ON A CANARY ISLE" For the *Daily News'* Travel section (November 20, 1986)

"As my plane banked to land, I was sure our pilot had strayed a few million miles off course. I looked down on the multicolored craters, swirling lava fields, and grotesque volcanic cones of what could only be a lunar landscape."

Read the article HERE

"CHOOSE PARIS SIGHTS -A LA CARTE" for the *New York Post* (August 9, 1988)

A French bus company has come up with a tour that accommodates the varied interests of each individual rider.

Read the article HERE

"WHEN CHILDREN MEET - 'UNEXPECTED WARMTH IN SUCH A COLD PLACE'" for the *New York Times'* Travel section (August 14, 1970)

"The end of the day comes far too quickly, and we begin the long walk back to the plane, Our group is stretched quite far apart now: my children are still with their new friends. As I walk along, holding the hands of a small girl who is showing me the way."

Read the article HERE

"VOYAGE TO THE BOTTOM OF THE EARTH" for *Long Island Newsday*

"The journey begins on a crisp wintry morning at Kennedy Airport when 50 of us leave on a flight to Buenos Aires, our first stop on the way to the Antarctic. After that, on gradually "shrinking" chartered planes that carry us over the vast

arid-brown flatlands of Patagonia, we finally arrive at the world's southernmost
town, Ushuaia, near the bottom of Tierra Del Fuego."

Read the article HERE

"TRAVELING WITH KIDS: ONE MOTHER'S ADVICE FOR MAKING
A TRIP SOMETHING SPECIAL FOR PARENT AND CHILD" (*Sojourn*
Magazine)

"For any parent, [traveling with your children is an] opportunity to share a
mutual growing experience, something that seems to be difficult in our increasingly
complicated and busy lives."

Read the article HERE

"WARSAW'S ONLY JEWISH MUSEUM: A FADING REMINDER" *The*
Polish Daily News

"Outside, small faded Hebrew symbols are the first hint of Judaism I have seen
in the month I had been in Poland. Inside, it is so dimly lit that my first impression
is that the museum must be closed, but as my eyes adjust, I see two old men sitting
at a corner table."

Read the article HERE

www.ingramcontent.com/pod-product-compliance
Lightning Source LLC
Chambersburg PA
CBHW031121020426
42333CB00012B/175